DATE DUE

DEC 16 1993			

Education for
Creative Living

Education for

IDEAS AND PROPOSALS O[

Creative Living

TSUNESABURO MAKIGUCHI

TRANSLATED BY *Alfred Birnbaum*

EDITED BY *Dayle M. Bethel*

IOWA STATE UNIVERSITY PRESS / AMES

Dayle M. Bethel is professor of education and anthropology at The International University Learning Center in Osaka, Japan.

© 1989 Soka Gakkai
All rights reserved

Manufactured in the United States of America

⊗ This book is printed on acid-free paper.

First edition, 1989

Library of Congress Cataloging-in-Publication Data

Makiguchi, Tsunesaburo, 1871–1944.
   [Soka kyoikugaku taikei. English]
   Education for creative living: ideas and proposals / Tsunesaburo Makiguchi: [translated by Alfred Birnbaum; edited by Dayle M. Bethel]. — 1st ed.
   p. cm.
   Translation of: Soka kyoikugaku taikei.
   Includes bibliographical references.
   ISBN 0–8138–0392–6
   1. Makiguchi, Tsunesaburo, 1871–1944. 2. Education—Philosophy. I. Bethel, Dayle M.,
1923– . II. Title.
LB775.M34139713   1989
370′.1—dc20   89–37830
                                                           CIP

Contents

Acknowledgments

It is a source of deep gratification to me that the educational theories of Tsunesaburo Makiguchi, the founder of the Soka Gakkai, our lay organization of Nichiren Buddhism, are herewith being introduced to readers on a worldwide scale. And I know there are many others who share my feeling. As Professor Dayle M. Bethel points out in the Introduction, the entire world at the present time is facing a crisis in education. In order to create the kind of humanistic world order that will ensure lasting peace and allow each individual to live as meaningful a life as possible, we must first carry out basic reforms in the educational system. My hope is that the present volume, which introduces to English-language readers the educational writings of Mr. Makiguchi, will help to clarify the problems that confront workers in the field of education today and will assist them in shaping effective educational systems and procedures for the future.

It was most fortunate that Dr. Bethel consented to undertake the task of supervising and editing this English-language translation of Mr. Makiguchi's writings, because he himself was the first to introduce Makiguchi's overall concepts to English readers in his *Makiguchi the Value Creator* (Tokyo: Weatherhill, 1973). Since the publication of that important work some years ago, Dr. Bethel has maintained a strong interest in Makiguchi's educational ideas and endeavors and has given unstintingly of his time and labor in the preparation of the present volume, for which I express my sincerest thanks.

My hearty thanks go also to Mr. Alfred Birnbaum, who undertook the difficult task of translating Makiguchi's writings into English and carried it out to so successful a conclusion, at the same time rendering invaluable assistance in the editorial process as well. Finally I would like to express my deep gratitude to Dr. David L. Norton, professor of philosophy at the University of Delaware, for contributing the Afterword that follows the translation. In it he has undertaken to evaluate from a philosophical point of view the implications inherent in the concepts and proposals regarding educational reform put forward by Mr. Makiguchi. Dr. Norton's appraisal constitutes further testimony, if such were needed, of the acuity of Makiguchi's insights and the high quality of his thought.

DAISAKU IKEDA
President of Soka Gakkai International

Preface TO THE ORIGINAL JAPANESE EDITION

The reader is here invited to consider my writings concerning the rebirth of a new, empirical science of education, intimately and integrally related to the realities of the life of learning. A value-creating education would aim at fulfilling the following essential conditions:

1. The streamlining of education in the interests of greater economy and efficiency. It is my conviction that if reforms were carried out on the levels of both policy and technique, today's expenditure of teaching time, study time, monetary costs, time, and so forth, could be cut in half.
2. The abandonment of blind, "whatever-comes" teaching methods for clear-sighted, planned, systematic, and acculturated education to facilitate the institution and management of education, accompanied by a coordinated learning to concord with action as an exemplar in the cultivation of powers of value creation.

Tsunesaburo Makiguchi's preface to the original book, *Soka Kyoikugaku Taikei* (pictured above), published in 1930.

3. Better treatment and selection of educational personnel in order to enlist the quality of educators necessary to carry out the above changes. Hence I have proposed the institution of an examination system for elementary school principals and fundamental reforms in normal school education.

4. The rescue of the educational system and teaching methods from the hands of unrealistically oriented pedagogues so as to render education actively productive and creative, that is, to bring education in line with real-life work activities. Thus I have called for special balance of mental and physical training under the guidance of professionals in society at large in a half-day school system.

5. The running of the schools as miniature participatory societies in accordance with sociological perspectives on society at large as a fountainhead of moral education.

What follows is the sum of countless memories, considerations, and reflections I have amassed over the course of my daily duties. Where some more mercenary members of the profession spent their every free moment brooding over monetary concerns, I have prevailed in grinding out ideas from my own experience and jotting these down in the form of notes. Now, after some thirty years as an educator, I find I have collected a mountain of little papers, some admittedly rather uninspired in conception, but others I would be loathe to throw away. The realization that sooner or later I would have to organize this mass of notes has continued to plague me. At the same time, I know there is no way that I could possibly do so, because of the busy public and private schedules of my days. It would take considerable time just to sort through it all, let alone select and discard, unify and structure, the ideas. Already I have been sitting regretfully on this stack of papers for more than twenty years.

Thus, although I can only reproach my own irresponsibility in bringing unrefined ore to market, I believe even more strongly that it is the scholar's duty to link into the proper channels and make his ideas public.

Indeed, I have been over all of this time and time again, so many times that the whole of this thinking has largely jelled into a full-fledged system of pedagogical theory in my own mind. The ideas are, I believe, sound enough that had it not been for the inhospitable harshness of the environment, they would have already borne fruit. As it was, however, they have remained stunted from the struggle to barely stay alive, though perhaps it is too much to expect others to accept this as an excuse. I just simply could not discard the product of several decades of experience that potentially belonged to all of society. Call it, perhaps, my scholastic conscience, but I found myself driven by the same sense of urgency that led me to write my previous *Geography of Human Life.*

Of course, whether society will want my ideas is another question entirely, one for which there is ample room for discussion. When I think seriously about these matters, I have to admit to myself that the results of this line of thinking may not be realized in my lifetime. Nonetheless, I have come to burn more and more with a fever to do something — and the sooner the better — about the deplorable state of the nation's education. Just the thought that through this effort might possibly come the difference in saving our million or more students from entrance difficulties, "examination hell," unemployment, and other contemporary neuroses has brought it all into focus for me. I can ask no more than that my thirty-odd years of hardship not have been in vain.

Toward this end, many of my young colleagues have been extremely kind and supportive of my efforts, consoling and encouraging me, helping proofread the material, and generally assisting me to bring the project as far along as it is today. Among these is my close friend of many years, Mr. Josei Toda. Mr. Toda has secured some small measure of funding and has made every effort to convince me of the value of carrying the project to completion. By now, we have almost reversed roles, for I am the one who now is often found dragging his feet. Mr. Toda has been a singular light in the struggle to develop a value-creating pedagogy. In addition, many other able and renowned figures have extended their sympathy and endorsement beyond all expectations. I should like to see the drive toward educational reform continue indefinitely with such able companions as I now have.

I now submit these writings for inspection and criticism to a younger generation of educators, asking only that they be accepted seriously and given a fair hearing. Education is, of course, an extremely complicated phenomenon in modern society and problems will not resolve themselves easily or quickly. We should not jump to conclusions, for if the problems are deeply rooted, effective solutions will be difficult to find. But if by chance something in my proposals does ring true, I can only hope it will be put to good use in the betterment of education, thereby proving of some service in the alleviation of a major national problem. We will be confronted with many urgent problems in our efforts to reform education. It is my hope and my expectation that Soka Kyoiku Gakkai will play a central role in these efforts. It is therefore to you, my learned friends and seniors, that I offer my most profound thanks on the occasion of the publication of this book.

October 1930

Foreword

HISTORICAL AND CONTEMPORARY SIGNIFICANCE

Very few Americans have heard of Tsunesaburo Makiguchi. He was born into poverty in 1871 in a small village in northwestern Japan. By the time he was three, first his father and then his mother, who later attempted suicide by jumping into the Japan Sea holding Makiguchi in her arms, abandoned him. He was raised by an uncle, Zendayu Makiguchi, whose name he eventually assumed. At the age of fourteen or fifteen he moved to Otaru, where he lived with another uncle. Too poor to attend high school in Otaru, he assumed a job with the local police department and studied for a government examination that would qualify him to take college entrance examinations. So impressed was the police chief with Makiguchi and his work within the department that he took him with him when he moved to Sapporo. Two years later, in 1891, Makiguchi entered the normal school as a third-year student. He graduated two years later and accepted a position as a supervising teacher in the primary school attached to the normal school. While a student at the normal school, he was subjected to the rigid

PHOTO: Makiguchi as principal of Shirogane Elementary School in Tokyo, early 1920s. For the definitive study of Makiguchi's life, see Dayle M. Bethel, *Makiguchi, The Value Creator: Revolutionary Japanese Educator and Founder of Soka Gakkai* (New York: John Weatherhill, Inc., 1973).

discipline that was expected to produce obedient teachers; and later as a teacher in the school, he was expected to be a model of discipline. It was as the result of an incident associated with an apparent breakdown of discipline that Makiguchi was forced to resign his position at the school in 1901.

The next few years were characterized by serious financial hardship for Makiguchi and his growing family but also by significant intellectual gains, which resulted in the publication of his first book, *Jinsei Chirigaku (The Geography of Human Life)*. After holding a number of positions, including one with the Ministry of Education, in 1913 he became the principal of Tosei Primary School and for the next twenty years worked as a principal and/or primary teacher in schools throughout the Tokyo area. It was from random notes accumulated during this period, reflecting his thinking about his work and experience, that *Education for Creative Living* originates.

Makiguchi began his career during a time of great debate over the direction of the new Japan and the social role and responsibilities of education. On one side were the traditionalists and the Confucianists who argued that loyalty and obedience were primary virtues to be inculcated. Education, like Makiguchi's own normal school training, was to produce good "subjects." On the other side were those who argued that schooling would best serve the future by educating citizens of an independent mind. To Makiguchi's great disappointment the traditionalists, riding the crest of a growing nationalism and militarism, triumphed and dominated the educational discourse until the conclusion of World War II.

Makiguchi's life and work stand in opposition to the traditionalists in both education and religion: "Building anew will necessarily first entail tearing down." In the education arena, where because of lack of respected academic credentials, among other reasons, he forever remained the outsider, he consistently and openly attacked privilege and ultimately sought to abolish the university system and restructure the entire school system top to bottom. Moreover, he was an outspoken critic of teachers and of the educational bureaucracy, headed by the Ministry of Education with whose policies Makiguchi frequently and publicly disagreed. It is little wonder that Makiguchi found so few allies and so many powerful enemies. In his later years, perhaps because of a growing disenchantment with education, he turned to religion as an arena within which to pursue his reform agenda. Here too, particularly following his conversion in 1928 to Nichiren Shoshu Buddhism, controversy surrounded him. For his intransigent opposition to the state-supported religion of Shinto in 1944, he was arrested and jailed in Sugamo prison where, at the age of seventy-three, after seventeen months of confinement, he died of malnutrition.

Education for Creative Living is of both historical and contemporary interest. As with the attempts of other educational radicals of the past, Makiguchi's struggles for reform stand as important social and political commentary. Not surprisingly, his was a brand of radicalism rooted in time and circumstance. He was heavily influenced by the intellectual climate of the times particularly as shaped by the rise of industrialization, growing class antagonisms, and the struggle to come to terms with issues associated with science and evolution and their meaning for life. As that of so many reformers, his thinking reflected the naive faith in human perfectability and progress through science characteristic of the progressives of the era, along with a sense of great urgency that much was at stake in the success of their proposals, "so long as [schools] do not seek to remedy the moral ills of society, I fear that they will, in effect, only add to the problems."

Parallels between Makiguchi's work and that of other reformers of the period, who shared many of his concerns, are easily identified. For example, I noted numerous similarities with the writings of Harold Rugg, an American contemporary. They shared a deep faith that there was a new era in education and in society they could see on the horizon, which could be hastened by appropriate actions undertaken by rational people of good will. Echoing evolutionary views, both appealed to organic metaphors to explain their ideas in which social systems were viewed as organisms. Within these organisms each part had an essential and complimentary role to perform for the health of the whole system; thus, there was ostensibly no necessary or inevitable conflict between part and whole, individual and society. Both believed that education held the key to social and economic progress: "The reform of educational policies is the way to revitalize society as a whole," as Makiguchi put it. Both believed in the power and potential of scientific reason to lead to truth and to produce a consensus around the truth that would enable progress. Both sought rationalization of the system of education and centralized planning. And, echoing themes grounded in Eastern traditions, both desired balance and harmony in life, "the full development of human personality...mind-body unity—a harmony of part to part and part to whole."

Moreover, like John Dewey, with whose works he was familiar, Makiguchi sought to ameliorate dualisms, the either-or type of thinking that reflects dogmatism and blocks mutual understanding, and to build schools intimately linked to community and life. Makiguchi also was grounded classically. Parting company with Dewey, he thought the physical and social universe to be orderly, based upon universal laws quite separate from human cognition: "The application of scientific procedures of observation and classification to the human world reveals an all-encompassing purposive order."

Although the issues Makiguchi addressed were of immediate concern as, for instance, his response to the various educational reform proposals released during 1931 (discussed in Chapter 3), many of them are still with us; and it is with respect to these that *Education for Creative Living* is of contemporary interest. I shall note just a few of the problems he grappled with that persist: He was dismayed by the lack of purpose in education, arguing that purpose, ultimately, ought to arise from "what people themselves see as the purpose of human life. Purpose in education must coincide with the larger life purpose of those being educated." He thought this purpose to be happiness, as he defined it, which represents a uniting of the private and public good and comes only through "full commitment to the life of the society. . . [through] sharing in the trials and successes of other persons and of our community." Surely there is no more pressing issue facing education today than that of purpose.

He was troubled by the domination of education by examinations, a domination that has only strengthened in the years since his death, and by the emphasis of teachers on memorization of facts, what Paulo Freire disparagingly calls "banking education." Such education is not only irrelevant and boring but ultimately miseducative, Makiguchi argued, and destructive to the individual and to the society, both of which must be forward looking; education must connect to life as it is lived and enrich it.

Recognizing the impossibility of learning all facts, which are innumerable, he was concerned that education come to emphasize process over product in learning where the teacher functions as examplar and guide: "It is the function of education to guide unconscious living to consciousness, valueless living to value, and irrational living to reason." Unfortunately, there were few such qualified teachers. Generally speaking, Makiguchi asserted that teachers were lacking in appropriate academic backgrounds—a topic receiving much attention currently—but, more importantly, they were lacking in character—a topic that deserves attention but is not receiving it. To remedy this situation he suggested a number of changes in teacher education, particularly those tied to developing apprenticeships.

And too, he was highly critical of educational theorists, and urged that teachers become students of their own practice and that of other practitioners. Theory, he argued, always arises from practice. There was an additional problem: Too little effort had been put into organizing the insights gained from the study of practice so that they might be extended and developed into useful rules and procedures. This as well is a problem that only recently has begun to receive the attention of educational researchers. These are but a few of the persistent issues that concerned Makiguchi.

As I read *Education for Creative Living* I found myself in frequent disagreement with the analysis, particularly with Makiguchi's epistemology, with his implicit conservatism, and with several of his specific proposals; and at times I must admit I was a bit amused by his naïveté—a feeling enabled by nearly six decades of hindsight. Despite this, I have been consistently impressed by Makiguchi's sincerity, obvious courage and intellect, and the remarkable optimism that endured despite the anticipated failure of his reform proposals. These are hard times for education and educators, perhaps in some respects not too dissimilar from Makiguchi's own; and it is a time that needs educators who possess qualities like those Makiguchi possessed, educators who are courageous and hopeful despite an awareness of the complexity of the problems of reform.

Finally, while reading, I was reminded of the importance of attending to the works of educators from earlier eras. Sad to say, we educators have notoriously short memories; we are shoulder deep in rusty and discarded bandwagons without even knowing it. There is much to be learned from writers like Makiguchi who offer us the opportunity to gain fresh insight and understanding into the problems we face if we will but take advantage of the opportunity. If nothing else, they can help us ask the right questions.

ROBERT V. BULLOUGH, JR.
Associate Professor of Educational Studies
University of Utah

Education for Creative Living

Introduction

This is a particularly appropriate time for the educational writings of Tsunesaburo Makiguchi to become available to international readers. Throughout the world, education is facing a crisis. And this is especially the case in some of the advanced industrial countries, where both private and government-sponsored committees and task forces are engaged in intense debate as to the causes of educational disarray and equally intense attempts to find solutions to educational problems.

In the midst of the din created by conflicting opinions, arguments, and counterarguments, Makiguchi's insightful ideas and recommendations for educational reform offer a refreshingly clear and usable framework within which to view our present educational dilemma. His analysis of education in industrial societies cuts through the seemingly irreconcilable disagreements over such issues as basic skills education and individualized learning and goes to the heart of the larger and more basic issue of the nature of human learning itself.

Makiguchi's ideas about education and his attempts to institute educational reforms through his own work as a teacher and principal in the Japanese educational system must be viewed and evaluated within the context of the Japanese society and culture within which he lived during the early decades of the twentieth century. Japan was, during those same years, caught up in the larger, worldwide process of industrialization, which was then in full swing in Europe and North America as well as in Japan. Makiguchi struggled with the same kinds of educational problems and realities faced by educators in other industrializing countries. Although a discussion of that larger process of industrialization is not

3

possible within the limits of this introduction, an understanding of the impact of industrialization on the economic, social, political, and educational institutions of a society is a prerequisite for understanding Makiguchi's ideas and recommendations.[1]

Basic Themes in Makiguchi's Writings

Makiguchi was deeply troubled by the inadequacies he perceived in Japanese education. His concerns about education could perhaps even be described as an obsession. His struggles to understand the complexities of the educational system of his society and to institute reforms became the central meaning of his life. Out of these efforts there emerged six basic themes or areas of concern that together form the core of Makiguchi's educational ideas and his proposals for educational reform.

PURPOSE IN EDUCATION

The process of formulating purpose in education was the heart of Makiguchi's thinking. It was in this area, Makiguchi believed, that Japanese education had been most deficient. He insisted that a society errs when it leaves decisions regarding educational aims and goals in the hands of scholars and philosophers. Too often in the past, he contended, educational goals were formulated by scholars and philosophers who spent their time engaged in abstract thought far removed from the realities of daily life. It is essential, he wrote,

> that we redirect pedagogical studies to relate to actual teaching situations. We must stand the process of theorization on its head. Instead of allowing scholars "high up" to pronounce upon what goes on "below" in the schools, disturbing the stratosphere with this and that theory only to blow over before the next prevailing wind, educational practitioners grounded in their own everyday experience must inductively abstract principles that they bring back to their practice in the form of concrete improvements.[2]

Thus, for Makiguchi, a first vital step toward educational reform was the development of a recognition that purpose in education must grow out of the needs and daily lives of people. In carrying through on this conviction, Makiguchi made intensive study of the lives and daily activities of individuals, families, and communities a major element of his professional life. This closeness to the realities of people's lives as they actually lived them is reflected throughout Makiguchi's writings, and it is these realities, he concluded, that must be the source of purpose in education.

HAPPINESS

Readers of Makiguchi must be alert in order to avoid a communication gap that his choice of words may create. This is especially the case with his use of the word *happiness*. When Makiguchi insists that the realization of happiness is the primary purpose of education and that all educational plans and programs must begin with this basic understanding, he has something more in mind than a shallow, ego-centered hedonism, which use of the word *happiness* often conjures up.[3]

The idea that for Makiguchi happiness is more than a preoccupation with one's own immediate satisfaction becomes clear when he stresses that a prerequisite for happiness is the development within each person of a social consciousness that enables understanding and appreciation of the extent to which all humans are indebted to the society in which they live, "not just for their basic needs and security, but for *everything* that constitutes happiness."[4] The tragedy of education in modern Japan, according to Makiguchi, was precisely that it had failed in the development of social consciousness within students, its most important and most basic task, and had succeeded, rather, in creating exactly the opposite, a happiness-destroying preoccupation with immediate personal and material satisfaction.[5]

CREATING VALUE

A third basic theme in Makiguchi's educational thought is the perception that human beings are creative by nature. It is the essence of humanness to be creative, and humans will express this creativity in their behavior unless that creative potential is stifled or destroyed. In summarizing his views about education in 1930, he wrote, "We begin with the recognition that humans cannot create matter. We can, however, create value. Creating value is, in fact, our very humanity. When we praise persons for their 'strength of character,' we are really acknowledging their superior ability to create value."[6]

The basic question, then, is toward what ends and in the interests of what values human creativity is to be directed. Makiguchi contends that with proper education, that is, education that enables each individual to perceive life in the context of its nurturing community, human beings will choose to use their creative capabilities both to enhance their own lives to the fullest and to create maximum benefit for their community. This is what he means by value creation. In Makiguchi's thinking, a fully alive, happy, fulfilled person is a person whose existence centers in creating value that enhances to the fullest both personal life and the network of interdependent relationships that constitutes the individual's communal life. Value-creating education is education that provides guidance toward that end.[7]

THE NATURE OF THE LEARNING PROCESS AND THE TRAINING OF TEACHERS

Transfer of knowledge, according to Makiguchi, is not and can never be the purpose of education. The purpose of education is, rather, to guide the learning process and to put the responsibility for learning into the student's own hands. Education as a process of guiding student learning is the bedrock of Makiguchi's pedagogy. He contrasted this approach to human learning with traditional education, which was firmly grounded in a perception of the human learning process as the transfer and organization of knowledge. He described the rote learning of the Japanese education he knew as

> that uneconomic method of education taken for granted the world over. It is surely one of the oldest and most primitive schemes ever invented by humans. Each student copies exactly what the teacher does. It is the very image of fishing peoples who have always fished with poles and know nothing of nets; farmers who continue to work the soil with a spade and hoe passed down from previous generations, never thinking to improve their tools.[8]

It greatly distressed Makiguchi that Japanese education in his day still clung to this outmoded and ineffective approach to learning.

Makiguchi noted that the perception of education as the process of guiding the student's own efforts to learn is not new but is merely a restatement of ideas formulated by Comenius, Pestalozzi, and others centuries ago. The problem with Japanese education as Makiguchi saw it was that this basic principle of human learning had never been put into real practice. He placed a large share of the blame for this state of affairs on teachers, and one of his primary concerns centered in the preparation of teachers who could be effective guides for students in the learning process, rather than simply transmitters of bits of dead knowledge.

Makiguchi concluded that force-feed methods and the information-organizing approach to human learning were responsible for the deplorable conditions, inadequacies, and ineffectiveness of Japanese education in his day. Teachers, he insisted, must leave fact-finding to books and assume a supporting role to the student's own learning experience. Teachers must choose between force-feeding students and guiding them in their own efforts at self-enlightenment. Teachers must decide if they are to be organizers of information or arousers of students' natural interest and curiosity. What teachers decide about this, Makiguchi believed, would be the single most important factor in reforming the educational system and, beyond that, in changing the entire conception of the how of education.

THE NEED FOR A SCIENCE OF EDUCATION

Closely related to his perception of learning was Makiguchi's conviction that education must become a science. In this emphasis he was, certainly, in tune with his time. Science, during the early twentieth century when he lived, was nearly universally hailed as the great liberator of humankind. Positivism was the road to the future. Makiguchi's interest in science, however, was more than a sharing in the prevailing intellectual climate. Rather, he was convinced that educators must discover and be guided by universally applicable principles of human learning if there was to be any hope for improving education.

> I refer here to the positivist approach: instead of tossing dogmatic and all too contradictory assertions back and forth, a body of positive proof is accumulated and handed down so that, even granted certain individual variations in interpretation, like conclusions can constantly be drawn. Nothing need be taken on blind faith. Positivism says that we are to take the daily realities before us in education as our working knowledge, then wield the scrupulous scalpel of the scientist to dissect out educational theory; that is, to yield constant

truths at the root of educational practice. Only then will education embrace an integrally systematized body of knowledge.[9]

Thus, for Makiguchi, science was a systematic, objective means of arriving at underlying principles of human learning upon which a sound educational system could be established.

Makiguchi's perception of science and its relationship to education is further expressed in the following comparison between education and medicine:

> For though medicine and education ought to rightfully be brothers in applied science—the one administering passively and preventatively to the body; the other actively and constructively to the mind—the breach between the two could hardly be greater. This, I believe, is due to the one already having a long history of development to a point at which it constitutes a real science with established technical principles, while the other still fears to tread on scientific grounds and even doubts the possibility of becoming scientific. And so educators continue to keep their noses to their immediate day-to-day tasks, sticking strictly to tradition and custom, essentially groping their way in the dark. This is the result of adhering to the philosopher's method of abstract thinking, rather than the scientist's method of inducing findings from actual experience.
>
> When will we learn? Although educational objectives may well have to rely on philosophers' or sociologists' deciphering of larger human-life objectives, once those objectives are set it is a mistake to let these learned scholars go on to questions of methodology. The very history of science says nothing if it does not tell us this.
>
> Here and now, what we educators need most in our daily instructional activities are answers to the questions of how to improve methods in the future, how to promote ever greater efficiency in education. With sixty years of experience behind us since the institution of modern education in Japan, how much longer will we keep deferring the establishment of pedagogical priorities to imported ideologies and philosophers? Herein lies my sense of urgency in calling out for reforms to break through the current stalemate in Japanese education toward the founding of value-creating education.[10]

Makiguchi believed that scientific objectivity would enable teachers and educators with widely differing views and ideas about education to share together in a thorough reexamination of the Japanese educational system and that out of that experience agreement on educational goals and practices could be arrived at.

> Ultimately, the lack of real-life value to contemporary pedagogy bears sad witness to the educational community's neglect of questions of underlying value structure. Let us, then, re-examine our ideas in education and restructure them with a view toward value principles. Let all educators rally to the establishment of a new pedagogy under the banner of these directives:
>> Begin from actual experience!
>> Aim towards goals of value!
>> Make economy of means a working principle!
> We are faced today as never before with the challenge of creating a full-fledged science of education, a pedagogy crystallized out of the bitter lessons of vast trial-and-error experience and tempered to focus on goals of life-value.[11]

EDUCATIONAL ROLES OF SCHOOL, HOME, AND COMMUNITY

The most revolutionary of Makiguchi's ideas and proposals, given the centralized nature of the Japanese educational system, was related to his contention that the school had usurped educational roles and responsibilities that rightfully belonged to other sectors of society, that is, the home and the community. Effective education, Makiguchi insisted, can only be carried on as a three-way partnership between the school, the home, and the community. At the heart of his program of educational reform, therefore, was a proposal to create a completely new education system in which school, home, and community each were to be responsible for a specific part of the educational task. The key element of this proposal was the reduction of the time each child would spend in school to a half day, allowing time in the child's schedule for learning activities in the community and the home, including apprenticeships and other types of work responsibilities fitted to the nature and needs of each child.

Makiguchi made far-reaching claims with respect to his value-creating half day school proposal. He insisted that its adoption would lead to better education at a fraction of the cost of continuing the traditional educational system. But though he considered budgetary and economic factors important, they were secondary. The most important result of his proposed system, he believed, would be the changing of bored, apathetic students who studied only when forced to do so into alert, eager, and self-directing learners. The fundamental idea of half-day value-creating education, he wrote, is that

> study is not seen as a preparation for living, but rather study takes place while living, and living takes place in the midst of study. Study and actual living are seen as more than parallels; they inform one another intercontextually, study in living and living in study, throughout one's whole life. In this sense, it is not the better economic budgeting of school programs, but to instill joy and appreciation for work that becomes the main focus of the proposed changes.[12]

When statements such as this are placed within the total context of Makiguchi's ideas of value, society, the individual, and the nature of the learning process, the revolutionary nature of his proposal for reforming education becomes clear. He was proposing nothing less than abandoning the existing educational structures and practices of Japanese society, built up over several centuries of industrial development in Western countries and transplanted to Japan in the years following the Meiji restoration, and replacing them with educational structures and practices based on an entirely different concept of the learning process and the relationship between the individual and the society of which the individual is a part within that process. In the existing system of education, built up out of the experience of the industrializing countries to produce persons suited to operate the machines and carry out the responsibilities dictated by the needs of an elitist-controlled production-consumption process, the school constituted the center of the learning process. Heretofore discovered facts and information constituted the curriculum to be transmitted to students. And educators in their several roles — teacher, administrator, theoretician — served as intermediaries standing between learners and the facts and information to be learned.

The conception of learning presented by Makiguchi radically altered this traditional view. In Makiguchi's scheme, the individual learner, not the school, is the center of the learning process. The nature of the individual and the social fabric (local, national, regional, and global) within which the individual exists constitute the basic curriculum. Educators are guides whose primary role is to encourage and motivate the learner in the pursuit of self-determined learning goals and understandings and to assist the learner in removing obstacles that might hinder the learning process.

These educational principles and goals stand in sharp contrast to contemporary educational policies and practices in Japan. If Makiguchi's proposals for educational reform had been adopted and taken root, they would have profoundly changed the nature of Japanese education and society. But those proposals were not adopted, nor were they even seriously considered in Japan for two reasons. First, probably because he lacked university education—his higher education was limited to normal school training—Makiguchi was ignored by the Japanese academic community. Following the publication of the first volume of *Soka Kyoikugaku Taikei* (Value-creating educational theory) in 1930, Makiguchi had opportunity to lecture and present his ideas at various places. He hoped to receive recognition and to initiate discussion and debate about his proposal. But his efforts were met with silence. He was simply ignored by the university-educated elite, which controlled the educational affairs of the society. Several years later Makiguchi described the disappointment he felt at that time: "Having started with a lecture at the educational conference held at Tokyo Imperial University in 1931, I presented my theory of education to the academic world. However, there was no reaction. Because of the present situation of education in our nation, I was deeply disappointed by that fact."[13]

In spite of this rejection by the educated elite, Makiguchi's ideas might still have received a hearing if it had not been for a second development that was occurring at the same time. That was the increasing militarization of the country. While the educational establishment rejected Makiguchi's ideas, some highly respected and influential persons in Japanese society rallied to his cause. Among them were such distinguished leaders of Japanese society as Tsuyoshi Inukai, prime minister of Japan from December 1931 to May 1932; Magoichi Tsuwara, minister of commerce and industry; and Itamu Takagi, professor of medicine at Tokyo Imperial University. These and other prestigious individuals strongly endorsed and supported Makiguchi's ideas and proposals.[14] There is every reason to believe that with this kind of backing Makiguchi's proposals for radically changing Japanese education would have in time at least been given a fair hearing. However, this situation ended with the increasing militarization of the country, particularly after the assassination of Prime Minister Inukai in 1932. There was no place in the new, military-dominated regime for the kinds of educational ideas and convictions that Makiguchi represented, and he was thereafter barred from all educational activity.

The task Makiguchi set for himself remains unfinished. Force-feed education has continued to be the dominant form of education in most, if not all, of the countries of the world. The continued reliance on force-feed education is leading to the consequences that Makiguchi predicted. These consequences are particularly evident in Japan and the United States, and in those countries alert people are pressing for a fundamental rethinking of the meaning, purpose, and practice of education. This book is presented to the members of the international community with the hope that it can make a useful contribution to these discussions.

Makiguchi and students at Shirogane Elementary School.

The Editing Process

Some aspects of the translating and editing of the book should be clarified. It should be understood, first of all, that Makiguchi's *Soka Kyoikugaku Taikei* is not a book but a collection of notes that he jotted down and accumulated over a period of thirty years. It was these notes, with little in the way of editing, that were published as *Soka Kyoikugaku Taikei* in 1930. Makiguchi apologized profusely in the preface to the book for publishing unedited notes.[15] In explanation, he expressed deep concern about the detrimental effects the education of his day was having upon children. As he went about his daily teaching responsibilities, he wrote, he constantly carried this concern with him and often jotted down notes as ideas for more effective education occurred to him.

Makiguchi described his extreme frustration at this point in his life. He desperately wanted to save future generations of children from what he believed were personality-destroying consequences of then-current educational policies and practices. He was convinced that his ideas, if given a chance, could lead to desirable changes in education. But he was without resources. He had to keep working every day and had no time to spend on preparing his notes for publication. Confronted with this dilemma, he finally decided to publish the notes with only a limited amount of editing. Instead of being able to sift the wheat from the chaff (or as he expressed it in his idiom, "sift the stones from the gold"), as a scholar should, he was forced to present the unsifted material.[16]

The realization that the book we were charged with rendering into English was not a book at all but a collection of notes led us to the conclusion that in order to be true to Makiguchi and to the spirit of the assignment, that is, the preparation of a coherent statement of Makiguchi's ideas and proposals on education in the English language, we would have to do the sifting and integrating of his notes that he was not permitted to do himself. This is what we have attempted to do. We believe that this book represents the expression of his ideas in a form in which he would have expressed them himself if he had been in a position to do so. We would note further, however, that we do not see this book as the final statement of Makiguchi's ideas on education. It is our hope that in the years ahead a new generation of bilingual scholars and researchers will further examine and analyze Makiguchi's writings and their implications for educational policy and practice.

One further reality about the book that should be noted is that it represents an unfinished work. At the time Makiguchi was preparing his notes for the publication of the four volumes of *Soka Kyoikugaku Taikei*, he envisioned additional volumes that would further develop and report the results of the application of his ideas. However, these additional volumes were never written.[17] After he was dismissed from active school work and barred from further participation in his country's formal educational system, Makiguchi turned increasingly to the religion of Nichiren Shoshu both as a source of motivation and as a vehicle through which he could carry on reform activities. His later writings dealt primarily with religious themes, and his earlier intentions with respect to further developing and testing his educational ideas and proposals were never carried out. Thus, if upon reading Chapter 5, the reader is left with a feeling of incompleteness, this is the reason. The book *is* incomplete because Makiguchi did not finish, for the reasons discussed above, what he initially set out to do. It remains for contemporary educators who are challenged and inspired by Makiguchi's contributions to educational thought and understanding to test and implement his proposals for a more humane system of learning.[18]

Criticism and Evaluation

In *Makiguchi the Value Creator*, I summarized areas of weakness that I perceived in Makiguchi's ideas and the limitations and handicaps he faced in his efforts to reform Japanese education.[19] A further criticism has been brought to my attention in an excellent study of Makiguchi made by Koichi Mori.[20] Mori argues that Makiguchi's pursuit of happiness as the purpose of education and life focused on a search for individual, subjective happiness within the limits of the existing social system, without in any way criticizing or questioning existing social policies and structures. Makiguchi, according to Mori's analysis, perceived society as something that individuals should obey. For Makiguchi the nation was equal to the government then in power: "It is impossible to expect any criticism against the government of that time from such understanding of the nation and society. Makiguchi identified the government policies with the will of the people."[21] Mori concludes that Makiguchi was naive in this respect and that his proposals for reforming society through educational reform did not take into account the extent to which existing power structures in a society can deny to individuals opportunities for self-expression and creative behavior.[22]

There is some justification for Mori's criticism of Makiguchi on this point. Makiguchi seems to have perceived existing social systems as givens. And, it seems, he did not see or was not bothered by this apparent contradiction in his thinking. Mori credits this to the ideology of the emperor system, with its perception of the nation as a family. Makiguchi, he argues, was so imbued with this ideology that he never questioned it.[23]

While such limitations and blind spots as those noted admittedly exist in Makiguchi's writings, they do not, I believe, in any way detract from the value and significance of his educational ideas and his proposals for educational reform. They do make it clear that Makiguchi was not all-wise or all-knowing. He was simply an ordinary human being who cared deeply about other human beings and who identified with the hurts, needs, and longings of his fellows, particularly the young. It was this concern, I believe, that led Makiguchi to focus his efforts and creative abilities on developing understanding of human learning and the social institutions most directly related to the learning process. And it was that effort that led to the formulation of his value-creating pedagogy.

I would submit that in his struggles to understand the nature of the human personality and the learning process, Makiguchi was anticipating the work of philosophers, educators, and psychologists in later decades of the century, particularly the work and conceptual contributions of Abraham Maslow, Erich Fromm, David Norton, Carl Rogers, Robert Theobald, and others. His work stands today as another verification of the validity of the principles and assumptions being expressed by these latter-day scholars, and their contributions to our educational understanding provide evidence of the genius and significance of Makiguchi as an educator.

Tsunesaburo Makiguc

1

Reflections on Purpose in Education

In education, as in any human endeavor, ends determine means. Thus, appropriate educational methods follow naturally from the purpose of specific educational programs. The problem with today's education is that it lacks clearly defined purpose. No arrow can be expected to hit the mark if the target remains obscured, yet this is precisely what has happened in education—and the ones who suffer most directly from the blind and ill-devised teaching practices resulting from this lack of attention to purpose are the children.

The task of formulating and clarifying purpose in education cannot be left up to the arbitrary judgement of theoreticians. Rather, the formulation of purpose in education must emerge out of the realities of daily life. It must take into account the entire scope of human life, but at the same time it must consider the specific needs of family, society, and nation. The purpose of education, when approached within this kind of comprehensive framework, leads inevitably to happiness as a central factor in human learning. It is the central theme of this book that the realization of happiness is the primary purpose of education and that all educational plans and programs must begin with this basic understanding.

The question, What is happiness? has been a favorite subject of philosophical discussion for centuries, but in order to arrive at an understanding of happiness with which I could be satisfied, I started observing and analyzing the "mode of living," or the daily activities, of people in various situations. In this way I ultimately arrived at the fundamental principle of value as the basis for happiness.

Formulating Purpose in Education

MEANS TO FORMULATING PURPOSE IN EDUCATION

The first step in formulating purpose in education is to determine how purpose is to be arrived at. My contention is that the task of deciding on the purpose of education cannot be left to scholars and philosophers. This has been a major error in educational planning up to the present time. I do not mean to detract from the important contribution that such persons make. Their role is an important and necessary one. But the point I want to make is that a major concern in formulating purpose in education should be the recognition of what people themselves see as the purpose of human life. Purpose in education must coincide with the larger life purpose of those being educated.

We still understand very little about how the human personality grows and develops, but it is obvious that humans are not born with predetermined goals. On the other hand, the human individual is not altogether aimless, either. My studies and observations lead me to believe that there is something innate that guides the life of each individual, yet something that is common to all. Whatever this innate something is, it shapes the unconscious notions of purpose that tend to pull the child toward some way of life. Needless to say, this innate something cannot be perceived by the external observations of another person, nor is it accessible to any of the senses. Even so, it is there in the mind, dimly discernible within the total life of the individual.

In view of the complexity of the human growth process and our lack of understanding of that process, it is small wonder that most attempts to construct life philosophies have simply sidestepped the main issues and rested on precedent, that is, the subjective views of earlier scholars that are untested but have been accepted uncritically out of deference to these great predecessors. But how did they arrive at their views? Presumably either by intuition or by deduction from even earlier premises. In either case, we are left with only the untested judgements of these scholars for which no proof is available.

There is a further problem here, also. A philosophy of life that developed out of the needs and demands of a particular society in the past may have been appropriate for that society at that time. It does not necessarily follow, however, that the same philosophy of life will be relevant for our society today. We have made the mistake of perpetuating many outmoded ideas about the purpose of education as if they were relevant, and because of this we are confronted by serious problems in contemporary education.

Just as an arrow shot without a clear view of the target cannot be expected to hit it, so effective methods in education cannot be devised if the purpose of education itself has not been clearly established. The central issue we have to address ourselves to, then, is how we can formulate clear and relevant purpose upon which to develop our educational programs. The task before us is especially difficult because the nation's educational system has already grown to overwhelming proportions, yet there is no clear purpose to guide it.

This situation calls for serious study and clarification. We need, for one thing, to determine what society expects education to do for its children. This involves at least two aspects: the aspirations that parents have for their children, and the expectations for the next generation held by the society as a whole. Parents who truly love their children would not think of using them as a means to their own happiness. This can be illustrated by the famous story of the judgement of Lord Ooka of Echizen when he was faced with a conflict between a mother and a stepmother over custody of a child.[1] Whereas the latter saw her own claim to the child as most important, giving no thought to the child itself, the real mother valued the child more highly than her own need to have it back.

A society must be equally concerned about the individual needs and well-being of its children. If society considers only how it can profit from the educated, the result will be disastrous for both. The purpose of education as formulated by the society must be in agreement with the needs and the goals of the individual. Education must be conducted in such a way that society does not use the educated as means to its own ends and vice versa. The reason for being of the one must be recognized and accepted by the other.

A nation or society is, after all, its people; it is a society of individuals. Where there is individual growth and fulfillment, there will be prosperity, enrichment, and health within the society as a whole. On the other hand, when the individual is stifled, the society weakens and deteriorates. A society prospers when its elements, or individuals, are united in their value commitments and disintegrates when wide divergence develops in those commitments. In view of these realities, it is crucial that family and society work together in establishing the purpose of education.

The importance of education in modern society can be attested to by the degree to which governments everywhere have become involved in the educational process. First taking over the actual responsibility of teaching from the home and local community, then gradually unifying and systematizing educational practices with associated changes in organization and scale, they have come to give it such priority that educational policy calls for lengthy parliamentary debate, and its implementation requires a massive administrative infrastructure.

This reorientation and institutionalization of education has inevitably brought about major changes in the educational process. But do people express the slightest doubt that it is all for the best? Even as more and more of the responsibility for their children's learning gets taken out of their hands, do parents actually give thought to where the educational system is leading their children? Does every family support the system out of a conscious awareness of the purpose of children's education? The answer to such questions, unfortunately, seems to be no. Most families send their children off to school without a thought as soon as the children reach school age. They do not question, or even consider, the final goal of the educational system. Though they may at times express dissatisfaction, their reactions remain largely passive. It is rare for parents to take the initiative in studying how to improve education. This pervasive silence about their children's education upon the part of parents tends to be interpreted by educators as tacit approval of the status quo. This is not enough. The active identification and affirmation of common aims for education are an absolute necessity. Without them, it will be impossible to arrive at any universal understanding or agreement as to the purpose of education.

HAPPINESS AS COMMON DENOMINATOR

There would likely be general agreement that in sending their children to school parents' primary concern is for their children's happiness. Though there have been many arguments concerning the meaning of *happiness*, no other word can better express the heartfelt wish that is common to everyone. Interpreting just what this means proves difficult in practice, however. It is often said that education should serve as a preparation for adult life. A simplistic version of this view holds that the three R's should be enough. Others criticize education for not being relevant to the real world. These people argue that education should be more responsive to popular opinion. All too often, however, both views tend to narrow perspectives to a nearsighted utilitarianism that emphasizes only what might be useful *after* the children are grown, neglecting entirely what children find relevant or interesting or even comprehensible during their formative years. Thus, most teachers, thinking only of adult needs, tend to keep cramming their students with information that has no meaning or relevance for their current lives. It is little wonder, then, that children are not interested in their studies and, more often than not, fail to understand them. The compulsory English curriculum as it exists in the Japanese educational system is a first-rate example of this.[2]

The detrimental effects of force-feeding a small child can be easily seen because of the small body's inability to metabolize more than it can digest. The excessive bulk passes through the child's system, an undigested waste. Or worse, it may lodge in the digestive tract, slowly putrefying and poisoning the whole system. Unfortunately, the effects of psychological toxification in children caused by the forced learning of masses of unintelligible information are not immediately visible. Consequently, the detrimental effects of this poisoning process in children's lives are not recognized. The situation is serious, but when we search for the causes of the problem, we are faced with the paradox that teachers and parents alike see themselves as providing for the future well-being of the children even though they make them miserable in the process.

The question as to whether the present educational system provides adequate preparation for adult life is not at issue here. And, furthermore, it is not a prerogative of professional educators to decide that preparation for adult life should be the purpose of education. Sooner or later, everyone concerned with education must come to realize that schooling that sacrifices children's present happiness and makes some future happiness its goal violates the personalities of the children as well as the learning process itself. This line of reasoning has led me to the conclusion that the purpose of education is to enable children to become responsible, healthy cells in the social organism, to contribute to the happiness of the society, and, by so doing, to find meaning, purpose, and happiness in their own individual lives.

Of course, I am aware that this simple conclusion is not readily accepted by some scholars. It is well known, for example, that Kant and his followers objected to taking students' own happiness as the goal of education.[3] Unqualified though I may be to contest a great philosopher like Kant, I nevertheless propose happiness as the purpose of education, based upon observation and systematic analysis of a purpose of life common to everyone. Within this context, I submit that the purpose of education should be derived from the purpose of life itself; and the purpose of life is deduced and recognized by the general public from their own lives as they live them, not by philosophers and theoreticians. No doubt Kant's objection stemmed partially from traditional thinking that the purpose of education must be established by philosophers and scholars, and partially from narrow interpretation of the concept of happiness in his day.

At any rate, my central thesis is that the most important consideration in formulating purpose in education is the happiness of the students themselves. What this means in practical terms and how we can go about the task of defining both the overall purpose and the specific aims of educational programs are matters to which we must now address ourselves.

Happiness as the Purpose of Education

THE MEANING OF HAPPINESS

Happiness is such a common and familiar term that it would seem to need no explanation. Still, upon closer examination, we find that people hold many different views as to what happiness is and what is meant by *happiness*. If happiness is to serve as a basis for determining the purpose and aims of education, it will be necessary to develop a more precise definition of what we mean by *happiness*.

Trying to explain happiness with words or idealistic philosophical conceptions would likely cause misunderstanding, since happiness is based in a person's experience rather than in theory. Thus, since happiness is something that we experience in our daily lives, a few actual examples of happiness will be more effective than wordy explanations. In order to better understand the concept of happiness, we will examine its antithesis, unhappiness, and cite a few commonly held misconceptions in an effort to better delineate its general contours.

It may be appropriate to ask first if there is an ideal or purpose in life other than happiness. If so, it likely is based on an understanding of the concept of happiness different from mine or it may mistake an element or component of happiness for the whole. The word *happiness* can be interpreted in a variety of ways, depending on the experience of each individual. It is difficult to come to a common definition. Some persons might regard great monetary wealth as happiness and be satisfied; others may feel happiest with a high position or status in society. Many other examples could be listed, but they all stem from incomplete understanding of the concept of happiness.

I was once asked by a distinguished scholar if the entire goal of a person's life could be explained by such a simple word as *happiness*. Clearly he did not think so. But if we conclude that the word *happiness* is not satisfactory, is there any other suitable word to take its place? Other goals may seem to exist for humankind, but it is difficult to find a goal more encompassing than happiness. Some people may resist accepting happiness as the purpose of education because they consider it a selfish, personal goal, but as we examine it rationally as a social phenomenon in the following sections, we will find a broader definition of happiness that is a responsible goal of life.

Thus, one realization that emerges from our consideration of happiness is that those persons who opt for some single sense of meaning in their lives, whether it be accumulation of wealth, achieving high social position, or something else, have confused the part for the whole, and in so doing have settled for something less than total well-being. Such choices can be attributed to an arrested development in forming a conception of happiness, a fixation upon some particular aspect of life to the exclusion of other equally vital human possibilities. This phenomenon leads us to see that we are talking about happiness not as a fixed mark to be achieved but as a sense of *becoming*. It is this dynamic, growthful nature of happiness that most concerns us educators. For implicit in the pragmatic orientation of education "for living, of living, and by living" is the understanding of both living and learning as *process*.

Our understanding of happiness has been enhanced in recent years by the development of the discipline of sociology. As indicated earlier, Kant was opposed to making happiness the purpose of education. However, I believe that he would have thought differently had sociology been developed at that time. Kant's concept of happiness does not include a societal element. Prior to the development of sociology by Auguste Comte, society was not an object of cognition and hence was not taken into consideration by Kant.

With the new conceptual tools provided by the discipline of sociology, we can now, for example, more clearly distinguish between subjective and objective elements present in happiness as commonly conceived of by the members of a society. The very same environmental factors, that is to say, objective conditions, may yield two entirely different reactions from two persons or even from the same person on different occasions; one set of circumstances will one time bring happiness, and unhappiness another. Moreover, we are all well aware that people may show every outward sign of well-being, much to the envy of all around them, and still regard themselves as unfulfilled and unhappy. Or again, the opposite situation may hold true. Thus, it is obvious that there are at least two sides to this question of happiness.

If we further break down the objective element into individual and societal requirements for happiness, we find that although neither can wholly exclude the other, the latter is particularly important. True happiness is not to be had completely on one's own terms. We do not live alone. Directly or indirectly, the social environment impinges upon the individual, and any friction is bound to cancel out the seeming advantages of insisting on having things our own way. Instead of mere self-seeking, we must bear in mind that individual well-being entails cooperative and contributive existence within society if it is to last any length of time. Our lives will always be tied in with those of others. To ignore this is to fall into a narrow egoism. Such extreme subjectivity has no place in deciding the meaning of happiness, especially not as the purpose of our children's education.

We cannot shut ourselves off from the concerns of the community. Even wealth cannot buy total isolation except at an inhuman cost. High walls and security guards to protect the most beautiful mansion might make carefree living possible for a while, but one day we would have to wake up to the mean and narrow-minded person we had become. Where is our happiness then? True happiness comes only through sharing in the trials and successes of other persons and of our community. Hence it is essential that any true conception of happiness contain the promise of full commitment to the life of the society.

HAPPINESS AND WEALTH

If we are to arrive at a meaningful definition of happiness, it is essential to examine the relationship between happiness and wealth. No single element is so disruptive and damaging to the happiness of individuals and to the well-being of the society as a whole as that of wealth and the uses people make of it. Certainly there are few other aspects of life about which there is so much confused thinking with such disastrous results. Alfred Nobel put it well when he insisted that although it is possible to inherit property, it is impossible to inherit happiness. This is one of the most important lessons we can hope to learn in this age of ruthless competition and materialistic obsession. Rich and poor, management and workers alike may find no more vital realization, especially if it allows even a moment's pause in all the hatred and violence, than to reconsider what is really of value. If we could state these realities in such plain language that the message would reach everyone, I believe that people would begin to think about improving conditions in society, actively seeking the means to do so, and eventually bringing happiness to all.

But, unfortunately, at present most people seem to operate on the premise that if you can't take it with you, then at least your children can take it on. The rich continue to amass wealth as though happiness could indeed be endowed along with status and property. Yet the more people stash away, the more it seems not enough, all because they have convinced themselves that their holdings will magically translate into happiness for their children. This is an illusion. It is more often the case that leaving great wealth for one's children results in their inheriting unhappiness rather than happiness. And the greatest irony of all is that the rich do not even enjoy what they do. They needlessly sacrifice their own present happiness in driving themselves so they can buy that illusion. Careful consideration beforehand would have brought the realization that the sheer meanness required to amass a fortune would just as surely get passed down to very unhappy children. Those who wish to prove it for themselves are welcome to spend their whole lives trying to get the better of the flawed and unequal system of private ownership while working through the system. But what a waste of one's possibilities.

As we begin to realize the ultimate emptiness of sheer material pursuits, we come to sense that it is better to find joy in giving to others than to live in fear that others are going to get ahead of us; better to discover peace of mind through coming to know the source of our being than to squander our lives foolishly on material accumulation. With such clarity of vision would go the responsibility of helping others who are still starving for money or who are caught in the web of materialism to recognize their delusions. But the starting point is for each of us to rid ourselves of our own illusions about wealth and so help to pave the way to peace through economic security for all.

If these realities regarding money and wealth were understood, people would not waste their lives simply accumulating wealth. Persons who realize these truths feel gratitude and find joy in giving money to others. Such persons strive to achieve a state of being happy and at ease through gaining insights into the central and enduring values of life instead of foolishly wasting time on material pursuits.

Helping people develop this clarity of vision is extremely difficult, however. History is filled with examples of the folly of single-minded pursuit of wealth, but unless one has already attained some degree of insight, one is blind to such examples. But just what is "some degree of insight?" Here is where we are faced with what seems to be a paradox. For developing the clarity of vision and the insight to properly assess the role of material things in life requires leisure and a capacity for spiritual reflection, which seem to come only with the wealth and social status for which everyone is striving. But it is exactly at this point that we need to think more carefully. While developing this insight and understanding regarding material things appears difficult for common people, I believe that if people can be helped to acquire a truly social consciousness, the misconceptions they have held in regard to material things will become clear to them. It is on this heightened social consciousness that we must focus our attention, then, rather than on the insight arising from leisurely reflection which is available only to a limited few. As I will stress later, it is precisely the development of this heightened social consciousness that is a primary responsibility of true education.

HAPPINESS AND VIRTUE

There is an old Japanese teaching that holds that good fortune does not drop out of the sky unexpectedly. Neither does it spring forth from the earth or suddenly visit us from afar. Good fortune comes by the workings of virtue and so is only another name for our original state of mind. True blessings come to those who humble themselves, apply their labors to the family good, and uphold the Five Relationships.[4] Conversely, ill fortune does not just happen either. The calamities that are our undoing and steal away our very lives come about from inverting the natural order of the world through our own selfishness and inconsiderateness, our disloyalties, our impiety, marital quarreling and sibling rivalry, and forsaking family duties. True curses befall those who lead cursed lives.

Whether or not one accepts this reasoning in its entirety, it must be admitted that there is some truth in it. The fullest experience of life does, indeed, come only when happiness and virtue coincide. The egocentric accumulation of wealth, as noted earlier, is a delusion, a delusion that, far from leading to happiness, leads rather to emptiness and disappointment. If our society condones and encourages virtuelessness and false values in the lives of its members, we must remake society so that happiness and virtue do coincide.

Such a revitalization movement would deal with current problems of social inequality, for these are a part of the same disparity. It is a particularly grievous flaw of our present society that the possibility of unlimited private holdings encourages discrepancy between private and public good. The sad truth is, if anything, that the unequal distribution of wealth is growing steadily worse. This must be checked on the one hand with external constraints, by redefining governmental policy, and on the other hand with internal constraints, by convincing peopie of the ultimate valuelessness of private holdings in excess of what they actually need.

HAPPINESS AND HEALTH

Finally, consideration of happiness as the purpose of education must take into account the relationship between happiness and health. Health is the physiological foundation of happiness. All too often this simple truth gets overlooked. Yet, of what good would be vast riches or noble status or even the most thorough scholarship if our body or our mind is not sound enough to enjoy it? Health is the first condition and the symbol of well-being.

Happiness, then, depends on health, but health in turn depends upon positive activity. Individual energies are often wasted by aimless living, apathy, or unconstructive activities. By the time people reach adulthood it is usually too late to change; patterns of behavior are largely set. But children and youth can be shown how to channel their energies into constructive activities. They may be directed toward a life of value creation. This is, after all, the reason we have education.

Educational Purpose and Society

EDUCATIONAL PURPOSE IN SOCIAL CONTEXT

If education is to achieve its goal of happiness and fulfillment for all, it must transform the apathy of unaware, egocentric social existence into a consciously thought-out commitment to society. Education can and must make people recognize the extent to which they are indebted to the society and state in which they live, not just for their basic needs and security, but for *everything* that constitutes happiness. There is nothing for which we are not indebted to society. Our society makes it possible for us to have food, shelter, and clothing, as well as protection of our property and our very life. Society is a kind of organism within which we live. We enjoy benefits from it to such an extent that, without its protection, we could not maintain life itself for even a short time. There are many people who are unconscious of the benefits they have received from society and who are concerned only with their own private lives. Such people are unwilling to put up with the least inconvenience. They loudly claim their rights but ignore the responsibilities that accompany those rights. It is the faith of the educator that, once aroused to an awareness of how society provides for everyone's happiness, these same persons will not only be encouraged to consider the ways and means of living in harmony with others but actually come to cherish the moral laws of social existence and realize there really is no better route to their own happiness than through being a productive participant in their society. Without this reciprocity a just and humane society is not possible. Only when people begin to perceive that their life in society in fact does make for the best of everything, will they take it upon themselves to work for the good of all toward the creation of an ever more ideal society.

Education seeks to engender the personal character needed by the members of a society that will enable them to become creative participants in that society. But for education to perform this socializing task, it must, as suggested above, raise the individual consciousness above limited focus on personal rights and privileges of private life to accept the duties and responsibilities of collective social life as well.

The purpose of education, then, is to change an unconscious social life into a well-planned, rational one. In other words, education is an important aspect of the socialization of the individual. Durkheim said it well when he wrote that "education is the systematic socialization of a minor."[5] Educators, whose primary task it is to help bring this about in individual lives, should accommodate their own daily lives to their society above everything else and contribute to the society in every way they can.

THE INTERDEPENDENCE OF PERSONS IN SOCIETY

The concept *human* includes not only a sensory, tangible, physical form but also a spiritual aspect that is different from the physical form but has its basis in the physical. Likewise, the concept *society* goes beyond the visible circumstances of persons living in groups and focuses on that intangible body of interrelationships that is the organizational basis for their living together. Society is not a mere aggregation of people but their mental and spiritual union. Imagine a pen, a bottle of ink, some pencils and paper, and some books piled on a desk. On the physical plane there may not be much difference between this collection of objects and a human household where parents, children, and perhaps some servants co-occupy the same space. But that is where the resemblance ends. Removing one or two items from the desktop does nothing to affect the rest. On the other hand, except for chance assemblies of people, human groups possessing any degree of permanence acquire an element of emotional or psychological interdependence.[6]

Even in a classroom situation where students carry out their assignments with little interaction or notice of each other, if one day one student is absent everyone immediately senses there is something different, something missing. The empty place soon calls for conjecture; maybe that student is sick today, or maybe there is some other reason. So it is with even the most tangential relationships in our lives. How much more keenly do we feel the loss of someone with whom we have had close ties? Or just imagine how let down and upset the whole class might be had they been especially counting on that one student's presence.

The forces that hold people together are subtle but implacable. A physical analogy more in the nature of things might be found in the forces of molecular and atomic attraction, which, although imperceptible in and of themselves, may have obviously solidifying effects upon individual particles. Laws of attraction and repulsion likewise govern human socialization. The mutual attraction and bonding between particular individuals, perhaps encouraged or reinforced by some common external threat, not only demands certain behavior from those individuals but also affects the configuration of the group.

Thirty years ago, in my *Geography of Human Life*, I attempted to explain the concept of society as a network of interdependent relationships. Although my understanding of society has grown in the intervening years, the examples I used then still seem relevant. The following paragraphs are from that earlier work:[7]

> The word *society* is being used in a variety of contexts and carries such meanings and connotations as "educational society," "economic society," "socialism," and "socialist party." Sometimes people make such references as "for the society," "social sanctions," and so on. In more common usage, it may mean "the world," "the community," or "the public."
>
> If a person accumulates wealth through shady transactions for purely selfish gain, that person will certainly receive society's retribution. On the other hand, if someone undertakes a great endeavor for the benefit of society without the slightest thought of personal gain, society recognizes that deed and praises it. A person's action is greeted with either praise or condemnation; one feels joy from the former but fears the latter. Those with some sense of ethics bear themselves accordingly. What is this entity that applies sanction, praise, or condemnation? Although we cannot see it as a physical body, we should be able to perceive this entity through its actions. We could define *society* as a human organization in which people share their lives in a certain lasting relationship and in which each of those persons constitutes a member of that society.
>
> How can we delineate a society? Suppose a large audience assembles to hear a speech, but among them is a drunk who interrupts the course of the speech. The popular voice of all present would immediately criticize his action so that he would be forced to leave. The assembly of that audience is a small society, the members of which assembled for a common purpose and are temporarily asso-

ciated through the same interest, which keeps them together. Take our families as another example: Families consist of parents and children, husbands and wives, brothers and sisters, and perhaps servants. All members of the family share their daily lives, perform certain duties, and, over several generations, share life together. If a member should fail to carry out these duties, it would disrupt the peaceful order of the household, throw it into confusion, tax its prosperity, and eventually threaten its unity. This, too, is an example of a small society. Now, consider a school, be it a small school with less than one hundred or a large school with several thousand students, where there are teachers, students, administrative staff, custodial staff for maintenance, and a principal above them who is responsible for the entire operation. All play their role in making it a functioning school. This is another example of a society. Likewise, a small village, town, or city each constitutes a society. On the national level a country represents the most fully developed society thus far. Yet the concept of society is still not limited to these examples. Sometimes it signifies a group of people with common ethics or heritage regardless of national boundaries or, in an even larger scope, the entire world community. Hence, the delineation of a society ranges from a group of several people up to the entire world, and the concept of society varies from instance to instance, depending upon the example. Nevertheless, we can observe that the concept of society always includes the following conditions:

1. A society consists of various individuals, similar to living organisms, which consist of individual cells.
2. A common purpose — conscious or unconscious — is held by all those individuals.
3. Members of that society share a spiritual bond or interaction over some period of time, analogous to the relationship between the cells that constitute a living organism.
4. All of the individuals assemble and share experiences together at a prescribed place.
5. All of the individuals link together to form an organization, as parts of living organisms unite to form an entire body.
6. Each member shares duties necessary for the continued activity of the group, similar to the functioning of organs in a living body.

SOCIOLOGICAL INSIGHTS ON PURPOSE IN EDUCATION

By way of summary, we may reiterate that society is an organic and psychological grouping of individuals who share a common purpose. Although we speak of psychology, it is not our individual being that we are concerned about but our social being, that is, the side of our character, beliefs, customs, feelings, ideas, and the like that is accountable in group contexts.

It is this social being that modern education seeks to engage and develop. In the past, pedagogy was built on a foundation of ethics and psychology. But this classic, philosophically oriented pedagogy is largely irrelevant as far as the needs of educational practitioners are concerned. Thus, for practicing teachers the importance of ideas and understandings in the field of sociology cannot be overemphasized. It is extremely fortunate for us that Hisatoshi Tanabe and his colleagues have undertaken the translation and introduction into Japan of the book *Sociology*, written by the American sociologist, Lester Ward, as well as the works of Emile Durkheim, founder of the French school of sociology.[8] All of us who care about the quality of education should read such works as these carefully. Education today is a science, and the educator must meet the concerns of society, individual growth, and effective learning through a combination of sociology, psychology, ethics, and pedagogy.

Modes of Human Living

THE VARIETIES OF HUMAN LIFE EXPERIENCE

Education is a human means of human cultivation. Its ends should not be at odds with human ends. Naturally this is not a random proposition. As stated earlier, purpose in education must be determined on the basis of the particular goals and the larger life purpose of the people in the society. Recognizing, however, that there are probably as many variations of purpose in life as there are people of different backgrounds, social classes, and standards of living, how do we proceed to formulate universal human goals? One fruitful approach is to survey the many ways of life among people past and present, in the West as well as in the Orient, staying as close as possible to everyday realities and summarizing them into specific commonalities of human behavior. These may be weighed against our own lives and the lives of others, and if they are truly universal, they should hold true for everyone.

The application of scientific procedures of observation and classification to the human world reveals an all-encompassing purposive order. Just as we can identify cycles and periodic laws that operate over the vast range of natural phenomena, it is possible to identify within the gamut of details and the nearly arbitrary course of human events certain recurrent patterns that prove reliable across the breadth of human experience as the bases for interpersonal relationships, human resource management, and social planning. The essence of human nature can be distinguished from nonessential idiosyncrasies, allowing us to formulate concepts or laws to live by. Thus, various types, or modes, of life experience emerge from the way we live our lives, and they can be helpful conceptual tools in the task of formulating purpose in education.

Various attempts have been made to formulate and classify varieties of human life experience, such as the classifications of behavior motivation proposed by Eduard Spranger and J. F. Herbart's levels of interest.[9] I have yet to be fully satisfied with any of these classifications, however. The Spranger classification, for example, while commendable for its grasp of human life as a psychological progression, fails to see the society for its members. If a psychoanalysis of the individual motives for behavior were our primary concern, such a classification would no doubt suffice. However, as soon as we recognize the basic reality that society is indeed greater than the sum of its members, the classification falls short, and we are left without any way of extrapolating truly human goals. The ground rules we are laying for education demand a higher order of analysis that will more clearly reveal the interplay of individual roles in the life of the society.

MODES OF LIVING AS STAGES IN HUMAN DEVELOPMENT

These considerations have compelled me to search for classifications that are more socially oriented and can better cover the range of human life. Although I have been struggling with this problem for some thirty years, ever since I published my *Geography of Human Life*, I do not feel that the classifications I have developed are in any way final. I offer them here only in the hope that they will challenge others to join in the effort to delineate a clear and undistorted picture of human life.

Let me note again for purposes of clarity that *mode of living* refers to a continuous pattern of activity that is necessary to sustain life, a sociological division of labor, so to speak. Each individual, while acting as a constituent element of the society as a whole, takes on an appropriate portion of the total functions supporting the lives of others and of that whole, and in return each is entitled to some form of support from other members. Imagine, for example, a person living off in a hidden valley or on an uncharted isle, totally removed from any necessity of involvement with other human beings. That person would be forced to carry out all the various tasks of subsistence entirely single-handedly. The decided advantage of cooperative living is that we are assured of all the necessities of life — and more — with a fraction of the work. It is to this participatory aspect of human life that the classification of modes of living addresses itself.

The first and most obvious distinction to be drawn among the ways in which people experience their lives simply recognizes two types of activity: unconscious activity and conscious activity. No one can afford to be conscious moment by moment of everything in life. If people were to pay attention to each and every movement they make, they would never get around to the higher concerns of human consciousness. Such simple procedures are handled as a matter of automatic reflex without need of impinging upon the higher sensory nerve centers of the cerebral cortex, though they would constitute the overwhelming portion of the day's activity if actually taken into account. This fairly self-evident fact of life takes on greater significance when considered in light of the course of human growth.

If we carefully observe the developmental process of human life, we realize that we do not start this unconscious, automatic reflex from birth. Observing a baby just learning to walk, with intense concentration given to every step, we adults realize that our own unconscious, repetitive daily activity must have started with such diligent, conscious practice. Thus, as a result of this capacity to relegate the more tedious mechanical activities, human beings are able to spend more energy in higher, more complex levels of conscious spiritual activity. Clearly there is an economy of mental activity here.

Bringing our scheme of differentiation a step closer to educational application and teaching methodology, we may liken the stages of awareness of one individual to the two poles of governmental organization: centralized government (the conscious life of a nation) and decentralized or local government (the unconscious life of a nation). Under an absolute authoritarian regime, the central government involves itself in each and every decision made. This overinvolvement often results in the neglect of important governmental duties to the detriment of the entire nation. As with the course of individual growth, such centralized attention is inevitable at first, but eventually it proves convenient to grant local authorities some autonomy and to relegate administrative duties to them.

In reality, daily lives cannot be clearly divided into these two categories, conscious and unconscious, but rather into incremental degrees of semiconsciousness between these two poles. By dividing them more precisely, we can identify certain distinguishing characteristics. All living things, plants and animals alike, are driven by the desire for life and the dislike of death and carry out life activities accordingly. This life activity is clearly distinct from the mechanical activity of nonliving matter or other natural phenomena that follow purely physical laws. Even the most humble forms of life—such as worms, slugs, and the like—exhibit defensive or fugitive behavior when in danger of their lives, although they seem to lack mental activity on the order of human consciousness. Netted eels dumped out on the bank of a river make every attempt to escape back into the water, and they appear to assume an attitude of resistance toward humans trying to catch them. Coming to still more complex forms of life such as birds and animals, we clearly observe behavior intended for self-preservation, such as fighting against enemies. Humans have subjectively inferred the presence of consciousness behind such behavior, without any means of communicating with these forms of life. But actually, they are not conscious in the same sense of the word as are human beings.

Applying these analogies to human life, it seems appropriate to make a four-part classification of the types of human behavior:

1. Plantlike behavior   Sleep
                                       Unconscious activity
                                       Absence of self-awareness

2. Animallike behavior   Conscious activity
                                       Absence of self-awareness

3. Individual behavior   Self-awareness
                                       Individually oriented activity

4. Social behavior   Self-awareness
                                       Socially oriented activity

Plantlike Behavior

Sleep halts only one portion of the behavior humans display in waking life. Despite the appearance of reducing all activity to the primal minimum required for survival, certain bodily functions such as digestion actually become more pronounced during deep sleep. The most obvious difference between sleep and waking life, however, is the total absence of consciousness in sleep; the sleeper is unaware of any activity at all. Dreaming is readily distinguishable from waking consciousness, and so need not enter into our present discussion. The blind, physiological behavior of the unconscious sleeping state may be characterized as hardly differing from that of plants.

Animallike Behavior

The activities of our waking hours differ from those of sleep in that we are aware of what transpires, but there is as yet no uniformity or identity to that consciousness. Amid the undiscriminated stream of events, we are without any continuity, and we change moment to moment at the bidding of external stimuli. There exists greater possibility of making something known to the waking mind from outside than in the case of sleep, but it is still doubtful whether a "self" exists at this stage. This lack of self-awareness distinguishes this category from those following. In this odd, halfway state, there is the knowledge that some activity is taking place but no knowledge that we ourselves are doing it or that it yields some outcome. We see without really seeing, hear without actually hearing, eat without tasting. We must depend on others and are totally unaware of even the possibility of self-actualization.

Individual Behavior

While the aspect of conscious activity holds over from the previous stage, a major evolutionary advance is signaled by the advent of self-awareness. As if in acknowledgement of the famous teaching of Socrates, "Know thyself," we are preeminently concerned with ourselves at this point. Although from early childhood we may pay a certain amount of attention to our surroundings and circumstances, and may even help others, as a fact of human nature our whole way of life, our very being, identifies with the goal of satisfying individual needs and desires. In this early stage of self-awareness our behavior is self-centered; moreover, this individual orientation is markedly emotional, then rational by stages.

Social Behavior

A growing awareness of something above and beyond the individual sees the actualized self as instrumental or elemental toward the greater goal of social realization. This becomes the focus of our consciousness at this stage.

Another similar classification according to branches of the sciences suggests itself:

1. Physiological life	An unconscious state of individual existence
2. Psychological life	A state of conscious activity as yet without clear-cut goals
3. Ethical life	Having singled out the ultimate goals of human life, the state of fervent pursuit

Finally, pulling all these criteria together gives us one scheme of classification that might facilitate the establishment of purpose in education and the consideration of teaching methodologies for accomplishing that purpose:

1. Unconscious living	Plantlike, physiological behavior Unconscious activity without self-awareness
2. Semiconscious living	Animallike behavior Undirected sensory existence in dependency
3. Conscious living	Protohuman psychological existence Undirected emotional existence
4. Individually conscious living	Self-awareness identified with the goal of individual fulfillment and nothing higher Conscious pursuit of values of gain and beauty
5. Socially conscious living	Self-awareness focused on the fulfillment of the social whole Conscious pursuit of moral value

EMOTIONAL BEHAVIOR AND RATIONAL BEHAVIOR

The concept of modes of living can also help us understand how emotional behavior and rational behavior shape ways of life. These two modes of experience are distinguishable not only among persons but also within the process of any given individual's psychological development. Emotionality is the dominant factor in a person's behavior in early life, but as one grows older or more mature, emotionality is tempered by reason. Failure of this tempering to occur can strike a disharmonious note in relationships from simple social interaction to international diplomacy. Living in true social harmony requires the maintaining of conditions of peaceful cooperation with others, and this in turn requires a balancing of emotionality and rationality in personal behavior.

Insofar as we can determine, primitive humans did not understand reason. They managed well enough without much thinking, living by their feelings in the circumstances of the moment. And so long as things went smoothly, that was fine. When problems did occur, however, they could be disastrous. The fear that something might go wrong was ever-present, yet these primitive humans accomplished little toward protecting themselves, precisely because they gave no thought to planning for the future.

Civilized people, on the other hand, are distinguished by foresight and the idea of preparing against uncertainties. Herein lie the origins of the life of reason. When something happens, our first thought is to make sense of it in terms of how it affects our lives and to what extent. We seek to repeat favorable occurrences and to avoid or minimize harm. We think out the preconditions that might have led to these things and seek to identify their causes. Notions of causality have become second nature to us. But the real proof is in the replication of the chain of events. Such, of course, is the inductive method.

The life of reason might also be called logical living, for just as the laws of causality function in the natural world, the logical order of life in society will not permit living by subjective likes and dislikes. The person is to be pitied who, although understanding and accepting the validity of these laws of logical reasoning in theory, fails to follow through in personal life, gets immersed in mixed feelings, then loses all confidence in what society has to offer and must learn the value of reason the hard way, not once but time and time again.

CLASSIFICATION OF LIFE BEHAVIOR ACCORDING TO LEVELS OF INTELLECTUAL DEVELOPMENT

At this point we can be assisted in our pursuit of a universal scheme for classifying levels of human experience by referring to Auguste Comte's classification of three stages in the development of human knowledge. His classification explains the sociological aspect of life behavior in contrast to the levels of consciousness as discussed earlier:[10]

1. Theological thinking based on religious beliefs in the supernatural
2. Metaphysical thinking based on causal relationships, ontology, inner principles, and substance
3. Positive thinking based on scientific, empirical knowledge

This progression in humankind's general development can also be seen within the course of individual growth. As educators, we may readily superimpose this developmental scheme onto our observations of children's mental growth, so that we can categorize three distinct periods in their relationship to others and the world around them:

1. Imitative living based on belief and rote pattern
2. Self-determined living based on questioning and dogma
3. Rational, scientific living

During the first period, children show absolute trust in their parents and teachers and obey them unconditionally. It is the role of educators to guide children through this first stage to the second and, eventually, to the third. But all too often this growth does not occur, and thus some persons live out good portions of their lives in blind faith, accepting whatever anyone tells them at face value and modeling themselves entirely upon the dictates and examples of others. Ironically, even educators frequently do little more than mimic their superiors and the "authorities" on pedagogy. Time and time again we hear of bad teaching practices resulting from erroneous transmission or misinterpretation of theories that were believed to the letter.

Belief can be a dangerous thing, and often it is hard to say which is more detrimental, religion or science. Ultimately, though, neither should be followed blindly. For either to lay claim to truth, the order within the universe, which religion affirms as the workings of divine will, must coincide with the natural laws science arrives at from the opposite direction, via inductive experimentation. We should beware of the half-learned scholar who disclaims all others' beliefs in order to dogmatically proclaim his own.

Nonetheless, short of personal experience, belief may well seem the best teacher. It is not unusual for scholars and philosophers to take their studies to such an extreme that their illuminations fall on uncomprehending ears and effect no impact on anyone but that handful of persons who share their views. For the vast majority of people, anything outside the bounds of their own life experience remains unintelligible. People cannot be expected to appreciate abstractions that do not draw upon their own store of experience. The academic may indulge in academic questions, but it is a waste of effort to try to explain them to those who have neither studied nor worked in that field. The adult may well get the child to listen, but listening does not lead to understanding unless the child has the experience to appreciate what is being said. Still the adult often labors the point, and the child is cornered into belief, accepting without actual comprehension. This is acknowledgement of the authority of the person, not acknowledgement of the idea itself. The corollary to this aggrandizement of those older and more learned guardians of truth is to stifle the impulse to attempt solving the problem oneself, believing it is too difficult. Thus many persons do not even bother to look any further than what they have been told.

This tendency to accept blindly the views of some authority or other, even about the most crucial matters affecting our lives, is widespread. No matter how intelligent we might be otherwise, when we are confronted by things that we do not understand or that are difficult to interpret, we do not attempt to think them through ourselves but blindly accept the views of our seniors or others who seem to speak with authority. Even worse, some people depend on fortune-telling, astrology, the *I Ching*, and the like in making decisions about their lives. At the other extreme, we tend to gloss over the simple and commonplace, responding intuitively rather than on the basis of reasoned analysis. Usually we manage well enough, although we also end up having to cope with repeated mistakes, just as operational errors may work into the matrix of an experiment.

In contrast to this childlike tendency to simply believe, without self-reflection or critical examination of accepted views or ideas, the acquisition of experience brings awareness of contradictions and misconceptions, which, in turn, leads to doubts and skepticism. This realization calls for thought. Awareness breeds awareness. Only then can rational living begin. Thus, it can be seen that doubt and skepticism represent an intermediate state leading to rational, scientific life.

The purpose of modern education, then, is to guide children from the primitive period in which they are living to rational, scientific living.

This should not be taken to mean that rational, scientific living contradicts religion. People sometimes think that religion and science are not compatible. But this does not necessarily follow. Scientific truth that is established through inductive reasoning and proven by experiment must be recognized as truth and law within the universe. However, if all phenomena in the universe are manifestations of God, as some religions claim, and if the law of the universe is the will of God, then universal truths that scientists establish through all their painstaking efforts should be compatible with what religion teaches.

MATERIALISTIC AND SPIRITUAL LIVING AS INDIVIDUAL VERSUS SOCIAL EXISTENCE

The contrast between materialism and spirituality offers yet another perspective on human living. Although it is true that humanity does not live by bread alone, neither do the goals of ordinary human endeavor lie outside living itself. No matter how lofty the aim, the quest toward which human beings strive is a better life. People may work toward goals not directly related to the demands of living, but in actuality this is possible only when certain basic necessities of life are secured.

Needless to say, the particular demands of living vary greatly according to the individual, economic class, personal background, and so on. None of these are unique, however. There is no qualitative disparity, only quantitative degrees of orientation such that living at one level readies us for and in fact provides the means to the next. Living on the material level is everyone's initial step. For as the Chinese philosopher, Kuan-tsu, said long ago, "When the granaries are full then you can attend to matters of etiquette and integrity; when you have sufficient clothing and food then you can worry about honor and disgrace."[11] This observation of Kuan-tsu has universal validity. Higher concerns must first have a material basis.

But having recognized this necessary material basis for any kind of spiritual life, we can observe further that value is relative to living. The less people recognize the value of their own lives, the more they overestimate material things. Wage slaves and misers seem to value their money as much as their own lives. They fear for their money as for their very existence. Should they fall seriously ill and have to spend their entire savings on medical treatment, they would likely become acutely conscious of the preciousness of life. Yet as soon as the danger is past, they return to overworking and hoarding money, mindless of how that may shorten their lives.

On the other hand, some people are willing to die in pursuit of their ideals. Artists, for example, who pursue art for art's sake, will actually throw their lives away for the sake of art. A youth who has lost his love might feel that life is not worth living without his sweetheart. In such cases, the purpose of life and the means of fulfilling that purpose have been reversed. Normally, this reversal is a temporary condition that does not last for long. It does not, at any rate, represent an opposition between material life and spiritual life.

Another common misconception is the idea that a person's individual being is inevitably at odds with social existence. Although it may be possible to conceptualize individual versus social life abstractly, in actual daily living it is difficult to differentiate between the two. Every human being is made up of two dimensions that we can theoretically differentiate but that in effect are inseparable. One is a person's individual, spiritual existence; the other is the emotions, thought, beliefs, and habits that represent not an individual but the organizations or society to which an individual belongs. All these combine to form one's social existence, and it is the purpose of education to instill them into the individual person. This brings us back again to my earlier insistence that education must develop in each person a recognition of our indebtedness to society for the maintenance of our lives.

Within this framework, then, and using the absence or presence of social consciousness as criteria, we can perceive two radically different kinds of qualities of life:

1. Individual living focused on material self-satisfaction
2. Social living focused on spiritually uplifting the community

These represent two modes of living whose diametric opposition in both means and ends are readily distinguishable in modern society. And, of course, education should serve to promulgate the latter.

COOPERATIVE AND COMPETITIVE LIVING

Let me repeat what we have just established. Unconscious, individually oriented living focuses on personal material accumulation, whereas conscious, socially oriented living focuses on the spiritual enrichment of the community. This realization can help us to understand the existence within human life of both warm cooperation and fierce competition. For a long time this seemed inexplicably odd to me. How should it be that the same activities and involvements can lead to something so wonderful as mutual reliance and sharing on the one hand and to the hideous tyrannies of distrust and greed on the other? After decades of serious consideration of this matter, I came to the simple conclusion that competitive living is associated with individual consciousness, whereas cooperative living appears on the scene with the dawn of social awareness. As long as individuals think only of themselves, there is no room for ethics. For cooperative and harmonious ethical life to make sense, people must first be receptive to the needs of others. That is, they must already have awakened to an awareness of the meaning and importance of society in the life of the individual person. No amount of preaching will do any good otherwise. Though the individualist living unconsciously by rote pattern may take on the semblance of ethical behavior, everything from within that person's own experience remains in bitter conflict. Preoccupation with self still colors the world, and by no pretense of cooperation can one escape the specter of an anxious struggle for survival.

Cooperative living can develop only as individual persons become able to see their own weaknesses and strengths as well as the weaknesses and strengths of others. Out of this mutual understanding of each other's strengths and weaknesses there can emerge a genuine pooling of efforts that works to the advantage of all concerned. Through clearly recognizing the benefits of their mutual relationships, the members of a community lay the groundwork for the lasting trust that makes living in complete cooperation possible.

If education is to transform those who see life as a struggle to get ahead of others into persons who appreciate and value the rewards of cooperative living, it must raise social consciousness by helping students to know themselves through comparison with others. The school is the ideal environment for such guided exercises in social living.

MODES OF LIVING AS DIVISIONS OF LABOR

We will be better able to understand the nature of this task, and the role of the school in undertaking it, through a consideration of modes of living as divisions of labor. Sociologists classify human social behavior according to various divisions of labor observed among members of the group. One such scheme is as follows:

1. Political activity
2. Economic activity
3. Cultural activity

Other possible classifications might include legal, moral, religious, scholastic, technical, artistic, educational, and other activities, but these merely amount to subdivisions already provided for within the broader threefold framework:

1. Political activity	Legislative
	Administrative
	Judicial
2. Economic activity	Productive
	Exchange
	Distributive
	Consumer
3. Cultural activity	Scholastic
	Artistic
	Religious
	Educational

Economic activity provides the basis for political activity, and these two in turn serve as the foundations on which cultural activities take place. But where exactly do these fit in our construct of modes of living? We have, up to this point, established three classes of human behavior as progressive levels of awareness:

1. Unconscious behavior
2. Conscious behavior
3. Self-reflective behavior (individually conscious living and socially conscious living)

It will be noted that these are derived from phenomenological distinctions inside the subject's own consciousness. When we consider the situation from outside, a completely different picture emerges. Tracing these classes of living back to their objective origins, we clearly perceive two dominant strains within human activities. Laws, for example, are but the preventive and punitive framework of right against wrong, and government but the means by which right combats wrong, or, in other words, the means by which the whole of society seeks to keep or remove an evil-minded few from abusive power. Education and cultural edification, on the other hand, serve to preserve and encourage the rightful order of things.

As humans we are born into society. Every one of us should offer his or her services to society for the good of all in the best way individually possible. No one lives a life apart; no occupation arises independent of the needs of others around us. In the rightful order of mutuality, each person, each labor, is part of the whole. Although mere physiological and psychological subsistence might have been enough as far as the individual is concerned, entering into cooperative social living requires taking the ends of individual life and simultaneously applying them as means to the fulfillment of the greater common life. Needless to say, the means are many, varying according to the unique capacities of the individual and the special characteristics of the social environment. Seen objectively, the diversity of human activity thus falls into different classes of contribution to the life of the society, and under these general headings come the particulars of occupation. In the natural sequence in which they occur in human life, we find

1. dependent living by receiving the efforts of others, with as yet no self-awareness or self-definition
2. self-reliant living by one's own efforts, with self-awareness and defined private self
3. contributive living by extending one's efforts to others, with awareness of a greater self and public self-definition

Or, in terms of energy expenditure:

1. Dependent life	Beneficial life	Living by normal means of support Living by begging
	Extortive life	Living by violence Living by manipulation
2. Exchange life	Economic life Political life Cultural life	
3. Contributive life		

Normally, people live in accordance with society as a whole. When one realizes some factor is missing in society, considers that this lack is problematic to society, and then works to correct it, the general public naturally responds favorably. For example, if one offers a new invention or new merchandise, the public welcomes and gladly utilizes it. When enough profit is expected, one would establish a new business and make a living from it. Instead of dealing with particular individuals, one advertises to the general public and expects the public to pay a fair price. This is a typical example of the second category and can be considered as conscious exchange life.

In contrast, the first category, dependent life, and the third category, contributive life, are unconscious exchange life. In the first category, one is conscious only of receiving but does not intend to give in return. In the third category, one is primarily concerned about giving to society and does not expect to receive compensation. In this contributive life one strives for the prosperity and happiness of the society as a whole without any conscious expectation of reward. Persons who thus contribute to society without thought for their own lives will receive respect from society. Even though they may not receive corresponding financial support from the society, their effort is compensated in some form that guarantees their existence in the world.

In essence, then, this whole scheme of classification is divided into two categories: exchange of material with material or exchange of material with spiritual. Since each element of society is interlinked spatially and temporally, one element cannot live life in absolute isolation from others, that is, without giving or receiving. Therefore, behavior in society can be classified as the exchange of material with material, material with immaterial, and immaterial with immaterial; or, from another standpoint, as conscious exchange and unconscious exchange; or, from still another standpoint, as direct exchange and indirect exchange.

Even an infant, for example, protected in its mother's bosom with no power other than growth, can be a cause for cultivating parental love, thus contributing to domestic felicity and thereby contributing to the prosperity of the entire family. Hence, even the life of an infant cannot be classified as simple dependence.

These considerations suggest that the classifications discussed in this section are not exactly specializations or divisions of labor but rather categories of participation. In other words, if divisions of labor constitute a static classification of society, these categories of participation could be considered a developmental classification.

If we combine all of these elements in such a way as to focus upon classes of participation in social exchange with our earlier concern about becoming or self-actualization, we have a classification of human behavior as follows:

1. Antisocial interaction	Blind living as a parasite or puppet with no self-awareness
2. Pseudosocial interaction	Obscure living as independent individual with partial self-awareness
3. True social interaction	Enlightened living as leader or contributor with total self-awareness

MODES OF LIVING IN RELATION TO ENVIRONMENT

We must now go on to recognize that human living is defined to a great extent by the conscious physical and mental interplay between people and their environment. Hence it may be useful to categorize the living according to four distinct grounds for activity:

Ground for activity	Relationship	Governing law
1. Nature	Subjection Harmonizing Conflict Conquest	Physical law
2. Individuals	Conflict Cooperation	Psychological principle Social (public and private) law Politics Economy
3. Society	Participation	Ethics Morality Social mores
4. Universe	Cause and effect	Causal law Religious principle

Our attitude toward nature must first be one of recognizing that we are creatures of nature and subject to its physical laws. But do we seek simply to follow the "natural course" of things? Or do we seek to triumph over nature? A third possibility chooses the path of moderation, both harmonizing with nature and also utilizing it directly or indirectly for our benefit. We may even to a degree domesticate nature to our ends, gaining all of the advantages with none of the dangers of its conquest. The key here is seeking a relationship of calm intellectual interplay between us and the environment.

In our relationships with our peers we bring forth feelings and emotions. Moreover, because we are a relational object for others as much as they are for us, we seek to establish our own relative position or identity. This requires mastery of the self through will. Self-reflection allows us to discover the principles that govern our existence, and by bringing our actions in line with knowledge through these principles we can achieve a life of sympathetic communion with others. We uncover the basic commonalities of spirit and thought that underscore our sense of fairness, exchange value, self-gain, and the benefit of others — the foundations of our political and economic livelihood — though as yet self and others are blind to goals higher than those involving security.

It is through recognizing ourselves as belonging to a society greater than the sum of its members and by engaging our lives with the life of the greater unity that we attain the vision of ethics. We must from this point on behave in either conscious challenge or obedience to the collective social mores.

When faced with the ultimate questions of life and death, we stand humbled before the vast and unknowable universe. Even our wisest sages and scholars, our heroes and creative talents, are helpless specks in the totality of all creation. To weigh our tiny lives in the balance is to call up religion, although in fact our social existence can be seen as a part of this consciousness. Here we may discover the link between religion and morality.

MODES OF LIVING IN RELATION TO TIME

Finally, we must recognize the relationship between modes of human living and time. We live in the present, a point in time from which we may, nonetheless, review the past and make preparations to pursue our hopes for the future. However, some people use the present as a preparatory stage for the future. Others think only of the past and regard the present as an effect of the past. Still others become so busily absorbed in the activities of the moment that they consider neither past nor future. Such persons live totally in the moment, immersed in the undiscriminated stream of phenomena, the ceaseless rise and fall of places, objects, and events, leaving no room for looking forward or backward.

The detachment wherein we gain a balanced perspective of time comes only with time. This can be appreciated if we consider this matter from the standpoint of age development. In infancy the present and immediate past consume our attention, and we do not lift our eyes from our immediate circumstances to even consider the future. In youth, ideals and hopes soar, but foundations are lacking. All too often we stumble and fall for failure to give attention to where our feet tread at the present moment. In old age, on the other hand, material wishes for the future recede as our thoughts drift more and more to reminiscing. Our minds tend to stagnate, and we become more and more conservative in outlook.

These three types of activity can, then, be observed in the life span of any given individual. In addition, because of different circumstances of the individual from birth, and the interaction of social with spiritual life, either optimistic or pessimistic orientations to life are created. Thus, six different modes of life can be identified in reference to time:

1. Immediate stimulus-response action in the present
   a. Optimistic
   b. Pessimistic
2. Anticipatory and preparatory activity for the future
   a. Optimistic
   b. Pessimistic
3. Reflective and summative activity toward the past
   a. Optimistic
   b. Pessimistic

Education should contribute toward helping children and young people develop a positive, optimistic outlook toward life and an effective balance in their relationship to the past, the present, and the future.

Educational Purpose and Creativity

Having already established that the rightful purpose of education is the enabling of students to create value, I propose to consider the question of value in detail in Chapter 2. This leaves us with the still-undefined property of creativity to deal with.

We should first note that creativity appears to be a unique feature of human education. Although other animals receive guidance from their parents and may possibly come to surpass them in the skills acquired, their behavior is instinctive and goes on for generation after generation without any difference in their patterns of association. Behavioral changes in animals entail physical modifications in the organism — this, in fact, is what is meant by evolution — whereas human learning does not come to be structured into the bodily makeup or genetic information. The abilities one generation learns for itself do not get passed on to the next except through the medium of education. It is this comparatively open and unstructured nature of human learning that accounts for human creativity.

Humans cannot increase or decrease the quantum forces or matter found in nature. However, they can control them to create what is of value to themselves. Whether it is termed originality or discovery, we have the power to change the form of and to redirect whatever nature offers to the benefit of humanity. In doing so, we are guided by our own freely established or acknowledged purpose with respect to human life.

If education is to achieve its purpose of fostering the abilities of students to create value toward the well-being of all of society as well as themselves, it must diversify its efforts into three methodological areas: the nurturing of virtue, of benefit, and of beauty. Each constitutes but one side of the complete human personality; none is sufficient of itself. If there is to be full development of the human personality, this kind of threefold education is a necessity.

The Evolution of Purpose in Education

People everywhere in the world inevitably have their age of enlightenment when they begin to intuit a need, however vaguely perceived, for education. They begin teaching and in the process learn to teach. As initially dim perceptions of educational needs resolve into ever sharper conceptions of education's role in society, awareness of ends and means grows in unison with the increasing numbers of persons to be educated. Expansion follows expansion, bringing about growth and integration of content and methodology.

Two distinct trends can be discerned in the historical evolution of educational purpose. First, there is a trend away from concentration on particular skills and separate fields of study corresponding to bits and pieces of the human character and toward a more holistic approach to the total person. This is not to say that the three R's should not be taught, for the ideal person as conceived by both parents and teachers would of course find these basic skills necessary and invaluable. The issue is what is important to the integral person, not what the building blocks to be combined piecemeal are. Beyond the individual the trend continues to relate the individual to the regional environment and eventually to the whole of society. Likewise, we see education catering less and less to certain groups and classes in society and instead reaching out to all persons.

The second trend is toward a recognition that humans must be able to coexist with their environment, both natural and societal. Here three historical periods can be discerned:

1. The age of specialized education directed toward providing individuals with skills appropriate to their social class. Members of the aristocracy were taught the morality and literary skills expected of their status, warriors were trained in chivalry and martial arts, and merchants in business and bookkeeping skills.
2. The age of general education common to all classes as necessary to round out individual life. In this stage education is seen primarily as a means to one's own gain; individual existence is the central concern, and the importance and needs of social life are largely unrecognized. Common people consider the political process as little more than the means used by society's leaders to pursue their own gain, and, consequently, the common people resist "the system" in pursuit of their own unlimited individual freedoms.
3. The age of total education in conscious acknowledgement of individuals as constituents in the overall body and life of the society. The true realization of complete social well-being is seen as the greatest good. When the members of a society achieve this condition, its he-

roes and leaders no longer perceive the common people as the means to their own individual ends but offer their contributive efforts to meet the needs of society.

When we analyze our own experience in Japan in terms of these historic trends, we observe that education traveled vertically downward, spreading from class to class along lines of political control and influence. Parallel to the general broadening of economic bases for material affluence, what was once the exclusive prerogative of the aristocracy eventually filtered down through the lords and warrior classes to the populace at large, though by the time learning had reached the common classes, the feudal system itself was breaking down. The limited emphasis on inculcating the morality of feudalism had likewise expanded into a more egalitarian view of education as providing everyone with knowledge and skills for the tasks of living and modernization. During the transition from the Meiji (1868–1912) to the Taisho (1912–26) periods, educational purpose was clearly conceived in terms of utility. Cultural concerns and objectives still lay further ahead in the course of democratic growth.

Today in Japan, peer pressure and fashion constitute the major motivating factors in the lives of most people. Such mindless imitation still is the strongest incentive to learning for many. Thus, we can see that Japan is still in the second stage of historical development as far as the evolution of educational purpose is concerned. The question that faces us now is whether education in Japan can make the shift to the third stage, with its universalistic and societal orientation. In any case, henceforth our primary task and challenge is to promote the cause of total education.

2

The Fundamentals of Value

In approaching the question of value, the first problem we are likely to encounter, and hence the first order of conceptual clarification, is to determine the nature of value relative to truth. The issue itself has a considerable history, and many are the philosophers who have posited truth as a form of theoretical value or as an element within a truth-good-beauty continuum on which their value systems are based. However, this only begs the question and prevents us from understanding either value or truth.

A phenomenological examination of the distinct psychological processes of cognition and evaluation will do much to show how utterly different truth and value actually are. This necessitates the breaking down of the "self-evident" order of the values truth, good, and beauty heretofore accepted in philosophy before we build a newer, better model of explanation. Let us consider the possibility of establishing a science of evaluation to provide us with standards by which to weigh and set values, just as the conceptual framework of logic already offers us rules by which to recognize truth.

Value and Education

Both educational theory and economics, as branches of social science, find their object of study in value. Yet, with education, the

53

question of value is, if anything, more difficult. I have struggled with this problem for many years, and I still cannot claim to have arrived at any definitive answer. It is because the issues involved so urgently need to be addressed that I feel I must present what understanding I have.

One might ask why I focus on value and struggle so obstinately over such a difficult problem? I believe the effort is necessary if we are to make sense of education or, rather, if we are to create a system of education that makes sense in human terms. Human life is a process of creating value, and education should guide us toward that end. Thus educational practices should serve to promote value creation. The point is of profound importance, and the more we reflect on it in social context, the more meaningful the conceptual clarification of value becomes.

Human dignity arises from value creation. One scholar has gone so far as to proclaim that the creation of value is the highest form of human activity. Everyone has to play his or her own role in the workplace of humanity in order to create values to meet the inexhaustible demands of living. Education can do much to fulfill this fundamental human promise. There is no need to nurse regrets for past errors; rather, educators should intensify their efforts to revitalize education into something that will foster active involvement of persons in the creation of value. But the question remains as to just how educators can relate to the problem of creating value.

It should be readily apparent that for better or worse we are what we learn. There is every reason, then, to choose education for better. We have already seen that we live in varying degrees of conscious pursuit of happiness, fulfillment, and self-actualization, goals that shape purpose in education. To live to the full realization of one's potential is to attain and actualize values. Helping us learn to live as creators of value is the purpose of education.

The consideration of value must not stop at philosophical speculation, for such consideration can provide principles for determining the direction of education as well. Real education must deal with life as the learners live it. It is the failure to do this, up to the present time, that has made education ineffective and irrelevant. Value is a real-life concern with real-life applications. Educators must come to recognize how important value is to both human life and human learning.

Cognition and Evaluation

TRUTH AND VALUE

In order to clarify our concepts of value, we must first distinguish those concepts rightfully belonging under that heading from those to be excluded. Here it becomes crucial to differentiate between truth and value and to make sure that the relationship between the two is really understood. In seeking to discover a truth, we isolate some commonality or universal property from among the myriad objects of the universe. With value, however, we attempt to determine the particular or uniquely characteristic way in which some object differs from all others in its relationship to our own lives and to the life of the community. Thus an expression of things as they are is recognized to be a fact or truth, whereas an expression of the relation between self and object is value. Truth remains purely a concept, the true conception of some object or of an interrelationship between objects. Value, on the other hand, takes on the character of an emotional bond bringing the object into human life. Totally unlike truth, which identifies an object in its essential qualities, value emerges as the measure of the appropriateness of the object for the evaluator.

Humans take no heed of things that have no bearing on them. They often go without noticing that such things even exist. It is only those things with some effect upon us that demand distinct awareness and acquire a sense of personal immediacy. And the more critical these things are to our life, the less we can afford to ignore them.

This is reflected quite graphically in the difference between wild beasts and domesticated animals – a difference resting precisely with the presence or absence of the human factor. At first, people left beasts alone as irrelevant to human life. Then something prompted them to notice a certain docile order and adaptability to the behavior patterns of animals and people started to keep animals around where they seemed useful, eventually taming them by conscious design. Experiments in domestication proved beneficial and practical, so the practice spread. The depth to which this symbiotic interdependence of animals and humans has gone on to penetrate and "civilize" our consciousness is testimony to the value we place on our dealings with animals. The human-animal connection has clearly been acknowledged as valuable.

By contrast, the concept of truth rests on verisimilitude, the expression of that which is as it is. Here we are to look on reality unemotionally. Regardless of what bearing it may or may not have on human life, truth is truth, while concepts of value cannot be formulated independent of some fundamental relatedness to the reality we live.

There is a definite epistemological progression to all of this. Reality at its most elemental begins with signals transmitted via the sensory organs, which are then assembled into images and further structured into ideas. The impact of perception on the system does not stop at mere sense stimulation, however. More than that minute amount of energy involved in the triggering, the perceptual information, once entered into the system, forces difference or change upon the life of the person. The living organism meets this challenge to the status quo either with acceptance or approval or with resistance and rejection; hence we are moved to feel pleased or displeased. The standards we establish on the basis of this process of subjectively relating the perceptual object to ourselves are termed values by societal consensus. And the ideas we abstract from those characteristics of greatest consistency and commonality among such perceptual objects are said to be truths.

Truth implies an objectified treatment of perceptual data so as to isolate like qualities, whereas value connotes a subjective reaction to the affective quotient or the quantity of influence that the perceptual data is felt to exert on our being. The cognition of truth is a yes-no proposition: This is true, and that is false, with no middle ground for passing judgement. On the other hand, the determination of value is entirely relative: This seems appropriate, and that inappropriate, in relation to our viewpoint, laying no claim to a discovery of true identity. Truth does not vary with the person or the times, but values cannot be separated from people.

The difference in human terms could not be greater. Truth cannot be created; we can only bring out what is already latent in nature. We can, on the contrary, create values, and in fact values are there for the making. All natural materials utilized by humans in daily life were originally used exactly as they were found in nature without seeking further value in them. But as the centuries passed, experience, inventiveness, and sheer effort on the part of humanity wrought marked improvements and commensurate increases in utility. Such has been the course of progress up to the present day.

When we speak of creation, we refer to the process of bringing to light whatever has bearing on human life from among elements already existing in nature, evaluating these discoveries, and through the addition of human effort further enhancing that relevancy. In other words, creation reworks the "found order" of nature into an order with special benefits for humanity. Strictly speaking, then, *creation* applies only to value and not to truth, for truth stops at the point of discovery.

Of course, there are times when we may just discover value. To highlight things that were simply never noticed before and make them apparent is an act of discovery, not creation. But when someone brings together previously unrelated things to the manifest benefit of humankind or builds upon earlier works to increase their relevance, that is called invention, origination, or creation.

Even from this rather brief survey of the issues involved, it should be clear that truth must not be mistaken for value nor vice versa. Blind deference to what our seniors and predecessors may have believed does not make anything true. Truth does not allow us to select the theory we favor most among the literature in the offhand presumption that each must have its own merits. We are not choosing lenses for a camera. But neither should we discard one set of values as wholly invalid merely because it contradicts another, as if they were mutually exclusive, true or false. Values may coexist to some degree where appropriate; truth is solitary.

Truth demands proof. No matter how eloquent or profuse the explanations, without actual evidence the truth of the matter must remain in question. Furthermore, the correctness of a proposition is to be ascertained through careful, rational consideration, not how we feel about it. Proper studies, as the term implies, need to maintain a propriety free from emotional leanings, free from our likes and dislikes, lest the universal self-consistency of the matter be forfeited. Feelings are rather the province of evaluating how we as the subjects of our own emotional universe interact with things; they cannot be more than that. Hence it profits us little to try to recognize truth via evaluation. Indeed, what a waste of effort! To forget this is to court disaster.

Let us take an example. Suppose there is news of an earthquake or a fire. Those with some stake in the existing situation would first want to check out the facts. Did such a thing take place or not? If it did, the reports were true; if not, they were false. There is no leeway here for judgement good or bad. Aesthetic evaluations are uncalled for. The truth or falsehood of the news is not a matter of degree. The most we could possibly say is that some aspect of the event itself was better or worse than it might have been. We are free to compare among facts: Twenty-degree water feels warm to hands used to ten-degree water but cool to hands with a thirty-degree acclimation. That much is relative.

Yet this is something quite apart from likes and dislikes, and something else again from their subjective basis in beauty, good, and benefit. These know no universality. What is beautiful to some is but an eyesore to others; one person's gain is another's loss. And although good and benefit actually differ only slightly in essence, neither are they invariable. They involve subjective judgements, whether by the society as a whole or by individuals. This difference in the scale of the evaluator is, incidentally, all that distinguishes the values of benefit and good. Benefit and detriment evaluate the means to each person's own survival, and good and bad the intentional activities of people with respect to the continued well-being of the society as a whole.

It is a common human trait not to like what we perceive as bad, ugly, or detrimental, but this says nothing about the truth or falsehood of the things we regard. It will not do to call a waterfall a river; that would be a false label. On the other hand, the reality of the waterfall goes unchanged regardless of what we call it. It is what it is. Only the verbal description is in question, and that is either accurate or misleading. The point is that once reality has been identified as a waterfall, it remains a waterfall for purposes of human communication, irrespective of what it might mean in the balance of human life. At any rate, no one ever liked or disliked something because it was true or false.

Contrary to the widely accepted notion that it is human nature to strive for truth, pure truth would be of no value to people. The classic three-point philosophical ideal of truth, good, and beauty is inadequate when truth proves to be unconcerned with value. Concepts of good and beauty are not in the same category as truth. Value concepts cannot bring us any closer to the ultimate reality of anything, whereas truth is by definition an ultimate concept in itself. We are powerless to explain any further in words what truth is; we can only know it via our intuitive faculties. With value, we have something else to turn to, for behind it there is the concept of subject-object relationship. Value cannot be proven through intellectual activity. The strength of the relationship between subject and object that quantifies value must be tested in actual practice. Only then can we know for sure how much the object affects us.

In light of the above line of reasoning it should be eminently clear that ideological mixtures of truth and value such as the pragmatist doctrine that views truth as "theoretical value" are fallacious. Pragmatism explains it thus: The more universal the validity, that is to say, the greater the applicability, the higher the value approaches that "theoretical value" called truth. Saying that truth and value are in essence the same, differing in degree but not in kind, we have plunged into the worst sort of semantic morass. We will find ourselves confronting statements to the effect that on the scale of value, something can be true because it is useful. The imprecision here is obvious. To clear up this misuse of language, we must either demonstrate that utility in human life alone is enough to make things true, or draw a sharp line between truth and value so as to render them into distinct logical types or conceptual categories. Short of embracing extreme utilitarian reductionism, nothing in our daily life would seem to support the necessary inverse equation that truth makes things useful. All of us surely know facts that are utterly inapplicable to our lives.

The pursuit of truth inevitably goes on whether or not it yields anything particularly useful. At the very least, we must grant that all the great discoveries and major inventions since time immemorial were not necessarily motivated by a view to material welfare alone. But then neither should we jump to the conclusion that in their love for humankind, great minds are above dealing with practical concerns.

I will not say the pursuit of truth is selfish, for both verification and value creation are necessary, but without selflessly providing good for all, truth has no meaning. In this the humanist will concur with the pragmatist: We cannot live truth; we must live value. Life may give us access to truth, but it forges ahead on value. Life looks on at truth, but it comes in contact with value. Once again, values denote the extent to which things reach into our lives and touch us, as judged against the standards of beauty, good, and benefit, but truth keeps its distance in pure discriminative activity. And well we should exact a distance between them, too, lest the truth-good-beauty confusion resurface in some other form. At the risk of belaboring the point, let us reexamine the distinction from yet another perspective.

Truth is immutable, whereas value changes. Yet even this is not beyond challenge. There are scoffers, self-styled skeptics, who doubt the constancy of truth. Consider Ptolemaic cosmology. It was long revered as truth, but it was all too soon overturned with the advent of the Copernican theory. What guarantee do we have that our most cherished truths will not befall the same fate? How much more does this forebode ill for the temperamental trends of education? Certainly, not a few scholars maintain that principles of educational methodology and the like can never presume to be fixed and invariable truths.

But first, may we not take argument with the argument? Who among the doubters have such strong conviction that they would apply this same severity of skepticism to their own lives, paring down their daily activities to the minimum core certainties, perhaps halting them altogether? Is anyone so thorough in critical method as to doubt or even deny the most trivial details of reasoning? Where does common sense part ways with truth that truth ceases to be suspect?

Even a three-year-old child knows that a moving train will not derail save under extenuating circumstances. The consistent skeptic ought to doubt this. Place a kettle on the burner, and the water inside will come to a boil, eventually steaming away to nothing. No more commonplace yet forthright demonstration of the truth of causality could there possibly be. The day that people took to doubting even this, there would not be a moment's rest from worry. Never in all history has there been a fire that failed to boil water, nor has anyone found cause to think there might be water that would not turn to steam. Would any great scholar care to come forward to refute the truth of these facts, as Copernicus took it upon himself to challenge the old view? The fallacy of the skeptic argument is that the logic leveled against the extremes is not carried through to everyday life. Just what makes it safe to sit comfortably amid the furnishings of day-to-day conventions while proceeding to batter the very architecture of rational assumptions? How are commonsense truths excused from the ravages brought on by more theoretical truths?

Some would protest that they are not the same class of truth. But can there be two types of truth? We readily accept the reality of our daily life, so why should we doubt other truth when it is sufficiently proved? And what about the overthrow of the Ptolemaic worldview? It was surely believed to be absolute truth in its day, but it was overthrown. Such belief is not scientific proof, as was shown by Copernicus. But might not the theories we believe today be dashed to pieces at some future date by the appearance of a new and more exact truth? The argument could go on ad infinitum on mere conjecture, though there would be little point to it. To embrace uncertainty about every last fact would not necessarily bring us any closer to truth. At any rate, why should we immediately reject all truths because an unscientific belief was once toppled? The real misconception that leads to all this uneasiness is the undue reverence for truth as something lofty and profound. What then is the intrinsic nature of truth? My conviction is simply that truth is the expression of the object exactly as it is, nothing more. Hence the problem in doubting truths recognized via proper scientific study typically lies not with the truths but with some instability or irregularity on the part of the doubters themselves. We observe this frequently in the world around us.

Then what about value and how it changes? Unlike truth, as we have stated before, value knows no constancy or consistency. We all know from common experience that something can be of vital importance to one and totally useless to another or can at least differ in relative degree of necessity. And it is well known that the same object will change radically in value for even the same person over time. It therefore goes without saying that value varies according to the circumstances that surround it.

Whereas truth expresses the object as it is in essence, which is to say, in its invariable characteristics as ascertained through objective observation, value arises from the relationship between the evaluating subject and the object of evaluation. If either changes relative to the other, it is only obvious that the perceived value will change. The differences and shifts in ethical codes throughout history provide but one of the more outstanding proofs of the mutability of value.

Paradoxical as it might seem, there is no contradiction in this definition: It is an invariable truth that value changes. The object that changes (value) is not to be confused with the faithful representation of it (truth). And what is science if not the systematic organization of faithful representations of the world, of concepts found repeatedly valid and universal, selectively discerned and abstracted from our ever-changing environment? What real truths can there be but the unchanging principles obtained by the scientific method? Rather than a formal proof, this is only a popularized exposition, but it will suffice for now. I will expand upon the nature of truth in more detail later, but my present purpose is simply to sharpen the delineation between value and truth on the basis of the plain and immediate contrast of changing and permanent properties. In doing so, I realize that I am only rehashing the two-thousand-year-old debate between Socrates and Protagoras. The contention between those who argue for a fixed and absolute truth versus the skeptics who view people as the measure of all things persists even to this day. The pragmatists take utility for truth, echoing Protagoras in his challenge to a rarified, constant truth. I would interpret his assertion to mean that ethical codes can and will change through the ages relative to the reality of things, a truth that in itself remains unchangeable. What he said is undoubtedly true of value, for therein the person must be the measure of all. Be that as it may, it is rather strange that this bickering and juggling of words has gone on for so long, because this kind of problem can be easily solved by making a clear distinction between the concepts of value and truth.

I look at the world as it is today and find nothing so insidious as this confusion between truth and value, cognition and evaluation. Mixing the two constricts actual understanding and prevents people from assuming an attitude of clarity and responsibility toward their chosen positions. Even otherwise knowledgeable intellectuals fail to see the extent to which this indistinction permeates their everyday speech. They discuss matters quite fastidiously but take no heed as they arbitrarily pass judgement, merely couching their personal likes and dislikes in the trappings of learning. There is no end to the ways people can be misguided in their thinking and actions.

Some would suggest that morality might be legislated or that ceremonious recitation of precepts for education would actually promote learning. But however solemn or exalting the tributes paid to principle, without understanding there is but empty formality and sham. Value judgements properly follow comprehension of the facts. The distinction is especially crucial in education. This is not to say that we should not have precepts of education, only that we must really know them before we value them so highly. Blind obedience provides no way out and, more important, no way to increase what we already know.

Suppose a student asks his teacher, "What does this mean?" and the teacher snaps back the reprimand, "What do you mean? Don't you understand that yet?" The teacher obviously confuses evaluation with cognition. The student did not ask for an evaluation of his ability; he was asking for information or for instruction on a point he did not understand. Critical evaluation of the person, if made at all, must be made after comprehension. A teacher does not further learning by turning on the questioner and diverting attention to wholly unrelated points. By ignoring the intention of the questioner and what is really sought, such a teacher not only abuses the intelligence of the students but is not even teaching in any honest sense of the word. This, unfortunately, is the way of disciplinarians. The teacher who gets irritated and scolds the student because of slow progress, or who takes the cognitive process for granted and assumes the attainment of more understanding than the student has actually acquired, subverts the learning process. Such a teacher creates an ever more insuperable gap between the student and what is to be learned. Regrettably, similar leaps of judgement past the facts are encountered at every level of society—in government, in business, and in the home. People stray from the real pursuit of knowledge, of the facts, of truth; civil discussions turn into quarrels and strained relations, not so much because of slips on the subtleties of words as because of plain confusion over truth and value, cognition and evaluation.

To avoid any more confusion, let us summarize our discussion thus far:

1. Truth	Spatial concepts	Recognition of the intrinsic nature of form, substance, and reality
	Temporal laws	Recognition of the intrinsic nature of change and permanence

2. Value	Aesthetics		Judgements on beauty
	Advantage	Private gain	Judgements on benefit
		Public gain	Judgements on good

COGNITION AND EVALUATION

We can recognize within our mental life the two wholly distinct activities of cognition and evaluation. Because the two are generally taken to be one and the same, few pay attention to the differences, much less understand them. Yet as with truth and value, the confusion hinders our epistemological progress considerably, so we must duly distinguish the two.

The mental operation by which we know things intellectually is termed cognition. Evaluation, as the word implies, involves placing a value upon things, or judging. As mental phenomena, both are but manifestations of the same unified psychology, related but not identical. As we have already indicated, cognition, the perception of the thing among things, is objective, and evaluation, the perception of the thing in relation to the self, is subjective. With the former, we are dealing with universals, whereas with the latter, standards are emotional and may depend as much on mood as on the outward reality.

The objects of cognition need not, of course, be limited to fixed or stationary substances alone but may include variable dynamic phenomena such as the abstract notion of change itself. Cognition is therefore possessed of the capacity to contrast as well as compare and discriminate. It is the mind's working to compose an accurate picture of the world.

Cognition affirms for us whether something is or is not, identifying it with something that was previously encountered and noting sameness or difference. For example, the statement "This is a dog" compares the thing before our eyes against the mental store of things seen, disallows its resemblance to anything else, and places it among the class of things labeled "dogs," in that it embodies the characteristics of a dog. The cognition "A dog is a mammal" involves no new perception but merely likens and distinguishes two predetermined conceptual sets. In either case some point of reference is assumed; we can recognize only that with which we are already acquainted.

A certain amount of cross-referencing is implicit in evaluation as well. The operation of the mind in distinguishing, say, beauty and ugliness and in passing judgement on a perceptual object as like or unlike our conception of beauty, works the same as in cognition. However, here we do not attend to the what or why of the matter. Rather we go a step beyond the presumed existence or nonexistence, truth or falsehood, setting our mind on how much it relates to us positively or negatively. Thus, whereas cognition determines truth by sifting out contradictions, inconsistencies, and impossibilities, evaluation weighs value on the scales of relativity, complementation, and opposition.

Needless to say, the two processes are in continual interplay, but as a careful consideration of our daily life will show, there are three predominant patterns by which we deal with the phenomena of our living environment: We may make evaluations after having reached a thorough cognition, attempt cognition only after our evaluations, or evaluate things without any definite cognition at all. Perhaps we are shopping for some item for the home. Having first studied the market to learn what is available to meet our needs, we might arrive at the evaluation that an item is worth buying. Or we could simply desire it because it is in fashion or because others have recommended it. Many times this is done in the vague conviction that our evaluations are facts, mistaking them for cognition. Sometimes we will not even try to look into something until we know that it is "supposed to be good."

The same patterns hold in the case of evaluating a person's character. There are people who side with someone solely on the basis of reputation, without actually seeing or listening or getting to know that person for themselves. Even those who are not hasty to assert their views until they have looked into the situation in some detail may gradually shift in their opinions under the sway of the general consensus. At first they may hold a person in high regard, but later they conclude that where there's smoke, there's fire, and they come to think there really must be some fault behind the bad reputation. In most cases this is how public opinion prevails in society.

This can prove to be the source of numerous social weaknesses. Citizens who will not even give an opening to understanding unless they already favor a particular view will mindlessly believe every word uttered by some respected figure whether what the person says is true or not. Yet, on the other hand, every one of us lives in greater or lesser dependence on the judgement of others in areas outside our own expertise because no one can possibly come to an accurate understanding of everything all by oneself.

Nonetheless, people do tend to confuse cognition and evaluation. The problems occur in combination; thus evaluation often takes the place of cognition, or evaluation bases itself on incorrect cognition. Hence we have doctors and lawyers who become unduly concerned with cutting a dapper, well-kept figure because clients judge by appearances rather than inquiring into their actual abilities. The modish young woman's finery is likewise the measure of the degree to which she readies herself against the judgemental eye of onlookers.

Such imbalances between cognition and evaluation as these, however, are no reason to try to do away with evaluation altogether. If indeed, as I believe, cognition and evaluation are the only ways we can deal with the external world, then we would be foolish to discard either. We must use both to obtain the fullest, most penetrating picture we can.

Our existence in the world and of the world resists the wait-and-see attitude of the bystander that sets externals at odds with our internal state and effectively denies the inward reality of others. We must experience, but we must interact as well. Put this way, our dealings with the world more nearly approximate our own phenomenology:

1. Experience — sensory or intellectual activity
2. Interaction — sensual or emotional activity

Scientists from Galileo on have striven to adopt the former attitude, to purge themselves of emotional and subjective elements while maintaining a third-person view on the object of investigation as if it bore no relation to themselves. Every attempt is made to avoid empathizing with the object—understandable perhaps, because scientists do not want to make the sort of premature judgements based on subjective emotion to which the unscientific are prone. Yet the cure is often as bad as the illness. When taken to the extreme, this preoccupation with objectivity can lead scientists to arrive at the narrowest, most shortsighted conclusions because of lack of synthesis. Outstanding scientists may thus become intellectual reductionists and regard their cognitions as the entirety of the object investigated. They cling to principle and ignore feelings and hunches that arise even in the course of research, let alone further application toward value. What stays in their minds to clog their thinking is the dregs of knowledge—objective but dead afterimages.

This attitude is a negation of the real aims of science. If we are to learn all there is to know about the mental and physical world, we must fully develop a harmonious cooperation between experience and interaction, lest we find ourselves snared by prejudice. Bergson speaks to this point when he says that scientists, otherwise without access to the inner sanctum of things because of their viewing only the externals, must be provided with "sympathy" to know things, especially in their inner life.[1]

At first glance, pure unadulterated experience and emotive interaction would seem mutually exclusive; yet, fundamentally, the psyche is never dichotomized part against part. Reason and emotion are both parts of the same whole, just as reality is never actually divided. If we are to reflect the whole of reality, we must use the whole mirror of the mind. This echoes Dilthey's call for education to engage the whole person: reason, emotion, and will.[2] The search for educational means will also find in this a call for practices underscoring the mind-body unity by which we live in the world. But at the very least that, too, would imply the necessity of both experience and interaction, cognitive and evaluative activity.

Here, then, is how we might apply these ideas to a twofold scheme of educational orientation:

1. Sensory, intellectual approach to understanding—experience—
   thinking

2. Emotional, intuitive approach to understanding—interaction—
   feeling

Comprehensive orientation to life

Cognition

COGNITIVE PROCESSES

As we have seen, cognition employs the two opposite and complementary processes of differentiation and analogy to affirm what a perceived object is or is not. These functions at their most fundamental and primitive are apparent among animals. Fish distinguish which bait seems edible, and apparently even plants select the nutrients they need. There is no cause to insist on the discriminative abilities of plants, of course, but at the very least we can recognize a certain evolutionary basis for human cognition. Our consciousness is decidedly more complex, yet there are correspondences to what we see as instinct in the nonhuman world. If we see cognition as the transfer of outward physical reality into inward conceptual reality through the medium of language, however, it becomes an exclusively human phenomenon.

Implicit in the formal and verbal languages that govern our processing of perceptual and conceptual information are typing and recall. In fact, probably all that we are aware of as we seek to place some newly encountered phenomenon is that something brushes our memory and we discover various aspects of it that are analogous to past experience. Thus the mind discriminates identity from differences among temporal as well as spatial contingencies. And, much more than simple comparison and contrast, the mind undertakes to reason with its cognitions; that is, in addition to powers of discrimination, our cognitive processes draw on faculties of analysis in forming concepts.

Reasoning or inference is the progression toward a convergence of ideas or the serial development of concepts toward a unified picture of our world. This pursuit of mental synthesis attempts to penetrate beyond the outward appearance of seemingly disparate phenomena and get to the inner order among things: the underlying content and structure, the organism or mechanism common to individual objects of cognition. Here we are building principles and cognitive patterns through repeated recall and typing. We abstract parallels and latent commonalities, slowly gaining proficiency at our scheme of metatyping. We come to weigh seemingly conflicting cognitions in order to ascertain the "truer" truth. For example, we are able to recognize someone as the person we knew three years ago even though humans change every moment they live. There is something that remains fundamentally the same despite whatever else might change.

The varieties of cognition are endless, but our mental operations have their common rules: We first divide up our perceptions to isolate and identify particular truths, then reassess and restructure these truths into a larger truth by highlighting links between the most essential elements. But what is essential? How are we to distinguish essence from nonessence before orchestrating it all into a synthesis?

By *essence*, we mean that which remains constant throughout our observations of ever-changing phenomena. Such is not only the object of all scientific research but indeed is that which allows us to live in confidence and security from one day to the next. Were it not for this awareness we should be cast adrift on a relentless stream of random things and events. The sum of information obtained via the scientific method would be an unintelligible catalog of momentary cross sections through the flow of sentient existence—debris in the wake of ongoing being. In truth, this ability to generalize universals from particulars is our saving grace. Experience teaches us what we can rely on and what will not prove repeatedly true. We do not necessarily have to gain all this experience firsthand, of course, for others have left us distillations of their own experience. Whether in the form of writing, painting, sculpture, musical scores, or publications, we are the recipients of a vast store of cultural property that society preserves and exchanges over and above material property. What we do not learn from our own trial and error, we learn from those things of significance that others before us, through cognitive analysis and synthesis, have seen fit to weed out from inconsequentials.

Either way we must admit that learning plays an integral role in our daily lives. A life without learning is a life groping in the dark. At the same time, learning divorced from life is empty theory. We must check our knowledge against our own experience, especially if we ourselves are not the source of the knowledge. Somewhere we must make the intuitive leap, shifting our eyes from scant details of immediate familiarity to a more comprehensive picture. It is doubtful how much actual learning could take place through the mere restructuring of what we already know. Learning always implies an element of new experience. Otherwise our mental activities are bounded by the limits of memory, never to exceed them. We must keep ourselves open to new explanations and new experience if we are truly to live and learn.

To cling stubbornly to our own experience without going on to abstract law is an all-too-common failing of the uneducated, yet it is hardly any better when partial knowledge makes people cling to theory, forgoing the test of life. Ideally, when some experience leads to the discovery of a causal relationship, we should not let it go at that but should make an extensive survey of like conditions and glean the essential elements of that causal principle through contrastive analysis. Even so, we will not be truly convinced nor have an unshakable faith that we have uncovered the real essence of the situation unless we see repeated demonstrations. Only then does cognition gain the all-important aspect of understanding. This is perhaps the greatest paradox: We must relive our experience under changing circumstances in order to really know we have grasped the constant truth of it; we must reexperience things differently to fully fathom why they always happen the same way.

INTUITION AND REASONING

The human mind may come to cognition via intuition or reasoning. The former process is probably best exemplified by the vision of the poet or artist who tries to capture the essence of experience in the most direct and concrete means possible. And on the other end of the scale we have the scientist who works by the rational process of elimination. The artist focuses on the unique and particular, viewing the object of cognition as a whole. The scientist takes the opposite approach, focusing on common and universal elements in order to form abstract concepts.

Intuition and reasoning are often characterized as the passive and active faces of cognition. Artists are typically said to have heightened sensitivity or receptiveness, whereas scientists go about setting up circumstances to induce the action of principles they wish to investigate. In fact, however, cognition can never be completely passive; consciousness pure and simple is a prerequisite for cognition, but the two are not synonymous. Rarely is cognition a matter of mere photographic reproduction. We are continually adjusting and repositioning the lenses of our senses so as to focus and burn images into mind. We seek out ideas.

Even so, there is a telling difference between intuition and thinking. It is a question not just of relative concreteness or abstractness but of methodology. Granted, both are ultimately ways of understanding, of ferreting out commonly recognizable truth, but reasoning is hierarchically more advanced and structured. Reasoning takes intuition as the preliminary step and source of experiential phenomena, then systematically proceeds to exclude extraneous details toward abstracting a general truth. With intuition, only the specific resultant truth is accessible to conscious examination, whereas reasoning lays its entire doings out in open view. Whether or not we follow the scientist in actually formulating a working hypothesis, our thought processes naturally and inevitably obey a certain procedural course. The laws of logic codify that course, and even if we do not make a point of emphasizing the logical configuration of our own thoughts in daily life, we are constantly approximating the scientist's methods. Indeed, it is logic that guarantees the universality of our ideas, structuring the most exact course back to the facts of experience.

Value

THE CONCEPT OF VALUE

Now that the concept of value is no longer limited to economics but has gained usage in such diverse fields as art, science, ethics, and religion, it is all the more important that we understand how the word *value* is actually being employed before we settle on what it should mean for education. The aim in examining these operational definitions is to get beyond our habitual interpretations and idiosyncratic associations and to consider the word by means of objective analysis. In this way we may also correct for specialized or occupational connotations.

Perhaps the earliest usage was in the economic sense of "worth," that is, how sufficiently something answered a demand or gratified a desire. The grimy rags that would be undesirable and hence of no value to the wealthy might hypothetically satisfy a want for clothing among the poor.

As indicated previously, value stands as a quantitative expression of the relationship between the evaluating subject and the object of evaluation, which translates into micro- and macroeconomics as private or public profits versus costs. Again, that which profits the individual may be of "benefit" in one's subjective analysis but "bad" for the whole of society. Or, the reverse: Farmers, forced by government fiat to sell tracts of land when the trains are to come through, get cheated out of earning acreage, all for the public "good." Thus, evaluation is often more contingent on the evaluator than on the object. The same object may represent benefit or detriment, good or bad, depending on the scope as well as the angle of view. Care must be taken, however, not to confuse the *good* and *bad* of limited vernacular currency with the terms properly applied to individual actions in broad social context.

But humans do not live by economics alone. All that is of value cannot necessarily be quantified monetarily. Even so, we may recognize value via the greater coverage of ends and means. That is, for all intents and purposes there is nothing in our everyday experience the value of which will not stand the test of how well it serves as a means to our ends, tangible or intangible. Far beyond any materialist myopia, we also find it necessary in our daily life to nurture our vital being against fatigue, loneliness, and sorrow, those things that sap our will, energy, and growth. We need that spiritual food called consolation. Whether active or passive, conscious or unconscious, this need is a natural and real part of human life. As a means toward such ends, we seek value in the realm of aesthetic relief.

No one can deny the emotional factor in our value judgements. That which we hold in value gives us at least some sense of pleasure, though this is not to go to the other extreme of reducing our every sense of value to mere pleasure principle. Can there then be things that give us pleasure but yet should not be considered to have value? Clearly we are most susceptible to the intensity of sensual gratification. But when our pursuit of physical pleasures injures others, or when our actions out of self-interest infringe on the holdings of another, where is the value of what we do? Our sense of decency, if nothing else, shames us out of indulging in such conduct and causes us to look askance at those who do. Strictly speaking, of course, even socially disapproved pleasures have value of some kind for the individual. If this were not the case, no one would pursue them. But such value is outweighed in the balance. Thus, while admitting that a large variety of values exists, we must insist that values for education, especially, embrace the broadest view possible to promote the greatest good for all.

VALUE OF RELATIONSHIP

As we have seen, the mere relationship of cognitive objects to things and facts in the world is not enough to constitute value. A subject-object relationship is required before value can be created. Only those relationships whereby the influence of some object tends to reinforce or diminish, prolong or shorten, our vital being can be considered beneficial or detrimental, good or bad. We first become cognizant of the existence of such relationships, and then we assess their significance for human life. Moreover, the evaluation may proceed on a number of bases, which we may call the scales of economic, moral, and aesthetic value.

In defining value as the measure of the relationship between human life and its objects, how is value any different from what economists refer to as utility or effectiveness? To be sure, these concepts do touch upon the same subject-object relations but only unidirectionally. That is, unless we wish to speak of anti-utility, we pass up the discussion of negative value. I would prefer to use the less awkward breadth of the word *value*.

Things that can harm us certainly relate to us and wrest us from indifference no less than things that aid us, but in either case our evaluations bear on the strength of relationship. For example, water in and of itself has no value. It often goes unregarded. Nonetheless, as soon as someone wants a drink of water, it has bearing. Then water is seen to possess the capacity to quench thirst, just as the person is able to be satisfied with water. At other times, water means nothing but disaster to people, as when a flood strikes. The value is not inherent in the subject (person) nor in the object (water) but is manifest in the attracting or repelling force between them.

Yet, the definition is still assailable. We find philosophers querying whether the relevance of something might not be inherent in the object itself. Durkheim suggested that life has value to people because they themselves are living things. Thus, wheat would have intrinsic value in its nutritive relationship in maintaining life. Justice is a virtue because it upholds the necessity of life, and murder is a crime for the opposite reason. In many cases value seems to be simply an expression of an inherent feature of things as drawn out and wrought to a logical conclusion.

Such arguments, for all their merits, fail to explain phenomena of symbolic value. An obvious example may be found in the practice of idolatry. Throughout history there has been little in this world that has not been seen worthy of worship. Idols of wood and stone can hardly be claimed to possess inherently valuable features. Humans have attached religious sentiments to even the most pitiful of creatures. The accepted notion that an object of worship is that which stimulates the human imagination to the full runs aground on numerous historical contradictions. People have held faith in all kinds of things whose value had nothing to do with the objects themselves. And this is not just limited to religion. Such seeming contradictions pervade our moral life wherever there is the presence of a strong faith. A flag is only a piece of cloth, but soldiers risk their lives to protect it. Furthermore, luxury items are invested with exchange values far beyond any inherent qualities they may have. Their value comes from the socially recognized status of possessing them. Thus we are back to value as acknowledged by the subject for its relationship to us—direct or indirect—in representing an important element in our environment.

CONSTITUENT ELEMENTS OF VALUE

Proceeding further in our analysis of the concept of value, we must attempt to identify those features evaluated in subject-object relations as differentiated from the subject or object itself. We may begin by distinguishing connections that are perceived to be relevant from the total of connections perceived, and the subjective from the objective elements within these.

As we have seen, humans manage certain activities unconsciously while others merit conscious attention. Likewise, various phenomena and relationships are dealt with consciously or unconsciously. When our attitude toward these things is merely one of intellectual cognition, without engaging an emotional response, we do not perceive that they have any significant degree of influence on our being, and thus we perceive no particular value in them. We pass hundreds of people on the street every day but interact with only those few who rouse us from our neutral equanimity to amity or hostility. Moreover, our "sight readings" into the world around us are colored by such factors as our level of knowledge or our personal character, individual differences that focus our judgements on certain criteria over others.

Taking the continuity of our existence as the standard cognitive base for evaluation, we first distinguish what is useful to us from what is not. At this point, we forge the primary distinction between that which has value and that which has none. Circumstances are rarely fixed or evenly divided between black and white, however. For example, suppose we had ten sacks of coal and used only half of them over the winter, leaving five sacks untouched. At the onset of winter we had no way of knowing just how many sacks it would take to keep warm in the months ahead, so all ten were justifiably valuable. But when summer comes, the remaining five sacks serve no purpose. No immediate purpose, that is; for we may argue that there is the promise of potential usefulness next winter. It is only for the time being, in the midsummer swelter, that coal has no value, for within half a year it will be restored to its former value; or, rather, we will again find value in it. The swing of the pendulum to zero value and back is often only a matter of months. And at the proper juncture of person, time, and place, even things wholly forsaken at present may be experienced anew as valuable.

The utility principle of value as mere usefulness, however, ceases to bear up to the complexities of the real world—it is not a simple yes-no dichotomy. Evaluation entails more of an ongoing compounding of accounts, with value as the recognized current sum relevance that an object—material or symbolic, physical or mental—maintains in the balance of means and ends. In keeping tabs, we might define the polarity as active contributive value versus passive deterrent value, according to our innate and acquired habits of actively pursuing the fruitful and passively resisting the harmful. Or we might align it along the economic columns of credit and debit as positive and negative value. In terms more specific and familiar though, we stand good up against bad, benefit against detriment, and beauty against ugliness. Moreover, in some cases we relegate conflicting senses of value to different orders of reasoning, or defer judgement to some later date, as when a negative and positive value coexist pending two foreseeable outcomes.

Unlike absolute truth, value can and does change. The kerosene lamps that were introduced in the Meiji period (1868–1912) were regarded as a vast improvement over paper lanterns at that time but have since been superseded in value by modern electric lights. Even so, today's clutter could conceivably resume a treasured status as tomorrow's antique or temporarily come in handy the next time the power fails.

Value changes as subject and object shift relative to one another in either or both of two vectors. First, the object of evaluation may alter of itself, typically through the process of deterioration or entropy, as in the case of our previous example of coal, which turns to valueless ash once burnt. On the other hand, the subject's perception may undergo some sort of transformation. The human attention span is notoriously limited, and novelty soon wears thin. In economic ventures especially, this is a major part of what the market will bear before reaching a saturation point. Gossen first put his finger on the phenomenon by formulating his "law of diminishing enjoyment," whereby (1) the magnitude of enjoyment varies inversely with the prolongation of exposure, diminishing to a minimum threshold of indifference, and (2) renewed exposure to the same pleasure not only fails to regain the initial magnitude but also accelerates the rate of decline to indifference, that is, repetition lessens the period and degree of enjoyment.[3]

The Varieties of Value

A HIERARCHICAL SYSTEMATIZATION OF VALUE

Having rejected the classical model of truth-good-beauty values in favor of a new classification based on benefit, good, and beauty, it now remains for us to integrate these into an inclusive conceptual order. As a point of reference, let us define *benefit* to mean those values of direct relevance to the life of the individual as a whole. Benefit is at once entirely personal and responsive to the entire person. By contrast, aesthetic values directly address the senses alone and involve the overall life of the individual only tangentially. An aesthetic object stimulates the faculties of perception and arouses a pleasurable or displeasing emotional reaction evaluated as beautiful or ugly, independent of any concerns for integrity in the total context of life. Here then are lesser sensory or sensual values partitioned off from the larger self. Opposite these, at an even higher level where the relevance does not center on the individual but rises to influence the life of the individual's society, the collective moral values of the group constitute good. We may thus conveniently picture a hierarchical system of value as a pyramid with aesthetic values at the bottom and moral values on top:

1. Good — social value bearing on collective group existence
2. Benefit — personal values bearing on self-oriented individual existence
3. Beauty — sensory values bearing on isolated parts of individual existence

In each case, it is not so much anything inherent in the nature of the object evaluated as it is the criteria of the evaluating subject that dictate the level of relevance recognized between them. One person may size up the same object any number of ways, draw different correlations, and judge it worthy of praise or criticism accordingly. Placing the object on the scales of good and bad, we weigh its moral value; on the scales of benefit and detriment, or gain and loss, we balance out its economic value; on the scales of beauty and ugliness, the identical object is measured in terms of aesthetic value. It all depends on the standards of evaluation.

Our reaction in coming in contact with an object we find merely pretty or amusing is casual enough to demand little thought for our continued livelihood or security. We are removed from it all in the rapture and calm repose of aesthetic appreciation. If caution does not temper our enjoyment, we choose to follow our every desire toward it as a matter of our own free will. If, on the other hand, we consider the object out of our reach in its magnificence, we resign ourselves to the state of adoration or awe. But when instead we are moved to see the object as useful, convenient, or profitable, our feelings are typically less ecstatic and more actively focused toward utilization. In this context, we have discovered the object's economic value. Or still again, viewing the object through the eyes of society, it may be so universally good that it commands our love and respect. Related this way, it takes on moral value.

Moral evaluation is not necessarily limited to self-willed human actions, as is generally thought, nor economic evaluation to monetary concerns, nor even aesthetic evaluation to works of art. Evaluators of perspectives differing according to social standing, upbringing, and other background circumstances might well take someone's personal conduct, for example, as an object of aesthetic or moral criticism. A drunk's rude behavior is regarded with mild amusement by passersby. Children will even tease him. To them he is but a laughable farce. Nonetheless, persons of character who consider it their civic duty to uphold public morals will not content themselves to sneer or ridicule but will take it upon themselves to admonish the drunk to reflect upon his morally reprehensible condition. How much more severely, then, would the drunk's friends and relatives, persons with intimate personal ties to him, judge his actions? And in the end, if the disgrace weighs heavily enough to injure their self-esteem, they may pass judgement on him in the economic terms of individual detriment and make every effort to change his behavior. Similarly, when a husband and a wife quarrel, there is no way the dispute can be a matter of calm, detached observation for the immediate family, let alone the parties involved. However, an outside observer sees the occurrence on the aesthetic level, as a curious phenomenon that just happens, like anything else in the natural world, or perhaps as a matter of only passing interest. Thus, although moral, aesthetic, and economic values differ, their divergence lies not with the objects themselves but with the various reactive attitudes that evaluating subjects can assume.

ECONOMIC VALUE

The concept of value, first recognized as an economic phenomenon, is now seen to have implications for the neighboring fields of aesthetics, ethics, and general philosophy in that it helps to clarify what the original sense of value as profit or gain means in light of the larger scheme of value common throughout the many areas of application. In every case, value is understood to assess subject-object relations. The standard measure in economics is perceived as an infinitely incremental continuum between benefit and detriment, and these in turn are defined as elements tending respectively to prolong or shorten the subject's life.

Economists universally attempt to explain and analyze the concept of value in terms of wealth but then often proceed to confuse wealth with property. At the most casual level, the two appear to be the same, but comparison reveals a definite division of meaning. Property is usually considered to be one dimension of wealth. Wealth includes everything capable of gratifying the physical or mental desires of human beings.

Let me here repeat once again my initial thesis that humans are powerless to create matter; we can create only value. All economists essentially concur in this, although their terminology may differ. Even if there is no direct admission of value creation, call it wealth or property or utility, human labor can at most bring forth new uses in existing natural materials by recombination, restructuring, or repositioning.

Humans seek to obtain and utilize property as the object of economic activity, thereby enriching life in its material aspect. This is because we acknowledge its materially gratifying capacity, although this quality remains latent until set in relation to human desires. Utility manifests itself when something necessary for living happens to suffice to meet the demand. Desires and property gravitate to one another, either or both inevitably adapting so as to maximize their mutual relevance. Such changes naturally alter or remake the utility in accordance with the new desire-property correlation. As wants grow more intense, the utility of the desired property increases, and as the desire wanes, the utility decreases proportionally. Similarly, even if the demand stays constant, a fluctuation in the nature of the property will also cause the utility to vary.

Economics uses the term *value* in two senses: Utility value expresses each individual's subjective profit, whereas exchange value compares utility values in the open marketplace so that subjective personal gain attains a measure of objective acknowledgement from the general public. This quantified and standardized ratio then acts as an exchange rate governing property transfer, the objective result of subjective pursuits.

MORAL VALUE

The concepts of good and bad are uniquely social in that they represent judgements of the group in praise or reproval of its members. To define *good* as that which contributes to the public interest will no doubt strike some as simplistic, but what other term comes closer to actual usage? There is a sharp division between profit on the individual or family level and the overall advancement of the whole community formed by these individuals and families. For when private interests conflict with the public interest, the general consensus is that selfish gain in disregard of how it adversely affects society is bad. In such instances evaluation unmistakably sides in favor of the group. On the other hand, someone who holds the well-being of the group as a primary concern, subordinating his or her own life to the greater life will be hailed as virtuous.

Here we have a clear-cut dichotomy. On the one hand, individual gain common to all people is considered good, while gain to the exclusion of others is considered bad. As long as the perspective in evaluation is not in some way abnormal, that is, not deluded or deranged or perverted, what one individual judges to be beneficial will coincide with what the members of the group as a whole consider the common good. This is commonsense human nature.

At the root of all our value judgements is the drive toward self-preservation. Survival is an absolute value for us, from which branch out all of our other relative values. This instinct operates not only in humans but in all organisms; hence we may at the very least assume that for all their individuality humans have a common basis to their desires. Nonetheless, the only objective assessment of this commonality is in the demarcation of limits. There is an infinite variety of what people actively seek, but all share one point in common as to what they passively resist. Herein we may find that ultimate critical principle of morality as the bounds set by restraint. In the West this line of resistance is expressed in the Golden Rule, "Do unto others as you would have them do unto you." The adage is not above objection, however, for its active formulation suggests that what everybody seeks will necessarily be the same. There is no such universality to people's positive desires, nor is there universal applicability to this law as stated. Rather, it is the corresponding Oriental proverb, "Do not do unto others what you would not have them do unto you,"[4] that attains the objectivity of scientific truth.

Still, one does not become virtuous simply by not doing wrong; rather one is just spared the humiliation that would be one's lot as an immoral individual. Such inhibition cannot be construed as the single solitary principle behind all morality, although it does inform one side of ethics.

Crime may thus be defined, within this context, as antisocial behavior justifiable only in the narrow judgement of the depraved, the foolish, or the insane—conduct that proves troublesome to other members of society. Yet even those who seem unable to realize their desires satisfactorily without infringing on the rights of others who share the same living environment can often be persuaded to pursue their own benefit in harmony with the interests of society once they are brought to an awareness of their social existence. This, indeed, is one function of education and upbringing. Children may impulsively infringe upon the rights of others before their character is fully shaped, but dedicated families will tirelessly strive to iron out these problems by channeling the erring ways into harmonious reciprocity. Such education in the home works to raise up responsible individuals deserving of their right to life.

Law regulates the minimum level of morality. It does not ask people outright to do good; it just punishes them for doing wrong. Technically, the courts are not empowered to interfere with the affairs of those who do not do positive good; the courts merely prosecute lawbreakers in the judgement that such persons are to be treated as wrongdoers or criminals. Thus the authorities always focus their attention on an offending minority, seeing to it that no one infringes on the rights of fellow members of society. Judiciary administrations do not exist to promote good but are meant only as punitive afterthoughts. They cannot really deter evil.

Again, morality evaluates—from society's viewpoint on a scale of good to bad—the individual benefit deriving from a person's conduct. Law but regulates one end of that scale, passes judgement on whether a given act transgresses the lower limit of morality into the inhuman range, and exacts corrective measures accordingly.

Let us examine aspects of moral judgement in more detail:

1. Can the terms *good* and *bad* be applied to phenomena other than human? No, not as we are using the terms.
2. Then can all human acts be considered good or bad? No again. Only a certain part of the whole of human activity can be taken as the object of moral evaluation.
3. *a.* What class of human acts can be called good or bad? Only those acts that are willfully or intentionally conducted.
   b. What class of human acts cannot be called good or bad? Obviously those acts that are unintentional, for they are really no different from any other natural phenomena.
4. Can all willful acts be called good or bad? Still again no. Only those willful acts that affect society as a whole can be called good or bad.
5. *a.* Should that class of willful acts directed toward oneself be considered good or bad? Generally speaking no, although most societies hold acts such as suicide to be evils.
   b. Should willful acts toward nonhuman things be considered good or bad? Not unless they indirectly influence others or human society as a whole.
   c. Should willful acts directed toward others or society be labeled good or bad? Yes, this is the proper arena for the moral evaluations good and bad.

To summarize, when an entire human society opposes one of its constituent individuals, or when one sector of that society stands against the rest, value judgements of good and bad are warranted. However, in the case of any other opposition such as, for instance, an individual versus an individual, or one society versus another, such judgements do not obtain. (Interestingly enough, though, in the latter confrontation between whole societies, we revert to the relative standards of economic benefit and detriment.)

In approaching the issue of positive moral value, of good, it will be instructive to consider some precedents in the history of philosophy, most notably the Platonic ideal. First, we must note that Socrates disassociates good from pleasure or the gratification of desire. Likewise the immediate goals toward which most people aspire in their daily lives — achievements, health, riches, and honor — are relegated to means superseded by a final end, the ultimate good. In a dialogue with Polas, Socrates suggests that acts follow ideas and that when the idea is just, the resultant act will be good. But just when it seems that Socrates has narrowed his sights in on justice as the final determining principle in moral judgements, the question comes back, How are we to pass such judgements without first knowing what is right or wrong? Thus the most probing inquiry for Socrates is still the value good itself. The resolution he reached for himself was to see a certain inherent element of moral good in all persons and things, so that inasmuch as this ineffable good was universal, there could be no coincidence — a natural moral order was immanent in the world. For Socrates, we may suppose that this order was an all-inclusive unity, an organic whole within which the inborn good of each thing, each act, manifests itself in relation to the total inviolate good of life that had existed since time immemorial, untouched by outward changes.[5]

But whether we choose to posit good on the basis of justice or vice versa, the fundamental point at issue remains how we are to recognize definitively these values in the real world. This is something quite apart even from assertions pro and con on the supposed eternal continuity of innate good in humans and in all creation. In practice, there is little recognizable difference between the Platonic ideal and the Confucian Reverse Golden Rule. That is, the gist of the Confucian tenet is to provide the clearest possible statement of moral wrong — a definition so eminently applicable and down-to-earth that no one has to be taught how to judge fairly. Our innate instincts know the principle by heart and will never steer us wrong by it.

The many definitions and nuances of *good* that have gained acceptance over the years do not, of course, necessarily agree with our understanding of good as established in our discussion thus far, nor even among themselves. The staunch individualist will say that good is self-love, whereas the Christian finds good in loving others. In ancient Greece, the word *good* referred to strength, bravery, and generosity, and the Latin counterpart similarly meant strength and bravery, while the French idea of good implied valor. These old interpretations of *good* might sound far from today's usage, but no doubt such notions did make sense in those days when people had to be strong to make peace and security prevail in premodern society. It should be equally obvious, nonetheless, that the meaning of *good* does not stay fixed but adapts to changing social conditions.

Even more important, we should glean from our survey that whatever the time or place, it has remained constant that the social context acted as the determinant for what *good* was to mean. Once again, good can be established only by society. Furthermore, group good always takes precedence over the values of beauty and benefit whose locus is the individual and which can have only indirect influence on the whole of society through the constituent individual.

AESTHETIC VALUE

What constitutes aesthetic value? What is this quality called beauty that distinguishes it from benefit and good? As a form of value, of course, aesthetic value must first achieve recognition by standing out from the ordinary. But at the same time it cannot demand excessive concern, because the aesthetic sense of wonderment is limited to the periphery of our existence, barely grazing our perceptive faculties as a pleasing sensation or enthralling observation, never staking such claims on our consciousness that we are put on the defensive.

Some scholars hold that aesthetic value applies only to sensory objects, that is, to things in exclusion of such nonmaterial phenomena as a beautiful deed or a beautiful soul. Nonetheless, humans are subject to the same order of appreciative feelings toward actions, occurrences, and ideas as they are toward things, so I see no reason to dismiss these from consideration as aesthetic objects. For although so-called beautiful deeds as acts deserving of admiration might seem better suited to the category of moral value, we find ourselves captivated by stories and happenings that bear little relation to morality. Thus do we have literature, fiction, and nonfiction passed down to posterity for the sheer pleasure of reading or listening.

If not exactly beautiful, then, what makes something interesting? What I am trying to say will become more apparent if we contrast it with something uninteresting. Only slightly derogatory at worst, that which is uninteresting carries none of the repulsive connotations of ugliness. We remain wholly neutral and impassive toward anything that has neither a positive aura about it nor any detractive stigma. Thus we find that judgements of beauty and ugliness assume a threshold interest level.

Any phenomenon, sensible or insensible, animate or inanimate, can be taken as the object of aesthetic evaluation. It is especially important to note in this regard that aesthetic value increases in proportion to the degree of contrast—that is, the contrast between success and failure, pleasure and pain, and so forth—as long as the contrast or diversity does not destroy the unity or integrity of that which is being aesthetically evaluated. In other words, those things regarded as negative value from the moral or ethical viewpoint are sometimes the very elements that produce the aesthetic value, because of their strong contrast, because they are on the "other side." The dramatic range is the source of the beauty.

Human activities, although in every instance perceived via the same organs of sense, will meet with distinct levels of evaluation when attention is focused on different determinants of interest. Beauty and ugliness focus on the formal aspects, quantifying the sensational impact of the mere configuration and combination of things and events that rise and fall in time and space, whereas moral good and bad are invested in the life of the society as they impinge on the individual. Again, interest keynotes aesthetic value, which, if not deriving directly from consciousness of sensory benefit per se, at least may be seen to seek a plateau of passive ease from any harm. So it is that people find comfort and alleviate fatigue by breaking the monotony of their everyday life, diverting their minds, and raising joy in place of melancholy.

The Relationship Between Science, Religion, Value Creation, and Education

RELIGIOUS VALUE—A NECESSARY CONCEPT?

Winderband posited a "sanctity" value distinct from truth, good, or beauty and defined it as a function of religion.[6] Many philosophers have since followed suit, claiming this category of value to be essential to the establishment of any value system. Their view is that all types of value with which we are familiar on a daily basis—the beauty of our artistic life, the good of our moral life, the truth of our scholastic life (albeit we have now distinguished truth from value)—must be grounded in some absolute value. But where are the grounds for establishing such a religious value?

If religious value is conceived as the ultimate sacred refuge wherein persons are saved or liberated from the sorrows of the human condition, then does it not in essence occupy a place in society corresponding in our thinking to moral value? Or, from the point of view of the individual, a benefit value? Other than to save persons or save the world at large, does religion have any meaning in the context of society? Is not the saving or liberating of individuals an individual benefit, the saving or liberating of the world a moral good? Call it divine favor, call it a state of grace, but the words express the same idea.

Some may object, saying that experience of the divine transcends the feelings of individual benefit and social good, but I cannot but see the sacred as consonant and contiguous with these as simply their purest form. I am fully confident that the beauty-benefit-good value system we have set forth thus far can accommodate the entire range of values possible without need to generate a separate sacred value.

RULE BY PERSONS OR RULE BY LAW

In ages past, nations were subject to the autocratic rule of a person in charge, not to a rule of law. The unchecked whims and arbitrary notions of a ruler, an aristocracy, and ministers were followed dutifully whether or not they made any sense. Blame for unwise decisions and ill-fated policies was passed down the line in purges of violence. In such systems leadership is based on the principle of "Might makes right." Although some people may have raised a view of dissent from time to time, most were apathetic and accepting of their situation, either from lack of awareness of other possibilities or from fear of the consequences of rocking the boat. It took a collective awakening to the superiority of rule by law over rule by persons to establish constitutional government. And where now-constitutional monarchies have chosen to maintain a figurehead, this "ruler," too, is subject to the law. Such awareness of law and of an order inherent in human life is, likewise, the essential foundation on which science rests.

It is written that Sakyamuni said "Heed the law, not persons." This is the greatest guidance that Buddhism has to offer to the advancement of humankind. Here we are shown the way up from dependence to true freedom, from living in obedience to charismatic power figures to living in unison with the universal order. As we shall discuss later in more detail, to follow blindly the will of others or even of oneself is a form of personality worship. We are self-sold into bondage. And because such one-track beliefs and attachments are not based in reason, they are apt to be quite volatile and reactive. The most minor doctrinal or icono-graphic deviations may fuel sectarian disputes and religious intolerance.

Religions everywhere preach compassion, mercy, and reciprocity with an intense fervor that almost inevitably leads to interfaith warfare, all because they get entrenched in personality worship. There is no chance to rise above the life of person dependence. Just like the lover who has no eyes for anyone but his love, the devotee of a personality cult has not the least inclination to assume an objective scientific stance to calmly compare the various religions, hail the greater similarities, and reject the trivial differences.

Gradually, though, as we move through the process of acquiring ever more knowledge, the subjective emotional elements give way to more rational considerations. We gain a certain distance from the charis-matic figure as our consciousness of an underlying order grows more pronounced. The realization dawns that even that person we had so revered only shortly before is but one ordinary human being. At that moment, like a sunrise outshining the stars that appeared to gleam so brightly, the focus of that consciousness driving our very being shifts from persons related to our own individual loss and gain to the natural order and social laws that work equally for all without favor or dis-crimination.

It is this awakening to consciousness of an underlying order and a commitment to rule by law rather than by persons that gives hope for the future. To be sure we must recognize the difficult problems that exist in the world. A mature approach to these problems and to contemporary life is not to grieve over present misfortunes and inequalities but to see them as steps toward a more just and humane social order that can grow out of this rising consciousness. As the masses gain awareness of their alienation from the power that is rightfully theirs and realize the impo-tence of a divided, noncollective existence, they can unite to seek their mutual release from their former bondage. And the key factor that has been responsible for guiding human beings thus far toward this growing awareness and consciousness is none other than education. Hence, as we look to the future, it is education that must provide the necessary guidance. Now more than ever before, all levels of society, high and low, the governing and the governed, capitalist and working classes alike, must recognize the value of learning in overcoming the illusions of self-important individualism.

Of course, it will not be easy, for unless we face up to a great number of important issues as yet barely discerned in the depths of our beings, there will be no hope for education. Furthermore, there can be no rivalry or exclusionism among specialized fields of scholarship such as we have witnessed time and time again up to now. No matter how revered the "authorities" are in their own fields, a refusal to acknowledge the lessons of other fields generates more problems than solutions. Again, the real test of education from now on will have to be in the answers it brings to our lives. We cannot afford to relegate the task of translating abstract truths into real-life values to religious sects that spend their time fighting and quarreling over which one has the most truth. These "great doctrinal debates" amount to nothing if they do not steer us clear of avarice, anger, and ignorance nor directly combat illusions and dispel the ignorance that render our lives directionless. If debates must ensue, they should be free of emotional arguments and serve to strengthen adherence to the principle "Heed the law, not persons." Only through such rational practices will science and religion and, by extension, religion and education advance together in unity.

Personality Integration and Value Creation

EVALUATION OF PERSONAL VALUES

In order to be able to evaluate our personal values correctly, we need self-awareness and other-awareness working in unison. This self-realization is not merely the self-recognition that one exists, nor is it the sense of individuality stressed through comparing one's own qualities with those of others. Rather, it is the personal value of oneself as a whole engaged in the greater whole of society that matters here. Socrates called for the awakening of the individual to self, to see the divine within us. Under the motto "Know thyself," he rejected the revelations of the Oracle of Delphi and embarked instead upon the path of self-reflection or learning. By self-reflection, he meant going beyond the infantile or primitive state of nondiscrimination of self and others or of sheer other-awareness, to come back to examine oneself in light of what one has contributed up to that point, for better or for worse, to the lives of those others who share one's communal existence. Thus we may say that Cengzi, who "looked within himself thrice daily," led the life of self-reflection advocated by Socrates.[7]

Let me stress again that in order to be able to correctly evaluate our own character for ourselves, we must have the prior benefit of others' evaluations for comparison. Proper assessment of personal value comes only when we are able to choose from among the values realized by others and oneself, to compare them and assimilate them into a synthesis.

Human living is, in its highest and most representative aspect, conscious behavior. In other words, the human personality is a whole entity that is unified for its purpose. The person is that union, that something able to orchestrate various elements together into a space-time continuity we know as life, a unity that lasts as long as it lasts, only to disband at death.

Naturally, that union we know as the person goes deeper than externals. An inner consistency is more true to character than appearances. Inconsistencies in someone's mental state as reflected in divergent behavior from one day to the next will cause others to distrust that person's lack of character. They will find it impossible to treat that person as a competent, self-sustaining equal and indeed will feel forced to see him or her as less than human, in the sense that a mentally disturbed person has in one way or another come undone—a mind lacking unity.

If, as we have asserted, the phenomenon of self-consciousness epitomizes all that is fully human (as distinct from other animals), then we must exclude infants, the mentally impaired, and the insane from the category of integral personal character. Even among persons considered normal and up to par on the whole, there are those whose lives are fraught with contradiction, though they try to cover it up, whose actions go back on whatever good intentions they have in mind. Their lives conflict moment to moment with their permanent objectives, and this lack of unity is revealed in their behavior. They too must be seen as lacking in character. Yet, there is no one who does not seek some kind of meaning in life. The search for meaning certainly ought to align itself with the best of means, but people may mistakenly choose means insufficient to reach that end. I regard these people not so much as wrongdoers as pitiable ignorants incapable of seeing any further than the immediate objectives at hand.

EDUCATION FOR VALUE CREATION

We may analyze our ideas of what makes for higher or lower, better or worse, personal character, but in the final analysis the nucleus of our evaluations is the ideals that different individuals hold in their orientation to life. These views on life purpose form crystallized cores from which whole systems of thought radiate outward as if from the facets of gems. These core beliefs on life purpose can be observed to reflect one of two basic attitudes:

1. Fully matured core beliefs on life purpose that gradually lead to increased or expanded being
2. Self-oriented worldviews that eventually collapse in on the self

Mature core beliefs and a clear life purpose lead to a sense of mind-body unity—a harmony of part to part and part to whole—and to a psychological consistency over time. The depth and degree of this unification in a given individual's life are the most important elements of personal character. Such a person is empowered to create value. It is the task of education to provide guidance toward this end.

As we seek to develop this quality of education, applied science can be of invaluable service by providing preliminary directives to orient our planning on how to create value. As with architecture, before beginning construction we must first draw up plans, budget the project to avoid the unfeasible or uneconomical, list all items required, and think through the entire process in order to avoid errors or actions detrimental to the project. *Anticipation* and *precaution* are the key words here, although such previsions must prove next to impossible for the inexperienced, for those accustomed to always act on others' orders because of an inability to systematize priorities on their own, and for persons who habitually deal with things in only the most momentary or circumstantial terms. Cumulative preparations depend not just on one's own experience but also on continual intake of the experience of others. One must be able to meet repeated circumstances, to draw on previously understood perspectives, and to summon up lines of thought that have had a history of success. The ability to abstract those elements and conditions indispensable for success out of numerous past advances and setbacks, whether one's own or learned from others, is the primary source of guidance. This is the essence of applied science, and the educator, as one entrusted with the vital social responsibility of working toward this most complex and profoundly important aim, the creation of human value, would do well to keep it ever in focus.

It is through discovering laws of causality for the process of value creation that applied science can best direct our efforts in education. Here applied science, through reexamining successes and failures up to now, can help us understand the causal relationships at work and, from these findings, formulate laws to help those in the future create values for themselves. Applied science ensures that we learn the lessons of history and do not simply repeat what has gone on before without critical examination.

How, specifically, does this apply to the business of education? Teaching day in and day out, yet unable to improve the efficacy of our methods, we teachers are often hard-pressed to discover just what should be handled differently. In such cases, we should reflect on the practices of our predecessors, consider their lessons, and pore over their records so as to learn what worked and what did not. This is no different from what researchers in medicine, agriculture, and other fields of applied science do.

Education is a science dedicated to eliciting personal values in teachers, who will in turn guide their students to value creation. The word *science* should not conjure up a cold and clinical image, however. Research in psychology or sociology must not be applied directly but needs to be tempered for relevance in teacher-student value-creation situations and practices. It must be a humanistic science that recognizes the needs of both teacher and student.

Rare and most exceptional are those individuals who can discipline themselves to learn completely on their own. Except for exceptional cases in which learners manage to set up their own programs or routines to bring value to, or rather from, the reality they experience, they must be guided. This guidance, once again, is the meaning of education. For the most part, this guidance entails the consciously planned labors of persons of character (teachers) working on the innate receptivity of others (students) toward the development of their personal character. It is the function of education to guide unconscious living to consciousness, valueless living to value, and irrational living to reason.

True education is no accident. Conscientious teaching engenders purposefully rational behavior. It encourages the sort of living that not only brings value to some few individuals at some particular time and place but also seeks to recognize universal laws of value for living. Thus education as a form of real-life guidance must constantly strive to get students to experience value in their own daily lives. Whatever is taught, the aim of creating value must never be lost.

Here, then, is where it becomes essential to discover causal laws for the processes of value creation. One effective way this can be accomplished is by studying the success stories of persons who embody the value-creation life-style, analyzing them in light of psychology, and by reviewing the hard-won victories of incisive mastery, rather than mulling over mediocre accomplishments, although such comparisons can prove instructive also.

Value creation stands as an educational aim deserving our utmost attention and earnest efforts. It is the very life of education, something we educators can and must work toward, drawing upon the lessons of all the other applied sciences. The breadth of the applied sciences not only affords no end of subject material for teaching but also repeatedly affirms the value of methodology and challenges all who care about the future of our society and our children to support rational efforts toward unified educational reform.

3

The Revitalization of Education

A New Direction in Educational Policy

THE CASE FOR REVITALIZING EDUCATION

The revitalization of education proposes nothing less than to build the ideal society of tomorrow by planning the cultivation of human resources today. As the artist works on canvas or marble to create new beauty, and the entrepreneur manages the transformation of raw materials into profitable products, so the educator is to survey the many shortcomings of contemporary society and set up programs aimed at shaping a better world for generations to come. This is truly the greatest, most urgent order of business toward the creation of value. It should involve everyone, gain the cooperation and endorsement of all classes and groups in society, and issue from actual teaching experience, not from theorizing in an ivory tower. Politicians must take up the cause of policy reform, solicit constructive criticism from the general forum of interested parties, and win the acceptance of parents before moving on to the next stage of implementation involving the teachers.

The task of creating economic benefit or aesthetic beauty from inanimate resources can proceed directly from the choice of materials to the respective formative processes, but when the value we seek to create is moral good from human resources, we must first cultivate those re-

91

sources. This consists of arousing an awareness of the collective life of society in each and every individual, because the degree to which people themselves take responsibility to work toward the common good and social betterment ultimately makes the difference.

Education properly addresses social ills. The metaphor is an appropriate one. If the physician is one who treats ailing individuals, and the politician one who administers to the body politic of the group, then the educator must also be seen as a doctor to society. But whereas the physician and the politician practice remedial medicine in the main, the educator is decidedly preventive in outlook. The former concern themselves with the present and problems as they occur; the educator looks to the future in an effort to steer clear of trouble altogether.

An equally compelling parallel can be found in the dual role of the modern family, that is, the satisfying of present material needs while raising the children for the sake of the future. In contemporary society, the educator has become a quasi-parental presence, taking on the second role of preparing the children for the future. It is essential, therefore, that families' concerns and desires for their children's education be communicated effectively to educators.

Class struggle, everyday strife, ideological upheaval, moral decay — seemingly insurmountable social crises stare us in the face. The burning question is how to stem this onslaught. The greatest obstacle is apathy. We are all only too familiar with the issues that plague this world in which we live, but until the troubles are upon us, until they become our troubles, they are simply "not our concern." The fires rage on the opposite shore, distant from our immediate circumstances until our leaders, lawmakers, scholars, and clergy alike are engulfed helplessly in the flames. What are we to do about this depressing state of affairs? Is not the greatest danger we face as a nation that the wellsprings that feed education will dry up, stranding us without proper leadership?

Obviously someone must forge the way out of our social crises, but though the reins are in the hands of would-be leaders among our scholars, politicians, and religious figures, far too often their ineptness cancels out any authority they might have had. And why should this be so? They tend to be either misinformed or tactless. But most counterproductive of all is that every bit of good counsel they give is negated by their own errant actions. Their pleas of "Do as I say, not as I do" generally fall on deaf ears. Corruption could hardly be more blatant than it is today. As power follows wealth, so politicians are at the beck and call of big business, and scholars and clergy in turn bend to the will of politicians.

What at first appears to be purist idealism on the part of education hints at a much deeper question: Whose vision of correct or incorrect thought are we to accept? While the government shuffles about behind the scenes hushing up "dangerous" views, who is to know what ideas are truly so terrible? Indeed what could be as insufferably frightening as the unchecked, soulless power of suppression?[1] In the heat of argument who is to say what is right or wrong? At the very least, we can see that debates drag on to tedious lengths for lack of any durable understanding of what good and bad should mean. And to make matters worse, one cannot even clarify the issues because of evasiveness on both sides. No one wants to discuss anything rationally.

In order to arrive at standards of good and bad, one has to reach people where they live out their values. This can never be entirely objective, of course, but involves the elements of emotion in evaluation. A knowledge of ethics and sociology can make significant contributions here, though not necessarily via the normal academic routes. Direct observation of ordinary real-life situations can lead to clearer understanding. The reader is invited to review Chapter 2, "The Fundamentals of Value," for greater discussion of this idea.

The question, What kind of education is best? is an important one that will be considered later. I want, first, to emphasize that there is no constructive way to combat either subversive or suppressive thinking save by education. Some otherwise knowledgeable persons would give the kiss of death to the whole of education as it now exists by pointing fingers at the failures churned out by the normal school system up to the present; but by the same token the idea of a totally uneducated populace is unthinkable in this day and age, especially given the degree to which citizens must participate in constitutional government. The way out of the problems of the present day is forward, not backward! Even the most cursory examination of the rather unremarkable examples of education in the Soviet Union and the Republic of China reveals that education at least makes for reasonable constitutional order. And even with the oversights and crises that do arise for failure to implement constitutional rule fully in those countries, it is, beyond the shadow of a doubt, the presence of educated elements that proves the saving grace, while difficulties occur only where those elements are lacking.

Let me repeat: The way out of our present dilemma is better and more—not less—education. Others may argue pro and con, but there is no denying society's demands for increased and improved education. And this includes the desire for better moral education.

Many leading thinkers have, in fact, voiced the view that proper education is the cultivation of social consciousness or a sense of community.[2] Political, economic, and other social efforts at reform are, at best, remedial cures. For thorough treatment at the source of problems, there is no other solution than the long-term revitalization of education. The future belongs to children and youth, and indeed their tender sensibilities are almost the only thing open to suggestion through education. Adults are typically so mired down in anger, avarice, and ignorance and so set in their ways beyond any ability for fresh self-reflection that attempts at the moral reeducation of adults are usually lost causes.

What, then, is to be done? Politicians and national leaders seem to feel that it is enough to state the goal of education as the fostering of social consciousness, and those responsible for the formulation of educational policy state the purpose of education as the fostering of national unity and the promotion of moral education. They have never, however, considered concretely how these goals are to be met and have left instead the entire burden of realizing these objectives with the individual teacher. As a result, years pass with no concrete proposals forthcoming and no teachers of a caliber to execute them should they appear. The result is our present deadlock in education. In this situation, is it really enough to direct vague words of encouragement at our teachers?

Ultimately, however, educators must recognize that they cannot expect solutions to come from elsewhere. They themselves must be in touch with the issues particular to their own time and place and must really grapple with the problems in their own minds. In such a context, failure is nothing to be ashamed of if it points the way to the source of the problems. We should see failures for what they are, get them over with and move on ahead. Our sixty-odd years of looking exclusively to Europe and America for ideas have failed us, but not without first showing us that mere mimicry will not solve the problems at home.

But lest my views become suspect and I myself be accused of trying to undermine the government's efforts at "guiding youth to correct thinking," let me qualify my remarks by saying that there is a time to tear down and a time to build. Without criticism, there is stagnation; yet to simply attack the status quo is to invite anarchy during that interval wherein the nation awaits a scheme of reconstruction to emerge. I believe that the socioeconomic situation of our country has become imbalanced in the extreme and that the time for change is upon us. Moreover, with proper commitment to peaceful and constructive means that do not threaten the unity of the nation, it should be possible to gain the understanding of the powers that be. In this way, educators can best work toward needed reforms.

Of course, to assume such an outspoken stance while the rest of the educational community merely bickers over trifling details involves a share of risk taking, but in this extremity is opportunity, and to go out on a limb for one's beliefs is to lend them argumentative leverage. And in this day when all has fallen to corruption and paranoia, the risk taking can be quite literal: The more vocal the appeal, the more likely the "troublemaker" is to be ushered out of the public eye. I fear that my efforts will be as futile as water sprinkled on a desert.

There is no getting away from the human factor, however, no dealing with our problems in the abstract. As all streams converge to the sea, so all dead-end standstills in our society can be traced to some shortcoming in human resources, which in turn points back to some failure in educational policy. Therefore the reform of educational policies is the way to revitalize society as a whole.

Here is a cause for real patriots to consider seriously. If we have learned anything at all from the World War, it is that legislators may do well to study the spread of social repercussions in order to trace back to the source of their own political aims: a fundamentally materialist position in support of industry. In recent years, in both Japan and the West, we have witnessed the phenomenon of the reeducation of adult workers to meet the current needs of industry, based on evidence of success in the reeducation of adults in the past war. However, in the long run, it is uneconomical and wasteful of human life to seek reeducation of adults without reassessing the basic orientation of children's education. The whole process will just repeat itself in renewed waste of human life if educational policy does not undergo a radical reexamination and redirection to meet the demands of the times.

THE IMPORTANCE AND UNIQUE POSITION OF EDUCATION

One tangible measure of progress is found in the steady increases over time in family, local, and state expenditures for the education of children. This reflects a pervasive awakening of parents to their responsibility for educating dependents. In the more industrialized societies, this awareness often reaches such critical proportions that parents make sacrifices for their children's education throughout their entire lives because the upward drive for learning is felt so keenly in the society and in the home. What this seems to indicate is that no matter how little is the conscious recognition of education per se, whenever people anywhere survey their world and compare the relative importance of everything in their environment, nothing ranks higher than the cultivation of human resources. It is an absolute supramaterial value.

Historically no one can deny the importance of the invention of means of transportation and communication, medical discoveries, and the harnessing of electrical energy, but nothing can top education qualitatively or quantitatively in extent of influence. Of course, this claim is exceedingly hard to verify in material terms except as represented in the investment of time and money toward students' education. Indeed, the expenditure staggers the imagination.

But in spite of these massive expenditures, we must face up to the reality that education in this country is outmoded and is actually damaging our children and young people. If people were not so busy with the cares of their everyday lives, they would realize this. A few people are becoming aware of the seriousness of the problem, and this is reason for hope. Some old people today, for example, are looking back to their youth when the Confucian classics and the like were, as a matter of course, a major part of the curriculum, though totally without value or application in retrospect. What a waste of time and effort! This clinging to outmoded, wasteful educational policies and practices can be observed in both East and West, and it is only thanks to the insistence of such revolutionary educators as Rousseau, Comenius, and Pestalozzi[3] that youth today have a lighter sentence to serve in the prison of meaningless studies.

Considering the great number of young people that educational reforms stand to affect, improvements in this area should be seen as having no less value than advancements in, say, medical science. Furthermore, considering the great number of children there are to educate, these changes should be recognized as increasing the responsibility of the teachers who are to implement them. As important as educational reform is, it can strike us only as singularly odd that antiquated practices have persisted as long as they have.

Once we have awakened to this, it is all the more imperative that educational policy be handled with sensitivity. Influence works two ways, and a mechanical or dogmatic staffing of schools with no understanding of the special needs of the local community could be worse than no change at all. In providing for public education, the state takes positive constructive action, but by the same token, education cannot be managed like other areas of governmental policy-making. At every level, from the founding of schools and setting of standards of practice to the provision of texts and choice of subjects for instruction, in every detail the state must make its aims clear while still maintaining close contact with the actual instructors.

Furthermore, it is unavoidable that the state, in the person of the minister of education, will specify the qualifications and credentials required of teachers, as well as relegate duties to a vast number of regional officials who will oversee, enforce, and promote the quality of education received. We are talking about standards of procedure and texts decided at the national level, not left up to the discretion of teachers alone. Education is now a national concern and must embrace comprehensive perspectives. We will consider this at greater length later.

Another analogy can be drawn to the only other government agency that deals exclusively with preparedness for eventualities, the military. Because the military is administered as an exercise in readiness on the outside chance that something may happen to threaten national security, here we find an active measure taken to ensure future self-preservation as opposed to all the other passive measures meant only to curb trouble after the fact. Needless to say, great care must be taken to act only when the circumstances merit and no sooner, for slipups can well prove irreversible. Scrutiny in judging the character of persons to fill decision-making posts is of the utmost importance, whereas common sense alone is enough for positions requiring only simple interpretation of rules. In other words, most bureaucratic offices merely call for someone who can passively understand and execute orders, but the educator—like a general—must actively take command. The average bureaucrat can keep pushing papers and, so long as no earthshaking errors ensue, will keep that job for years even without any visible accomplishments.

In the case of educators, however, entrusted as they are with the weighty responsibility of schooling tomorrow's citizenry and passing on today's culture to those who must assume leadership, it is important not only that they prevent harm from coming to others' children but also that they actively work to show each child his or her potential to realize an ideal life. The task for a teacher is not just to preserve and protect but also to stimulate and enhance, to look ahead and bring out latent character values. This is an awesome prospect for someone not painstakingly chosen for the job. The educator cannot be just anyone; he or she must be a model of the best society has to offer, a vision of everyone's ideal. And along with that, the educator must be outgoing in conveying that ideal while providing students with guidance and leadership over a wide range of academic and practical activities.

In review, the special characteristics of the educator's work may be summed up as follows:

1. Whereas other government administrators need only involve themselves with partial goals that apply to their own respective departments, educators must embrace the whole of the educational process and totally commit themselves to carrying through the larger goal in each specific case.
2. Unlike the characteristically passive, prohibitive nature of most administrative work, education requires active, promotional, and constructive effort.
3. Whereas the typical government administrator need pay only a minimum of attention to public welfare, educators must make maximizing the well-being of the nation their highest ideal and actively strive toward that goal.
4. Government administrators can generally handle all that is expected of them with only regular common sense. Educators, on the other hand, must answer greater demands; hence, in addition to common sense, a higher degree of character development and acquisition of special skill is needed. In this sense, society regards educators in much the same way that moralists and priests were once revered as guardians of the soul. Although that role has now been secularized, the expectations are still every bit as great.
5. Education is far more complex than other lines of administrative work. In contrast to the rather simple enactment of laws and orders, educators must fully understand both the fundamental educational principles involved and the special qualities of each and every child to whom these principles must be adapted. The consequences and power of influence are great, and it is no easy matter to spot successes or failures until considerable time has passed.
6. Whereas other work engages only part of the person, it is the teach-

er's business to find value in every aspect of the total personality, to lay a foundation of that whole person who will have the potential to undertake any and all fields of work. To this end, teachers must command two types of specialized knowledge: knowledge of all textual materials and subjects to be covered, and knowledge of methods and techniques by which to transmit, direct, and apply studies in the subjects to be covered. Neither area can take precedence over the other. Legislators and educational supervisors must have an understanding of this before they go about setting up educational policies.

If the nation is to have education truly work to best advantage to combat social ills, it cannot content itself with the all too labor-intensive yet essentially inconsequential workings of other administrative and enforcement agencies but must seek to delineate the most effective and resourceful policies possible.

One particular area deserving attention is the relative distribution of spending within education. Why spend so much of the nation's money on advanced education and scholarships for independent research when the seedling bed of primary education gets far too little fertilization? And in primary education, because primary school teachers are so important that they practically are primary education itself, it is shocking that more energy does not get put into improving and updating their skills.

Nor is it only that handful of persons in the employ of the educational system that need concern themselves with this point. Each and every citizen must realize what is at stake here if we are to establish an intelligent national policy toward education. Only when all of society understands the value and the mission of education will the government become responsive to educational policy. Provision must be made for external supervisory agencies and regulatory programs by which society and the nation can keep close tabs on budgeting and expenditures; internally, the whole educational organization must be overhauled and redesigned for greater effectiveness.

I am not talking about minor changes. The entire structure is wrong for the avowed ends. No amount of fussing with existing regulations will make possible the kind of improvements needed. As with society at large, the microcosm of education is at root the people who compose it; thus educational reforms must look to the people involved and seek ways to improve human resources. As the society begins to realize that human development is a greater wealth than monetary riches or property, it should naturally follow that the revitalization of education must first look at the human element in the system — the various roles educators are to assume. Short of this foundation, all reforms will be like trying to build a second story in the middle of the air.

If we examine our present educational system from a sociological standpoint, in terms of how it fails or succeeds to serve and promote the well-being of society as a whole, we can focus the question of educational reform on the idea of the roles to be played. Of course, in the most general terms reforms must involve, on the one hand, passive or conservative measures such as trimming operating costs down to a budget and, on the other hand, active or innovative moves to increase the overall effectiveness within those limits by prioritizing roles. Areas of insufficiency must be brought up to acceptable levels, excesses scaled down, redundancies streamlined, and disparities pulled into unison. Given the avowed aims, how essential is any one particular role to the whole system? To the other roles? How much does its retention or elimination affect the cumulative ability to attain those educational aims? In order to resolve such questions and issues, policy decisions need to be reviewed and redefined in at least the following areas:

1. Upgrading the role of the teacher in classroom practice
2. Improving teacher education facilities and practices
3. Readdressing administrative functions to educational needs
4. Establishing authority to coordinate educational practices
5. Establishing research facilities for educational studies
6. Providing for a mediating agency to settle educational disputes

Each of these items deserves discussion separately and will be taken up in turn at greater length, but first I would like to examine the relative importance of the teacher's role in the whole of the educational system.

The Organization of Educational Systems

To facilitate our analysis, we should first distinguish two general classes of roles played by educators: direct educational practice and indirect educational support. Teachers who stand at the front line of educational activities and come into direct contact with students engage in the former role. They are unquestionably the most important persons in the entire scheme of education, all other positions merely contributing toward heightening the effectiveness of their practice. They are irreplaceable. No matter how hard the other functionaries pull together and pool their resources, if the central role of the teacher in the classroom is not filled, nothing can be accomplished.

In the arts there is a clear-cut separation of roles between the artist as creator and the critic as evaluator. In education, we have the teacher, the practitioner of the art of education, and the educational thinker or researcher, a secondary but nonetheless essential role. The ideal teacher is one who is truly a master of the technical side of teaching, so thoroughly experienced that teaching comes as second nature, so successful at producing results that he or she is recognized and revered by all as an exemplary person. The awesome skill of a true master is perhaps more easily noticed in the arts or other disciplines because some tangible sign or record of accomplishments survives to be passed down. If the fame and technique of the masters of other arts are kept for posterity, why should education alone be different? Education is also an art, an extremely complex one, and one that should, like all other arts, be passed on to future generations. It is toward the creation of such masters in the field of education that our research must progress.

Here is where the similarity stops, however. In modern educational systems, the thrust of education does not originate with the teachers themselves. It resides in the central organ of the whole educational system that includes and empowers them. The teachers are rather only specialized cells in the total organism, comparable to nerve cells at the outer periphery of the nervous system.

If we push the analogy a little further, we note that the organization of the modern educational system cannot work independently of the rest of society any more than a bodily system can function outside the body. And just as one system or organ mirrors the others, we recognize a homology of center to distributive extensions. In a system as large and complex as that of education, the aim of nationalized public schooling can be achieved only through the complementary and cooperative organization of a two-part system: One part consists of the diversified outreach elements dedicated to direct practice and the realization of educational ideals and actual value creation; the other consists of the centralized managerial element to deal with administrative duties and research.

The last link in the organic vision of the relative organization of educational roles comes with an understanding of how the evolution of education and the evolution of society were not two separate processes but that the one grew out of the needs of the other. Just as originally the economic affairs of society were carried out directly without government intervention or direction from any central authority but came to require a center of leadership to regulate and coordinate society's business only as it grew more complex, so too with the business of education; what started as a wholly voluntary, private concern undertaken by local church schools or tutors gradually came into the province of the nation only after the unification of the state. Education having become a public concern, the state began to intercede on society's behalf to oversee and uphold the level of education and finally assumed control of education itself instead of merely subsidizing the private sector. The evolution of educational systems and the roles involved therein are considered in the following section.

The Teacher as Educational Technician

THE EVOLUTION OF THE TEACHER'S ROLE IN EDUCATION

To inquire into the nature of the unique mission of teachers in their remunerated service to society as the focal point of educational activities is to ask what society expects of them. What area in the division of labor constitutes their exclusive province? What responsibilities are they to fulfill? Such questions must be addressed first in any attempt to revitalize education.

The discussion of educational reform, of course, presupposes the clear realization that simpleminded assumptions about teaching do not work. No matter how long we bear with old laissez-faire ideas, it should be obvious that just bringing students into contact with an exemplary learned and moral human being in the person of a teacher in the hopes that sooner or later something may unconsciously rub off will never lead to a perfected educational system. Once again, nothing comes of efforts based on indefinite conceptions of what education should be. Let us, then, review the evolution of education in terms of the changing role of teachers and the corresponding development of adjunct educational institutions.

First period: the age of direct transmission of knowledge. In oral cultures, the three qualifications of the perfect teacher are extensive knowledge of what is to be taught, ability to transmit that knowledge, and exemplary personal character as a model for children. Breadth of understanding and a strong memory are the most revered qualities in a scribe culture.

Second period: the age of trial-and-error improvements toward transmitting knowledge in more readily absorbable form with the advent of printing technologies. At first, the choice and arrangement of lessons is left up to the teacher. Then, the boom in student population and the growth of printing industries leads to the use of backup texts, although many skills must still be acquired through trial and error. Much practical experience is lost because information is passed on only in the form of raw notes.

Third period: the age of specialized text production. Further increases in student numbers preclude finding enough learned and moral individuals to fill demands for ideal teachers. The government joins the search for more efficient means of teaching. Isolating one qualification of the teacher—the knowledge of lessons to be taught—from the total person of the teacher brings greater focus upon experience and command of teaching methods. In this division of labor, scholars devote their time to the compilation of texts, away from the actual task of teaching. Teachers need not be expert in the subjects to be covered to be effective as long as the text is authoritative and they are practiced in getting the message across. The printed word still takes excessive precedence in the teaching process at this stage.

Fourth period: the age of guided studies. Natural and social phenomena of the immediate living environment are studied through direct observation, with texts serving only as related reference material, much as stylebooks and grammars are used to supplement knowledge on finer points of an already familiar language.

But what does this mean for teachers today? It is obvious that we are not far advanced in our use of teachers to carry out the roles considered in the fourth period. In the most general terms, the work of teachers in this period is that of managing their students' interest so that the students absorb the material to be covered. But what does that really mean? For one thing, teachers no longer exist as pipelines for information but have become catalysts to the informing process; they stand no longer between teaching materials and students but to the side as conductors, seeing that attention is aroused, maintained, and compounded through proper pacing and additional explanations.

The basic intent is to get students to experience the validity of the lessons in their own lives. Of course, when students are very young, teachers may need to put extra emphasis on themselves, temporarily stepping in for other teaching materials and drawing out reactions. But as a rule we should never forget that the teacher is merely an accessory to the learning process. Teachers can never learn for their students; students must be allowed to learn for themselves. Conversely, there comes a sense of urgency to the prospect of teaching with the realization that no matter what teachers do, all will be to no avail unless they can get students to experience things for themselves.

This requires extreme sensitivity on the part of the teacher: an awareness of that unique natural and social environment in which he or she teaches, coupled with the selfless dedication to get students in touch with those things that can bring them happiness through the greatest realization of value in these real-life circumstances, through being well adjusted to nature and society. The teacher needs the sensitivity of a midwife to aid the self-actualization process without trying to control it, to be ready and standing by but not standing in the way.

We might see the changing role of teachers also in terms of the evolution of teaching materials. Here three stages can be detected. First is the stage of the textbook. In this stage, the teacher stands at the front of the class, employing books as the sole teaching device, verbally explaining and physically directing lessons. Second is the stage of reference materials. Concentration on textbook materials continues as in the first stage, but now it is supplemented by various enrichment materials such as pictures, real objects, charts, models, and the like. These are brought into the classroom to arouse interest and enhance learning. Third is the stage of experiential learning. In this stage the natural and social environment *as is* provides teaching materials, with the teacher acting as a guide, standing by to mediate the direct contact of students with the world around them.

There is a tendency to see the real importance of the teacher as a giver of notes. Teachers waste valuable time lecturing over material students might well read for themselves. Aside from writings not available in translation or extremely new information not in wide circulation, why insist on such antiquated and inefficient methods of teaching? To do so simply reflects a time before the age of mass communication when the word from the teacher's mouth held a powerful mystique. Seen from the evolutionary perspective, the coming trend in education is toward curtailing undue effort on the part of the teacher while at the same time conserving students' energies and learning capacities for better, less redundant uses. Thus, I foresee a major redirection in education from elementary to university levels.

Moreover, I predict that change will come not only by lightening the teacher's burden but also by actual reduction in teacher numbers. The elimination of perfunctory lectures readily obvious from readings would permit teachers to focus directly on study programs aimed at increasing student self-reliance in comprehension and application of textbook information. Nor will there automatically have to be one teacher per subject. A small number of selectively trained teachers per school with one teacher per several classes across comprehensive curriculum clusters should not only suffice to provide students with more overall guidance but actually reap superior academic results. The shift will be away from the heretofore accepted notion that a teacher must always be present, up in front of the class at all times, and toward the introduction of value consciousness in education. Self-study responsibilities and honor systems for students will be recognized as dear to the cause of education for value creation. This shift will no doubt entail the total reform of education as it stands, but if only for the sheer economy of such a move, I cannot help but feel the time is already upon us.

THE TEMPERAMENT AND QUALIFICATIONS OF THE TEACHER

On the basis of more than thirty years spent in the field of education, I would be hard-pressed to think of any single group of people who are more concerned with their own self-preservation and less concerned with service to others than teachers. Only rarely will teachers set their sights beyond looking after number one long enough to consider the life of the nation or society at large. I can only feel disheartened and ashamed when I observe how few in the teaching community would even think to engage themselves in discussions of how to best serve the public interest, when not a one misses the least opportunity to advance his or her own self-interest. All my experience has brought home to me the sad truth of Sakyamuni's words during more than forty years of preaching:

"Persons of either vehicle who seek their own salvation without trying to save others will never attain Buddahood."[4]

It is only when educators take stock of themselves as their brothers' keepers—or rather, as our children's keepers—that they become capable teachers. Educators are in this regard applied moralists. They must always stand ready to act as judges of good and bad and have the courage of their convictions to act accordingly. This is, of course, an awesome responsibility and not the sort of thing we want to entrust to just anyone.

What I am saying is that the notion of a profession called teaching presupposes that the teacher stand as an exemplary human being, a guidepost on the road of life. Any discussion of the ideal qualifications for teachers thus assumes that the holder of these qualifications be revered by society at large precisely for these. This should know no distinction from elementary to university education, regardless of the age or scholastic level of the students. When a person who does not measure up to these standards assumes a teaching role, it is nothing short of fraud.

We must now ask ourselves just what exactly the proper qualifications should be. One thing is certain. A respectable person for the job must be a whole person, someone with a unified personality, that is to say, someone whose words and actions match. The overall idea in teacher qualifications comes back to the question of character, of intellect in unison with personal conduct. This much, at least, has not changed from times past, nor will it change in the future, even in the face of cultural decline, political pressure, or the envious scheming of small-minded men. There is no reason to suppose that people will stop recognizing and respecting true character, for it is only human nature, and humans are not evil by original nature.

Assessment of teachers must not be carried out by harried supervisors whose busy schedules will not permit anything but the most superficial guesswork or snap decisions based on a few brief visits each year. Nor must it depend on those whose vested personal interests would bias their evaluations with ulterior motives. No, the most accurate means of getting close to the true value of a teacher is to run an independent check of the scholastic achievements of the students he or she has taught for the last few years. There can be no deception here; the teacher's influence will be all too plain.

Let us look at this another way. Why is it that nowadays the schools are in turmoil, unlike times past when "students walked three feet behind the teacher's shadow" because the sense of propriety toward teacher-student relations was so strong? Is it not because of the fraudulent credentialing of teachers? Has not the entire teacher selection process gone awry? Still, one cannot lay the blame there, for does it not all trace back to society's uncomprehending apathy toward the realities of education as reflected in uninformed and uncoordinated policies?

But again, perhaps we have no right to expect that there should be enough persons of real character to fill all the positions now required, for these are times when we have had to settle for less than average individuals even for police officers. It has all been too sudden and too haphazard. What did we really think would come of our rush job in establishing teacher training if not a flood of roughshod semiprofessionals? This is the cause of the current decline in education. Hence I repeat, it is essential that teacher selection seek persons of respectable character.

In order to bring about improvement in this situation, we need first to formulate standards of selection, followed by research into how best to implement these standards. As the bare minimum in teacher qualifications, I suggest the following points of emphasis:

1. Some degree of basic professional knowledge, that is, enough scholastic background to be able to apply educational theory on the job. Added to this, a good reader's curiosity and command of current topics to keep abreast of the world. And inasmuch as teachers are entrusted with elementary school children who have their entire life ahead of them, the position of teachers as educational professionals absolutely obliges them to have a reasonable acquaintance with educational theory. This is only common sense.

2. Before that, however, teachers must have a broad background in more general knowledge so as to be able to appreciate the specialized knowledge of their chosen profession and to conduct proper evaluation of subject material in context; that is, teachers should have a junior college education or more.

3. A sociological awareness in two respects. First, a teacher should be competent to function in that cooperative society in miniature, the school. Second, a teacher should possess a socialized character able to act as an effective model for students. Teachers must understand the aims of the group as a whole well enough to see beyond the limited perspectives of their specialization yet be able to withstand the

seeming cross-purposes of the total body politic. A sense of fairness and decency to form the core of the teacher's frame of mind must come from social consciousness.

Society defines the teacher as that person who, in the division of labor, is assigned the practice of education, with all the expertise that it entails. And just like a physician applying curative techniques, the teacher must be an educational technician. It is a fact that the professional is better at teaching than an amateur, which makes the teacher a teacher. The minimum expected, as we have seen, is that the teacher be able to guide students in their studies from texts; anything more must come from perfecting techniques with practice. Therefore, the urgent need is for a scientific scheme of training teacher candidates in educational theory from which stem technical principles, as well as providing practical how-to lessons in teaching. We cannot afford the uncertainty of having teachers blindly acquire skills over years of trial-and-error teaching any more than we can afford to be treated by barefoot doctors who have learned—how much, we do not know—solely from experience in the bush. All things considered, the primary qualification for teachers in their own studies is that they understand practical techniques of teaching together with the fundamental educational principles upon which those techniques rest.

How about the moral element, which we have seen as the most basic of all criteria for a teacher? Once again, this quality is harder to come by in the numbers needed for today's public education than is scholarship. We may have to settle for decent individuals; not moral giants perhaps, but not immoral either. In other areas of scholarship we will have to compromise and not expect every single teacher to comprehend all subjects, but about morals we cannot be so lax. For morality is the principle element at the root of educational theory, which in turn provides the guiding directives behind educational practice. Not one teacher is to be excused.

Much earlier we discussed Auguste Comte's three stages in the development of human knowledge, the ultimate stage of which saw persons who are no longer content to pursue their own happiness to the exclusion of others but actually offer of themselves in some form or another for the collective life of their community and country—and that not just in times of emergency but on an everyday basis. This attitude is more important than any other for teachers. It must permeate their thinking and bring clarity to their efforts to formulate educational aims. Unless teacher candidates fully awaken to this most central moral vision underlying social consciousness, educational theory, and, finally, teaching practice, they can only dole out hollow and ineffectual rote lessons.

Whatever else teachers and educators in general do, moral education is their most basic mission. Is this not the line that divides teachers from other value creators, such as artists and technologists? Thus the qualitative difference between educators and noneducators boils down to teachers' direct involvement with exclusively moral values in their value creation. If teachers and educators are to act as role models, then more than anything they are to be model individuals in the creation of moral value. Whatever else teachers' work entails, they must constantly be on the alert for actions and attitudes, however trivial they might seem, whose immorality or amorality threatens to break down the cohesive unity of their society.

I see social problems as stemming from poor education, the wrong roles learned from bad models. Clearly, when our leaders openly demonstrate their lack of morals, there is something wrong with our society. It is as if we have handed the keys to the vault over to burglars. In education as well, we hardly ever encounter magnanimous and civic-minded teachers actively contributing to the life of society. Instead, the greater part of the teaching community involves itself in jealous bickering, spreading unfounded rumors without compunction. They lack the courage to confront each other in an open discussion of the facts, much less to offer criticism and point out errors.

The original business of moral education was intended to promote public morals from the ground up. But do the supervisors or Ministry of Education authorities keep their eyes on this side of their civic responsibilities? No, the terrible truth is that they are utterly uncomprehending of the real meaning of education. Schools can excel in sports or drafting or crafts or whatever, but so long as they do not seek to remedy the moral ills of society, I fear that they will, in effect, only add to the problems.

For the same reason, no matter how hard school principals and teachers make it their daily concern to keep up appearances, balance the books, or flatter and cajole superiors, their inner unrest will show only too plainly in a lack of harmony. And this unrest will eventually spill out into society. I myself cannot simply remain silent and let the harm come to pass. Teaching must be brought under stricter supervision, and that means raising society's consciousness and expectations of teacher training and educational administration. No matter what is common practice in other professions, when the indifference and unconsciousness of teachers, for whom the distinction between good and bad ought to take precedence, lead them to turn their backs on right and wrong, it can only be called a blasphemy of the teaching profession. Unless the headwaters of education are made pure, we will just see the same cycle of erosion and dirty waters downstream repeat itself over and over again.

An Examination System for Elementary School Principals

My thesis in this section is that in order for principals to meet society's demands and deliver the full potential of elementary school education, we must establish not only a sizable body of standards of competency—to include both a command of teaching materials and a working knowledge of teaching methods, plus knowledge and skill in school administration—but also a rigorous system of examination to uphold these standards. I see this as a central issue in the whole of educational reform, for without radical pruning, the hazards stemming from ill-administered schools will only grow steadily worse with each passing year.

Up to now the selection process has been an altogether lackadaisical affair, with no real objective standards entering into the picture. Thus, as anyone might well imagine, the choosing customarily has proceeded on the general recognition of good common sense and worldly-wise experience, ability to meet spur-of-the-moment needs, or else some special talent for socializing and keeping up contacts in high places. Occasionally, of course, some good persons do happen to get posts in this way, but it is nearly always an accident. For the most part, the selection is made on the basis of conditions irrelevant to the main purpose of education; hence we find all too many principals who could not be less suited to their jobs. The dangers of this nonsystem do not necessarily go unobserved; it is just that no other approach presents itself as an alternative.

Any consideration of how to go about correcting the problem must first focus on the capacities of the educational supervisory system. As it stands, a mere handful of supervisors has to cover districts throughout entire prefectures, so they can only spend a minimum of time in each school. There is just no way they can be expected to get anything more precise than the overall gist of the school's state of affairs and staff quality. To be sure, these supervisors do not come into things unprepared, so they do get some idea of what is going on, good or bad, better than any layperson would, but still that is only on the most general level. So what they end up writing in their recommendations on contract renewals and job placement can scarcely be very concrete and instead tends to fall back on hearsay gathered here and there.

What is needed is a checklist of sorts: a set of selection standards by which to evaluate elementary school principals on the job. Next, the process of selection itself needs to be studied. Toward these ends, it behooves us to examine just what labors are actually given over to the hands of principals and whether these really constitute appropriate job requisites. At first glance this would seem only too obvious, but the fact of the matter is that society does not much appreciate the urgency of such systematization. Even the principals themselves hardly have any clear picture of what exactly they are supposed to be doing, so they generally bend to pressures from supervisory authorities. And if anyone thinks to criticize this charade of the blind leading the blind, no one has the courage to speak out.

What, then are principals supposed to do? We note two fundamental spheres of involvement:

1. Administrative duties, that is, overseeing the running of the school according to the rules so as to passively prevent regulatory mishaps.
2. Value-creation efforts, that is, actively working to increase the effectiveness of teachers under them, thereby allowing for more meaningful education to reach the children directly. What this boils down to is not so much running the show as removing the obstacles that would otherwise prevent dedicated and motivated teachers from taking the initiative in implementing their skills.

The active sphere of involvement ranks as the number one focus in the labors of elementary school principals. Other tasks — accounting, record keeping, coordination and compliance with higher supervision, and the like — all are secondary, of subordinate value. Everything branches out from the central aim of value, which is the life of education. Even if only relatively little time and effort go directly into active value creation, it is precisely that part of the work that cannot be eliminated, for therein lies the essence of the job. Other more repetitive and mechanical administrative duties might well be relegated to subordinate staff members. It would be easy enough to hand almost anyone the task of keeping records and making reports on the observance of set rules. The active provision of optimum conditions for value creation in children's education, however, is no ordinary busywork and so is not to be entrusted to just anyone.

Once again, what conditions are good principals supposed to provide? First and foremost must come stability. Just as the head of a household must first ensure the security of the home, and the ruler the security of the nation, the principal's first order of business is to bring a peaceful order to the school. For no matter how well external appearances are glossed over or how successfully public relations proceed, even the most celebrated principal will fall from popularity and soon vanish in ignominy if no lasting, fundamental order is established. Likewise, so-called award-winning schools most often only bask in the light of temporary or partial achievements and special programs. Far more attention must be directed to effecting lasting improvements through setting down basic standards.

Nonetheless, educational administration is of a slightly different character from other areas of public administration; hence reforms cannot proceed as they do in other parts of the government. Elsewhere, reform proceeds by universal application of ground rules of economizing and streamlining across the board, that is, by readjusting or eliminating administrative organs that have outlived their usefulness in their present form.

By contrast, money has in many ways ceased to be a limiting factor in today's education. For it is in education that modern citizens see their children's future. People today are more than willing to make that extra effort to make sure their children get ever more adequate education. Because they are no longer satisfied with the school facilities provided by public expenditure and, even more to the heart of the issue, because they hold strong reservations about the character of teachers and the educational system as it stands, what people seek is decidedly not simple-minded budget cuts or perfunctory force reductions but a total, progressive, and constructive reform based on thorough value-oriented considerations.

True to the aphorism "There is no plastering over a crumbling earthen wall,"[5] no amount of external support can remedy an inferior base structure. Now is not the time for a face-lift or a mere remedial patching up. Educational reform must be wrought from the ground up.

Everywhere the demand is for clean sweeps of administration, for weeding out the bad elements. And that is fine — eliminate superfluous staff and all who have outlived their usefulness if need be, but should we replace them with the unskilled and inexperienced? I would sorely regret losing whatever old pros we do have, teachers who have gained valuable expertise over long years of study and experience, just to jump on the bandwagon of streamlining administration. What sort of reform is it that throws out jewels mixed in with the other rocks and that does not distinguish between the skilled and the unskilled? We cannot have it both ways: We cannot rail against the supposed high salaries for proven educators and call for their replacement with younger, less expensive teachers, while at the same time decrying the shortage of quality educators.

Meaningful reform must proceed the other way around, for there is no dealing with the situation at the tail end once teachers of questionable effectiveness have already been chosen because of a lack of stringent selection criteria. Rather, energies must be poured into improving the quality of educational personnel. I guarantee that real savings will follow. If we succeed in enlisting superior human resources by painstakingly selecting personnel, and then make equally careful choices to find just the right persons capable of directing and coordinating these human resources, there should be no problem in reducing the supervisory inspection force instead.

We are now back to our original questions: How are we to go about selecting qualified teaching personnel, and what qualifications make one capable of overseeing their efforts? It is my belief that the best way to proceed from where we stand right now is to first establish an orderly examination system to select from among candidates for the job of principal those who fully demonstrate their confidence, dedication, and respect for the position. Then they should have a free hand in directing or weeding out the incompetent and unskilled, so that at the least there will be no further decline in the effectiveness of the educational staff, and, beyond that, in improving the effectiveness of the skilled. Thus, setting aside the issue of fostering superior ability among new teacher candidates for a separate proposal to be presented later, we will turn our attention to delineating minimum requirements for an examination system directed at identifying the leaders among incumbent teachers:

1. Authority of examination. After the example of examination systems for other professions such as law, medicine, and technical trades, a board of examination made up of educational scholars with at least middle school teaching certification from the Ministry of Education, together with scholars of sociology and other related disciplines, is to be responsible for examining candidates and current holders of principal posts.

2. Contents of examination. Essays will be used to demonstrate knowledge of educational studies directly related to the job of elementary school principal, with particular emphasis on scientific training and cumulative experience in educational methodologies. (Unfortunately, educational research at this point is still inexcusably weak on practical methods. We await the establishment of facilities dedicated to practical study of education—that is, educational strategies actually applicable in real-life teaching situations as derived from real practice.)

3. Intent of examination. The examination will ensure that persons placed in charge of schools and entrusted with the cultivation of future citizens will operate not out of blind intuition or dogma but out of rational and scientific understanding of their particular field.

All high-level occupations—physician, lawyer, pharmacist, and so on—demand a commensurately high level of specialized education. Elementary school teachers similarly need a high level of knowledge of their profession above and beyond a general middle school education. Only then will they be able to systematically manage their duties and effectively incorporate scientific findings into their practice.

The trouble with teachers up to now is that it has been easy enough just to get by. Because for better or worse educators deal with children unable to make value judgements for themselves and thus unable to level criticism in their own defense, educators have been palming off a haphazard job of teaching with no ill effects showing up until much later. Accordingly, even the most undistinguished persons could put in their hours without any further study on their part at all. And so too many teachers simply repeat the same tiresome lessons year in and year out for ten or twenty years, neither discovering anything new nor effectively creating value. Such teachers, who really have nothing to offer for all the time they've put in, inevitably end up as relentless dogmatists, relying on nothing beyond their own limited experience. It is precisely because there are so many nonteachers like this that principals charged with coordinating and directing them absolutely must have a higher-level command of curricular knowledge and practical skills.

Education has reached today's straits because it has been let slide for more than fifty years now. The problems that have amassed will not be corrected in a day. The ill effects are quite far-reaching and will require extensive multiple studies and concrete proposals. Now is the time! In this connection, we can start by implementing a testing system such as the one described above, which will help to set specific training requirements for principal candidates whenever new openings are to be filled.

Proposed Reforms in Teacher Employment Conditions

The big question in seeking to reform the employment conditions for public education personnel is to decide whether to please the educators or society at large, for it appears they are almost at irreconcilable odds. Although no educator would ever say that monetary provisions were by any means excessive, the rest of society as a whole finds it impossible to meet the seemingly endless demands within their standards of living. Set limits must be established as a median. We educators are surely grateful for the continual efforts of politicians to improve our lot, but all the same we need to go on to reflect that our salaries do come from taxes levied upon the common citizen.

Let us thus consider whether the present terms of employment are indeed excessive or not. Of course, this is governed by prevailing economic conditions and the overall prosperity or depression of society. There was a period in the middle of the World War, for example, when industry was booming, and teacher salaries were so low in comparison with those in business that many fine teachers were siphoned off into commercial enterprises. When the war came to a close and suddenly the economy ran into bad times, many sought to return to their old jobs. The economic situation keeps fluctuating, so it is difficult to lay down any one hard-and-fast rule. Needless to say, cost-of-living allowances must allow variance either way over time, but as to the current material benefits of our profession—our point of reference—I daresay none of us insiders in education could possibly claim that we are getting a worse deal than the rest of society at large. We have only to observe the fierce competition for matriculation into teacher training schools to realize just how good we have it. To put it frankly, our terms of employment are positively the envy of most self-employed business persons.

Why, then, should it be that we are unable to enlist adequate numbers of able individuals into the ranks of elementary school teaching positions? There must be some other reason. The problem lies not with present conditions but with the future. The starting salaries may be good — perhaps even a little too good — but then they go nowhere. In twenty or thirty years we see no scale of advancement comparable to, say, wage increases for those in other parts of the government, the military, or private enterprises. And there is no easy way under the system as it stands to approach the concerned local economies of the townships or districts for raises either. This is a major obstacle to recruiting good teaching staff. Therefore, reform must actively address not the lower limits but the upper limits of salaries, not the minimum wage question but the issue of maximum wages.

How, then, do we set the upper range for employment benefits? In the more advanced European countries, I have heard, conditions are made attractive enough to ensure that promising human resources will stay with the job for their entire career. Something along such lines needs to be worked out for Japan. That would prove the most appropriate solution, I believe. Of course, as mentioned previously, there as yet exist no objective standards for recognizing or evaluating human resources in education in terms of their actual capacities. Short of such standards it remains impossible to treat real excellence fairly. If the upper limits of the wage scale for educators is to be extended, we must correct for this lack of standards of excellence.

Moving on to more intangible aspects of the treatment of educators, we should be ready to recognize and respect real ability on whatever level and give credit where credit is due. Many are the educators well deserving of acclaim, yet they receive neither official recognition nor supervisory posts. In order for teachers to feel confident in their work and be able to exercise their skills fully, they must all be treated with the same spirit of respectful consideration that society extends as a matter of course to doctors, lawyers, industrial engineers, crafts persons, and artists. And they should not be subjected to excessive administrative interference or pressure. For educators, being recognized as competent professionals becomes a point of pride in themselves and their work, something all too unacknowledged at the moment.

Getting teachers to realize their importance, moreover, has implications reaching far beyond the immediate circumstances. Teachers must be made to feel that what knowledge and expertise they have acquired is worth passing on. Imagine what a loss it would mean to society if that valuable store of information — real cultural property — were never to reach the next generation of educators. There ought to be some system of acknowledging excellence other than the hierarchical ladder of job ranking. Failing that, the treatment of educators ought to at least be as favorable as that given all other representatives of officialdom.

Proposed Reforms in Teacher Education

GENERAL CONSIDERATIONS FOR REVISING TEACHER TRAINING PROGRAMS

The Ministry of Education proposal for improving teacher education is notable in that not a single person, from the minister himself on down the line, has ever attended a teacher training school. One newspaper account commented on this feature of the proposal as follows: "According to the plan it is expected that the new heads of the Ministry, none with any ties to the educational community past or present, will at last stand not on the side of the educators, but truly represent the demands of society."[6] This is a good move in some respects because it brings laypeople into discussions of educational issues. But it is the distrust of professional educators reflected in the ministry's action and the public's response to it that should be of concern to teachers. I am afraid that we have only ourselves to blame for this state of affairs.

Whatever the case, I submit that the measures called for will remedy present dead-ends on a short-term basis at best. I doubt that the proposal will have an effective life of more than a few years. I am disheartened to think that in their distrust of currently active educators, neither those who went ahead to decide on this plan of action nor the members of society who are going along with it care to look very far into the future.

How much better it would have been to have taken this opportunity to institute policies that reflect the basic underlying thrust of education instead of quick compensatory measures to counter the more circumstantial and peripheral shortcomings of the day. In other words, social realities are not the only deciding factors. The essential tenor of education must also enter into the calculations. This might seem the long way around to harried public administrators and engineers who must produce immediate results, but I for one would hope that a good physician would not only make a detailed diagnostic examination of the specific symptoms of whatever visible illness but also have the perseverance and foresight to render judgements based on a checkup of the patient's total physiology. The questions that need asking are those of relevance. We must recognize just how vastly and integrally related this one part of the life of society is to every other part as well as to the whole.

Only when we have succeeded in collectively and objectively evaluating what the total social situation truly demands will appropriately basic proposals to reform teacher education be forthcoming. This necessitates a complete about-face to fundamentals, that is, to a reassessment of the role teachers are to play in society. An accurate picture of what exactly teachers are to do will go far toward determining how they are to do it, which in turn will inform efforts to redirect education and, in particular, teacher education.

Teacher education up to now has operated on the naive assumption that knowledge of the curriculum is all that matters. The time has come to supplement this single line of thinking with a three-pronged approach:

1. General scholastics – curricular studies, to gain command of the various subjects to be covered
2. Preparatory techniques – methodology, to acquire experience and knowledge in teaching methodologies and means of directing studies in various subjects
3. Moral cultivation – character development, to foster awareness of the teacher as a role model in personal character, the foundation of the other two aims

These three aims can be further amplified by the understanding that before becoming teachers, teachers are first students themselves receiving instruction at each level:

	Scholastics	*Methods*	*Morals*
Student level	Organizing information and applying knowledge to real life	Acquiring writing and verbal skills needed to record and recall direct instruction	Acknowledging and actualizing moral principles after the teacher's example

Teacher level	Guiding information gathering and application toward value creation	Studying and utilizing techniques for relaying basic skills of retention and recall	Self-actualizing model character to serve as a basis for guiding moral value creation
Teacher training level	Providing information and directing studies in scholastic methods	Directing studies in general preparatory background knowledge	Systematically aiding character formation

Existing teacher education programs have, by and large, considered only the first area, scholastic knowledge. The technical and moral dimensions of teacher training are still a relatively undefined wilderness. Not only do we lack basic definitions of background knowledge for teaching positions, but the specification of necessary skills and technical knowledge is primitive at best, while the standards of assessing and selecting morally sound human resources in education have yet to approach those already instituted in such fields as, for example, the military.

Although this lack of attention to the technical aspects of teacher training might have been unavoidable in the days when educational studies had not yet recognized the value of providing guidance to teacher candidates in professional skills, now that we are certain that scientific educational research must be born of actual experience and relate to actual experience, we need greater emphasis on techniques in practice. To ultimately perfect educational theory, we must scientifically establish principles governing the ways and means of guiding studies. If the present blind trial-and-error business of teaching were thus transformed into clear objectives in student guidance, I predict we would see a sudden upsurge in successful concrete schemes of education sweeping away the uncertainties that have nagged us so long. Education would become more effective with each passing term, and as teachers themselves actually took interest in their teaching, they would become master practitioners in a profound art no less noble than any other professional accomplishment.

Technique, however, is not the only qualification for professional standing. It takes moral responsibility and social consciousness. Given that elementary school teachers are placed in charge of up to seventy students per grade level, and that each student is a unique and irreplaceable individual life the same as any adult, we know we do not want mechanically uniform results from inflexible application of technique alone. But once we reject the rigid production-line approach, discipline becomes a problem. Supervision of extracurricular activities, field trips, and the like, where real dangers to the students may be involved, aptly demonstrates the seriousness of the problem. If a student should be injured or killed, it becomes a major issue far beyond the limited context of teaching. To espouse total permissiveness only shows how little one knows of the realities of education. Teaching may be an art, but unlike artists, teachers are not dealing with inanimate materials. Teaching is ultimately a moral proposition.

Individual teachers probably differ little in the amount of effort they put into their job. The telling difference in what they do is rather a question of the relative degree, scale, range, and breadth of their acknowledged objectives. One teacher is not the same as any other in terms of effectiveness in teaching, and it is markedly inefficient to play musical chairs with teachers, moving them around to new assignments when conditions change. Far better would it be to train teachers with an eye toward ultimate objectives. To raise teacher consciousness is to increase the effective flexibility of each teacher to meet whatever conditions exist, thus eliminating the need for uneconomic reassignments and readjustments. In a real sense, maximized flexibility is what the teaching profession is all about.

Strategy in the attempt to remake the teacher education system will be determined on the level of those theoretical tenets by which we first take a stand. Failures up to now and our perpetual return to the drawing board do nothing if they do not prove this point.

When the school system was initiated, almost the sole consideration was how quickly great numbers of teachers might be produced to spread education nationwide; hence it was inevitable that energies focused on quantity rather than quality. But by now Japanese education has reached the limits of such thinking, and it is time for a reversal from the quantitative approach to fulfilling the qualitative potential of the facilities we already have. We have the numbers; let us be more exacting about teacher substance in our planning from here on. The following questions need specific answers:

1. Is teacher education only to vary in the extent but never in the kind of contents? Will it continue as an extension of existing general programs with some measure of improvement in the level of information but no additional specialized methodological studies or applied practical training?

2. Is there to be teacher education by force-feeding or by guiding teachers through their own process of discovery and application? Are teacher training schools simply to transmit as many disparate pieces of information as must be taught, or are they to serve as centers to facilitate teachers' acquiring of the knowledge necessary to effectively assist students in learning and discovery processes and to allow teachers to practice the associated methods?

It goes without saying that no one with a mere layperson's knowledge would feel comfortable deciding just what items of specialized professional information deserve inclusion in teacher training programs. Who, then, is to decide?

As one might suspect, academics are not likely to have any more perspective on such specialized concerns than the average person on the street does. Up to this point, the decision has fallen to a steering committee of teacher training school principals, as a result of the educational administration's conviction that they were the most qualified to judge. But asking them has proved no more conclusive than asking the manufacturers of a product for ideas on how to improve it instead of going straight to the consumers themselves. For innovative thinking, we should look not to the supplier but to user demands. So how about asking those who have been on the receiving end of teacher education, the active elementary school principals who are the real source of the teacher training school principals' insights anyway? Even here, however, we need to choose whom to ask. We would want the opinions of those elementary school principals whose superiority is proven through experience and a scientific grasp of the prospects for improving education. But before we can determine this, we need to reexamine the essential role of the teacher, the elementary school teacher in particular. At the risk of belaboring the point, let us consider philosophies of education embodied in the person of the teacher:

1. Are elementary school teachers meant to be suppliers of information or helpful guides to the processes of inquiry and learning? The real source of problems up to now has been the mistaken adoption of the former role. Socrates said long ago, "Knowledge cannot be transmitted," but somehow the meaning of the words has yet to really penetrate.

   Thus teachers have spent their time trying to implant information into their students' minds when what they should be doing is channeling student efforts into better ways of formulating ideas for themselves. Once this is admitted, the task of preparing teachers in the means of directing studies must become the highest priority in teacher education.

Moreover, directing knowledge acquisition should not be limited to the inner life of the mind in so-called scholastic pursuits; it applies just as much in the outward life of working in the world. Teacher education must recognize that the mental processes of cognition or knowledge formation manifested in on-the-job value creation and those involved in scholastic learning are the same. All areas of human activity operate within the triadic framework of benefit, good, and beauty. This is true of the teacher's job and of teacher education as well.

2. Inasmuch as it is the aspect of moral good that most concerns teachers in value creation, the second priority in teacher education must be to instill a greater measure of the moral elements in teachers' personal character than is present in the average person.

3. There is little variance from subject to subject in the curriculum on the above two items: Teachers need knowledge and training in methods of assisting learning and value creation, and they need cultivation of their moral character no matter what they are to teach. But of course, they also need some degree of academic background as a basic prerequisite. In other words, although this last fundamental has been overemphasized in the past, it is still a vital concern, if only a third-place priority.

The most fundamental issue and the deciding factor in resolutions to remake teacher training facilities is how best to raise consciousness of the teaching profession. Perhaps more than any other profession in the service of society, education is a complicated business, especially because it aims to foster character values. It requires a total synthesis of means and ends, large- and small-scale operations, short- and long-term planning, rough outlining and precise detailing, into systematic and orderly procedures. Thus, teachers need both the specialized educational knowledge of universals, as well as the all-purpose abilities to handle whatever might come up in practice. Such command of theory and practice and ends and means comes only with long years of training and study.

Still, most people do not recognize teachers as technicians who need thorough training and practice. Few even are the teachers themselves who give enough thought to this! It gets overlooked in determining employment conditions, in weeding out dead weight, in passing on and cross-fertilizing teaching techniques. As a result the oversight adversely affects the overall effectiveness of education severely. This much should be obvious by now.

The technical side of education is every bit as demanding as that of any other art or form of value creation. If anything, it is more complicated, so naturally it takes long years to perfect. But because there is nothing in education comparable to the master-disciple apprenticeship system, people tend to think that there is nothing to education ("Why, anyone could do that with a little headstart instruction and practice!"). Such thinking belongs to the age when scholarship was still simply a combination of latent skills, if in a somewhat more orderly form, already found in certain individuals throughout the populace. That is no longer enough: As all fields of knowledge now evolve in tandem with associated specialized technologies or techniques, so too in education has the time come to raise our expectations of teachers and see them as first-class technicians or artists in the service of society.

Unsympathetic and unaware of the real technical potential in teaching, educational administration has wrought incalculable long-term damage to society by dealing with teachers purely on a monetary basis, treating them like mere hired labor or office staff to be arbitrarily assigned and reassigned. Why have we allowed so sacred a calling as preparing our children and youth for life in society to be contracted out like so much menial labor?

If teaching is a technology or an art, then what does that mean? It is not something that just happens to come about from one or two chance successes but the product of compounded practice and experience meeting specified conditions so that particular results can be assured. The abilities that guarantee these results, when invested in a person, are said to be that person's special skills. Their attainment is what separates professionals from ordinary people. Ask them how they managed it, and most likely they themselves will not be able to explain—it is simply ingrained in them. Artists sometimes even amaze themselves with their own skill, and true masters go so far as to display a seemingly inhuman degree of perfection in their art. This is not limited to the so-called fine arts, of course, but applies to all human activities once a certain level of proficiency is surpassed. Why not, then, with education?

In most fields, the proven way to attain technical proficiency is to enlist as an apprentice under an expert and learn the basics until one is competent enough to fend for oneself in a competitive market. Typically this takes upwards of a decade of steady practice. If we are fully satisfied with the roughshod grade of teachers that the teacher education system has produced thus far, then that is fine; nothing more need be done. But if we want to have truly superior teachers, then we had better take a lesson from the apprenticeship system and have our teachers put in a number of years of proper study and practical training under those who know what they are doing. As invaluable as children are, as vital as persons of good character are for tomorrow's society, it is a tragedy that instruction of teachers has been patterned after material manufacturing and not the apprenticeship system. The proof is in the product. How can anyone expect someone to produce anything worthwhile without a good number of years of hard practice?

RECENT DEVELOPMENTS IN TEACHER EDUCATION ABROAD

A completely independent perspective on reforming the teacher education system, that of recent developments in teacher education in Germany and America, lends further support to arguments I have been making in favor of changing Japan's present system. I think it especially important that we examine what is happening abroad, because the questions that are now being debated by the Ministry of Education—largely centering on whether separate teacher training universities should be established or whether teacher education should be simply one departmental major within a more comprehensive liberal arts university—are not limited to Japan but are common to progress in teacher education worldwide. In America, perhaps the leading innovator, and even in Germany since the Great War, we find that neither proposal has won out entirely, but instead both approaches are being implemented simultaneously. Both countries have established special teacher training universities as well as university-level programs in larger institutions.

Perhaps because of their size, however, neither Germany nor America chose to follow one set policy nationwide. Which of the two approaches is preferred depends entirely on the region. In Germany, for example, Saxony, Thuringen, and Hamburg have not set up separate teacher training universities, whereas Prussia has. In America, areas west and east are different, as again is the south; programs even vary from state to state.

Some discussion persists as to whether one specific type of teacher, say elementary school teachers, are better prepared under one system or the other, but wherever either approach is used we should note that it is university-level training that has become standard practice, and all graduates are thoroughly tested before being granted credentials. Moreover, in Prussia, full credentials are not granted until after five years of actual service as an associate teacher. We have much to learn from other countries toward perfecting our own system.

Proposal for a National Educational Research Center

In this section, my thesis is that national funding be directed as soon as possible toward founding an educational research center along the same lines as the national or quasi-national research centers that already exist for the study of hygienics, chemistry, nutrition, weaponry, and the like or as the research and development facilities for industry, agriculture, forestry, and aquaculture in the private sector. There is no excuse for the failure to modernize. We have been implementing "new" Western educational practices for more than half a century now. We have forged ahead in these other fields, yet we still force our several million students to undergo the same unreasonable and uneconomic ordeal in the name of schooling. Nor is there any sign or hope that things will get better on their own. Common sense should tell us that the potential for harm here knows no limits.

Although a centralized national or quasi-national educational research center would undoubtedly be the best thing, if that should prove difficult, the most urgent needs might be handled by establishing regional centers on the model of local agricultural testing stations. In such a case, the ideal solution would be to establish private research centers funded by the donations of civic-minded philanthropists.

If I might offer an analogy on the value of this proposed national educational research center as an authoritative organ, I would compare it to a seismometer, which by virtue of incorporating an absolute "true" point of reference independent of its grounding in the bedrock plate can measure tremors therein. In much the same way, an educational research facility might be planned, set up, and maintained for testing, unaffected by the political, economic, and ideological shifts in its social grounding.

Education is an exceedingly complicated proposition; its rational and scientific systematization, a gigantic undertaking. To imagine that the meager experience and creative ideas of isolated individuals might bring it off is delusive. It will only be possible by obtaining the cooperation of knowledgeable parties from many disciplines in conscious recognition of the essential aims of education and by further orchestrating the various contributions toward those ends. In particular, the realization of quality education demands, first, dividing up the labor between separate organs for planning and implementation, then coordinating them in a mutual and harmonious manner. The central planning commission must strive not only to rise above the fragmentary accepted thinking of disparate interests among society's divisions of labor and to sweep away hard-set prejudices but also to bring together the invaluable legacy of lessons from past pioneers to shape the educational ideal. This planning organ must be enabled to provide the conditions necessary to make the ideal a reality. Nor can teachers as on-the-spot educational technicians peripheral to that central organ be satisfied with working in bits and pieces. They must perform their duties out of a comprehensive and consensual understanding of the whole scheme of education as laid out by the planners. This means that they must have an even better grasp of the ideas of educational pioneers as systematized in their cumulative writings. Only then will teachers break out of their blind lethargy to take heed of the aims of education, take pains to upgrade their own teaching methods, and prove whether the plans put before them by the planners are, in fact, appropriate. The real proof for both planning and implementing organs is in this process of self-testing, mutual criticism, and corrective evolution.

Correcting from the actual observed results also proves the surest way to avoid perpetuating uneconomic practices. It is simply bad management to stand by and watch how things develop undirected. Whatever the field, it will be seen that rational management is necessary for developing a unified organic structure; hence the move to establish research centers for planning in various industries. Inevitably they are seen as long-term investments: outright expenditures at first, but eventually paying back the original capital outlay many times over. This thinking is likewise behind the call for establishing an educational research center.

This educational research center would not stop at merely testing the practicability of applying rules down to the letter as in existing trial-program elementary schools attached to teacher training schools but would go one step further to ascertain whether the rules themselves make sense. Toward this end, freedom of research and freedom from external interference within the limits of the law must be guaranteed. By the same token, inasmuch as the process of education consists of assisting or directing students in their own learning processes, testing must be radically different from the rote experimentation that medical researchers conduct on animals, yet neither can it fall to staid repetitive trial runs of ideas developed elsewhere. Research must always be conducted on a strictly scientific basis, curbed by the moral necessity of making sure no harm comes to the children. We must assume neither the regimented stance of educational philosophy that seeks to find one set methodology for the human norm nor so-called liberal education's permissiveness, which tries to accommodate each and every individual's subjective experience as a unique thing unto itself.

In its physical plant, the educational research center would consist of three interactive facilities: a higher normal school aimed at fostering expert educational technicians capable of carrying out studies in value-creating education, an adjoining elementary school for practical testing and proving new ideas in value-creating education, and a census facility for recording self-reported and observed findings from teaching practice. My own ideal in the above may be outlined as follows:

A. Three basic aims must converge to realize the full potential of the educational research center:
   1. Study of the ways and means by which experienced teachers as expert technicians in value-creating education are to guide the teaching staff under them.
   2. Greater provision for value-creating education than for ordinary teacher training, with an aim toward instilling thorough competence in educational techniques.
   3. Maintenance of ideal operating conditions in the attached elementary school to provide control conditions for testing and proving theories in value-creating education.

B. Research center fellows are to be selected from among those elementary school teachers who have several years of practical experience and who, furthermore, show special interest in education itself. The standard items of consideration for selection are to include the following:

　1. Objective verification of thorough training and a superior track record of competence in educational techniques as an indicator of an exceptional degree of interest and dedication to education.

　2. Requisite scholastic background for teaching, as well as a highly developed skill in utilizing that background to the students' aid.

　3. Faultless work record and good peer relations with colleagues.

　4. Some piece of self-initiated research as an indicator of on-the-job innovative spirit.

C. Research center fellows must meet a standard of two years' practical experience directing actual student lessons and studies and must have attained scholastic ability sufficient to pass the Ministry of Education's certification examination for middle school teachers.

D. Research center curriculum is to include the following:

　1. Actual-site [in-class] training in teaching methods based on scientific instruction.

　2. Directed studies in principles and basic theories of education.

　　a. Studies in scientific educational research.

　　b. Directed studies in sociological foundations of educational thought.

　　c. Directed studies in psychological foundations of educational thought.

　　d. Directed value application of applied science.

　　e. Directed studies in the history of scientific thought.

　3. Studies in religion as the fundamental principle of human life, and religious guidance toward the ideal life.

　　a. Directed empirical studies in religion as the heart of personal character.

　　b. Life guidance toward "relying on principle, not on authority figures," according to religious teachings.

E. Directed studies for research center fellows are to be conducted as
follows:

1. After fulfilling their responsibility to instruct at the adjoining
proving-ground elementary school under the half-day school
program [see the section in this chapter entitled "The Half-Day
School System"], fellows are to spend the remaining half day in
critical evaluation and in various curricular studies, so that after two to three years of in-service training, they will have attained sufficient scholarship to pass the Ministry of Education's
certification examination for middle school teachers and will
possess the knowledge and skills to serve as a model in directing
elementary school teaching personnel.

2. Going beyond the prevailing condescending unilateral teaching
practices that reduce students to vessels for receiving information, research center fellows are to develop their abilities for
directing students' learning in various subjects via some form of
self-initiated research.

3. In order to foster personal values in students to enable them to
create the economic, moral, and aesthetic values of benefit,
good, and beauty to guide them through life, research center
fellows particularly need directed studies in how to assist students in applying principles of knowledge in their own lives.

4. Because the evolutionary or developmental perspective on history encourages interest and new discoveries in educational
studies among students and teaching personnel, a historical
consideration of the development of ideas and practices in
scholarship ought to be added over and above the regular upper
school curriculum, so that research center fellows might become familiar with evolutionary principles.

5. Because the essential aim of education is to help provide guidance in the life of society and to help set it on an ever-better
course, research into the real-life circumstances of the people,
that is, scientific study of social realities, is of primary importance. I believe this oversight to be one of the most serious
failings of education up to now. Therefore, detailed study of
various aspects of society should be one major concern of this
research center.

6. Training will be needed in unifying knowledge and action, word
and deed, ends and means. Because education seeks to guide

the transformation of undisciplined, unconscious, unplanned, and uneconomic living into conscious, rational, and economic living, educators, as models, should possess some understanding of the great moral principles expressed in religious tradition.

7. A healthy and whole citizenry depends in no small part on the moralizing influence of its teacher models. Research center fellows must have the courage to discuss issues of right and wrong openly without letting their own emotions hinder their objectivity.

F. The adjoining elementary school is to open its doors especially to underprivileged children. In other words, in order to instill elementary school teacher candidates with a pure and altruistic interest in education, the proving-ground elementary school should enroll the poor and needy to arouse interest in the mission of education itself and circumvent aims to ulterior benefits.

The reasoning behind all these recommendations is aligned with the Herbartian view that takes accepted notions of ends and means in education and turns them around. Whereas formerly the transmission of knowledge was seen as the aim of education, making the transmission process as interesting as possible, I hold that the true purpose of education is to engage interest and that presenting information serves but to promote that involvement. For the same reason, if the goal of teacher training is seen not as the implantation of knowledge en masse but as getting teachers to think for themselves, then obviously the best way to do that is to arouse their interest as the prime mover toward self-betterment. Only then will they in turn be able to guide their students competently. Learning is learning whether the students are children or teachers themselves. In either case, it is largely a matter of motivation. Personal interest and involvement, more than fame, more than personal gain, more than anything else, take the center stage in cultivating human resources.

Proposed Reforms in Educational Administration

LIMITING SUPERVISORY POWERS TOWARD SCHOOL AUTONOMY

The establishment of a legalistic structure of rights in education is a relative proposition. To make education more effective, we must not only clear away the inconsistencies currently obstructing the educational process but also clearly outline the limits of authority. Only by clearly defining the limits placed on rights and privileges can we hope to do away with unfair, excessive, and oppressive exercises of power in certain quarters, while at the same time upholding the just rights of all involved.

This has become an especially pressing concern since the nationalization of education, bringing in its wake the complexities of today's educational administration. Many parents of today's students received their education during the Meiji and Taisho periods, and so, being that much more aware of what goes on in schools, they are not likely to simply stand by uninvolved and let some supervisory administrator or honorary official with no direct ties to their school come tampering in educational affairs of the local community. For better or worse, it is now the community's own school, understood as an extension of home life. Parents have taken on a guardian role toward schooling, not merely providing school supplies for their children but actually going so far as to enter into discussion of the contents of education, searching out the causes of good or bad grades, coaching and encouraging study. And for the first time, we are starting to see education bear fruit. On the other hand, however, there must be something more that can be done on the educators' side. Given the sizable percentage of family living expenditure now given over to education, parents obviously have their rights, and educators an obligation. The astounding cost of education is a sum of innumerable sacrifices and invisible efforts.

By contrast, the hiring and dismissal of principals and teaching personnel has up to now been the exclusive prerogative of supervisory administrators, wholly removed from the parents and local groups. Such policies and procedures ought to have been left behind in the move away from autocratic bureaucracy to democratic participation through constitutional suffrage. As taxpayers, parents and local groups not only have the right but also the obligation to visit the schools and to see that their money is being put to good use. This is not something to be left to others but is an essential part of home rule. If this much be admitted, then from now on parents will have to take it upon themselves to make educational studies figure into their common knowledge, right alongside child rearing, sanitation, cooking, sewing, and so on. Fairness demands that parents serve as the final evaluators of educators in the same way that consumers have the only real perspective on the soundness of products, because to parents' eyes, children reflect the character and achievements of teachers with uncompromising vividness. Nonetheless, such evaluation can be realized only after parents have a general background in educational thinking as a standard basis of judgement. Once a majority of parents are informed, what better way is there for educational administrators to get reactions to their policy decisions than to ask local groups openly for their opinions, instead of conducting clandestine surveys?

There could be no better, more honest, or more straightforward way for local citizens to effectively express their autonomy than to establish school autonomy as part of their constitutional rights. Having at one point during my term as principal at Shiragane Elementary School in Tokyo already come close to acting on this conviction, I feel more and more convinced that we Japanese are ready and willing to make this move.

Admittedly, in the early, formative years of Japan's modern educational system, people had too little background to determine for themselves just how far the authority of the central administration should extend into civic life. Consequently, the administration overextended itself and took the liberty of posting superfluous and redundant officials in the name of coverage, so they could not help but prove a burden and a meddlesome nuisance to the common citizen. Then before we knew it, we were plagued with incompetent minor officials who specialized in abusing their powers.

If a clean-sweep reform of educational administration is to occur, it must start with a penetrating look at this fundamental issue. The question of limits to power concerns not only educational administration, of course, but here it becomes all the more critical that we never let the authorities forget their true role in the service of education.

A strong line must be drawn between old politics and new. The autocratic age in which people were to be kept on tap but kept in the dark has given way to today's age of autonomy, in which people keep tabs on how their taxes are spent. It may have been permissible and even expected in times past that officials actively and directly interfered in the public welfare, but even so, there had to be limits to the number of posts, if for no other reason than the sheer impossibility of infinitely extending finite funds. We have in some ways come a long way from those days, and yet the illogicality persists. Higher-echelon supervisors posted ostensibly to keep an eye on the business of school administration end up not only overstepping their rightful place and assuming others' powers but actually creating mountains of needless bureaucratic busywork for lesser officials. If anything, they guarantee inefficiency. The problem here is that what started out as an essentially passive administrative function meant solely to prevent the nation from going to ruin in a chaos of lesser autonomies instead became an entrenched part of the bureaucracy.

What is needed is a separation of duties and powers. If active directorial or supportive administrative functions are deemed necessary, a special office should be established for just that so that existing offices can attend to their given functions with no loss of goodwill. Otherwise, this kill-two-birds-with-one-stone approach, lacking definite distinctions, will continue to work against effective education.

In short, we must recognize limits to administrative powers in education as in other areas of government, keep these offices to passive, preventive roles, and eliminate pretensions to active, steering functions. At most, it is a question of moral, not legal dimensions. It would not be possible or desirable for police officers to actively encourage each and every citizen to do right, and it is just as unreasonable to expect the agents of protective prevention in educational administration to try simultaneously to manage the affairs of all other officials as well. That never was the purpose of supervisory school inspection anyway. Granted, inexperienced teacher trainees and substitute teachers in outlying areas might be in need of some overseeing, but what is the role of the school principals if not to provide such guidance?

Administrators, whatever the field, are to bring their attention to bear on the minimum operating requirements—whether the rules and regulations are being observed. Should there be no infractions, then they really have no business interfering and certainly are in no position to pass evaluative judgements on the competence of teachers. Other than the citing of regulations, or alternately their observance, the only scales they have for making judgements are utterly undistinguished commonsense notions.

Of course, educational administrators and educators themselves are both working to realize the same larger vision of what education is to be — the underlying ideal of all their efforts — but within the system aimed at that goal, their respective roles could not be more different. Like the physician who works to remedy present ills and the hygienist who seeks to prevent the causes of future illness, the immediate objects of their technical skills diverge, but their accomplishments converge in the greater perspective of parts combining to make a whole. It is only the complexity of today's education that demands such divisions of labor — just as with the development of medical science the general practitioner's role has been split up between various clinical practices. Yet this does not mean these functions are antagonistic, existing in independence and opposition. Rather, they are to realize a cooperative coexistence. Particularly because the technical side of teaching is such a delicate matter, susceptible to interference from all other areas of the educational system, limits must be set on the relative development of each area in order to create a horizontal structure of equal and mutually supportive relations between teaching and administration, instead of the present vertical hierarchy.

The question may then arise as to where exactly the authority to hire and fire teaching personnel should rest. This issue was debated at the 1931 session of the Committee on Restructuring Regional Administrative Finances, during which it was proposed that such powers be shifted from the Ministry of Education to the Ministry of Domestic Affairs. Which would be better? Well, if effective limits were placed on the administration of education as suggested above, the difference between the two ministries at the teaching level would be insignificant. The Ministry of Education claims that the Ministry of Domestic Affairs cannot comprehend the complexities and special circumstances of education. But on the other hand, this incomprehension might work to the advantage of educators by preventing excessive administrative intervention, keeping administrators at a distance. Again, if administrative powers were shrunk to the passive minimum level of prevention, the extent of comprehension should hardly make much difference. Why, even the Ministry of Education is only half comprehending at best! For the sake of autonomy, would not uncomprehending administrators who didn't interfere or pretend to know it all be better than half-comprehending administrators who put on omniscient airs and throw their weight around?

The way that administrators treat teachers is outdated and feudalistic. Yet teachers are educational technicians or artists, and even in ages past, lords knew better than to order artists around like commoners and instead treated them like honored company so that they felt encouraged to implement their full artistic abilities. On rare occasions, one does see some enlightened regional administrator treating an old-hand teacher with all due respect, but the point is that this ought to be the standard for all administrators in their relations with teachers in general.

How respectful a distance, then, is ideal? Comparisons between the administration of education and other areas of public service end at the point at which we acknowledge that, unlike the cases of police officers and judges who have to be transferred from post to post to prevent them from forming local emotional ties that would bias their judgements, teachers and principals cannot be shuffled about insensitively. For, unlike average bureaucrats who, however trustworthy, only occasionally have any contact with matters of personal character in their bookkeeping and paper pushing and thus can cause but minimal passive failures of omission, in education, supervisory inspectors and teachers deal with real people on the level of value creation. Whereas the former are to go by the book of legality, avoiding emotional or moral involvements (or at least keeping them private) in the interest of public fairness and social equality, teacher-student relations must, of course, be more than just fair across the board; they must go one step beyond the passive prevention of wrongs to the positive promotion of good through warm interpersonal relations tailored to the individual.

By guaranteeing teachers a reasonable measure of job security, the Imperial Elementary School Order has already contributed much to the recognition of teachers as occupying a special position not to be reduced to that of rank-and-file officialdom. Indeed, were teachers' responsibilities not protected from the power politics of school inspectors, the damage would eventually spread throughout the nation's citizenry. It is now common knowledge, even among those unacquainted with the inside story of education, that teaching is sacred as nothing else in society is and must be kept inviolate. Any teacher worthy of the name, worthy of respect as a teacher, must prove his or her ability to judge between right and wrong and to make a difference by choosing the right, not just giving lip service to it. The superior teacher is, in effect, the embodiment of moral value. If such a superior teacher were to be imprudently transferred, the shock to innocent and impressionable young minds would be more severe than most adults can imagine. For this reason, more than any other, it is my conviction that the powers of school inspectors acting on subjective whims should be curbed, if not curtailed altogether.

School inspectors have been granted a special position relative to the rest of the administrative functions of education, though it is not clear why. From the point of view of the educational community, they are a meddlesome nuisance; and from that of the national economy, an unnecessary waste of expenditure. If education were to remain in its present sorry state, there would, perhaps, be some justification for keeping them. However, I would prefer to plan a better future.

The school inspector system ought to provoke heated controversy once the stake it claims in society's future is seen for what it really is. Educators especially, once they realize their own vital role in guiding society, ought not to simply stand off to one side and let these policing agents have a field day. We educators should not keep silent, fearing for our own necks, but should reflect upon the system with detached open-mindedness.

Up to now, the proponents of the school inspector system have pinned the blame for the "less than convincing" results of education on a supposed shortage of personnel keeping watch over administration. Thus, government, in its incomprehension of the realities of education, complies by increasing the already superfluous numbers of inspectors at ever greater outlay of funds. Examples of this are all too numerous. The nation's finances are drawn upon as if unlimited, yet no corresponding improvement in the quality of education results. This is an imposition on the taxpayer.

To the layperson, the idea that both supervisory and leadership powers might be vested in a single figure sounds most convenient. Yet if we press such thinking to its logical conclusion, the ideal thing would be to have one inspector assigned to each school. This would amount to having two principals at every school: one to take care of regular office work and administrative tasks, the other to keep watch over teachers and provide them with leadership. Accordingly, teachers would have to take orders from two authorities, throwing the whole school into confusion, wasting funds, and even worse, jeopardizing the mission of education.

Perhaps in the case of short-term technical in-service training, it might make sense to call in a specialist for guidance, but where are these school inspectors' claims to mastery of any specialization? When they bear no special knowledge or experience or have even less knowledge than the norm, as is the case of too many inspectors, their pretensions to authority, their hard-selling of new educational ideas they themselves have only just picked up and don't really understand, become both offensive and detrimental. The original reason for having inspectors at all stemmed from a lack of confidence in the abilities of principals, for which they were to function in some compensatory capacity. If that be the case, then why not bring in specialists to address specific issues if and when they arise? What need is there to keep an office of superseding authority permanently dangling over principals' heads? Today's school inspector system is a throwback to the rotating teacher trainers who did the rounds of the school circuit back in the early Meiji period, when inferior teachers were still prevalent. Still, I would not say school inspectors are necessarily counterproductive, as long as there are schools that lag behind the rest and need some additional pointers.

But to carry this line of thinking further, the cases in which school inspectors would be a positive benefit are limited to those in which principals and teaching staff have proven their incompetence. And that argues not for any school inspector system but rather illustrates the need for a proper job-placement examination system for principals, as we have discussed earlier. The question of how best to provide leadership for teachers thus comes back to the promulgation of an examination system for principals, stressing a command of scientific research on educational principles and teaching methods. If this were done, principals would be immediately relieved of the unnecessary humiliation of the present school inspector system.

THOUGHTS ON A CENTRAL PLANNING AGENCY FOR EDUCATION

At least two major elements must be addressed in considering how to revitalize Japan's educational system. One involves reforms focused directly on upgrading the quality of teaching personnel so as to enable them to implement their abilities fully. The other is the establishment of a planning agency as the central organ of the system, an agency that would be empowered to draw up and organize long-range plans. Short of accomplishing these two aims, mere bifurcation of functions within the system as it stands will simply obscure matters behind cosmetic improvements and postpone real change.

The central agency would make a difference through active planning. Elsewhere, we have made the comparison with the idea of military readiness. Just as the general staff headquarters in the armed forces never fails to attend to strategic decisions even in times of peace, education must never lag in setting down and continually reorienting its directives if it is to keep up with all possibilities in the wake of changing times. It is a grave mistake just to leave this important task of forward planning to the Ministry of Education, which simply serves to enact previously determined policies, or to the Educational and Cultural Policy Council, which, in turn, does nothing more than support the ministry as a review board.[7]

Education ought to be thinking a hundred years ahead. Instead, decision are left up to politicians so nearsighted they can't see beyond what contributes to their own public image in the next election, which makes the actual educators even more nearsighted as they vie and connive to protect their jobs. For all the supposed suffrage of the electorate in matters of education, the realities of the system have hardly left the age of slavery. Planning for the next hundred years, a function that rightfully belongs to a central planning agency, cannot be abandoned to the interests of bureaucrats whose calls for reform do not really change anything. Under the present system, they cannot do much but evade the responsibility.

This being the case, it is only natural that educational policy should have fallen so far behind the times and run into a deadend. And just as obviously, we should not brood over past failures but get on with the business of actively planning long-term educational policy.

Here it is half a century and numerous reforms after our country's first modern educational system was borrowed almost directly from foreign sources, and yet amazingly nothing has changed overall. This is true, for example, of higher education, which was formerly geared exclusively to the needs of the privileged classes. Although this theoretically is no longer the case, everyone in education today, right up to the administrators themselves, still seems quite comfortable with the notion that students for public middle schools ought to be selected on standards of superiority specific to the middle class and above; hence the senseless tragedy of the "examination hell" of competing to get into the university.[8] Even today, when middle schools have come far toward spreading education nationwide, the roles of public and private schools have somehow gotten reversed. Although public education ought to work up from the lowest common denominator to meet the greatest need as a populist institution, its standards are so high that only those students with the best grades, who will need the least attention and cause the least trouble — in other words, only the elite — get admitted, while the rest are farmed out to the private schools by default. Indeed, nothing has really changed at all.

How long can these outrageous conditions be allowed to persist? Social consciousness is growing rapidly. Common citizens have begun to make it their business as taxpayers, members of local support groups, and parents to call for equal opportunities in education. If the curriculum is to come from the value creation of real life and utilize the whole living environment as text, then the entire apparatus of education needs overhauling. The age is one that demands rebuilding of the educational system in its entirety. This is why it is urgent that we move immediately to establish a central planning agency to decide on a unified long-range educational policy.

What, then, would this planning agency do? In general, it would survey the conditions of contemporary society and determine what will have to change over the next generation. It would be charged with seeking how to provide the best possible education for tomorrow's citizens, giving constant attention to planning the creation of personal values. Its task would be one of observing and making proposals, not implementing existing statutes as do other areas of administration. Nor would it do the research center scholar's investigative work of researching better, more effective methods in teaching. Rather it would work to set the larger framework within which teaching can take place. It would consider the internal structure of the educational system in light of its external relations to other government functions and determine how it can best serve the ends of the future well-being of the nation, and so the agency would develop long-range plans. On the basis of its assessment of the overall condition of the nation, the agency would act to coordinate the efforts of all organs within the educational system.

Of course, finding the right persons for the job will not be easy. Nonetheless, I propose that a network of persons from all walks of life, who understand the exigencies of education from a scientific viewpoint and who are open to new ways of thinking, be asked to keep their eyes trained on the horizon of the coming age. A council of such progressive thinkers is imperative.

AN AGENCY FOR MEDIATING IN EDUCATIONAL DISPUTES

The accepted traditions of Japan's educational community, developed under autocratic rule, cannot stay on top of the wave of innovations now overtaking the political and economic spheres. I have said this time and time again. Problems are cropping up all over, but the old feudalistic ploys will not work anymore. We can't just follow the leader right or wrong or put an end to things by sweeping them under the carpet. We need the resolve to face the issues and seek out solutions appropriate to the times. Three mechanisms must work together in any such scheme of problem solving: a mechanism of neutral mediation to settle disputes fairly, a mechanism for reprimanding offending parties, and a mechanism for bearing out the views of vindicated parties.

To some, an agency of mediation in educational disputes may sound dangerously close to the rhetoric of labor bargaining, but we must at least be prepared to run into conflicts within an educational system undergoing the strains of radical change. Ideological disputes are bound to occur, especially among young innovative teachers leaning toward extremist thinking. Autocratic directives by persons in higher administrative positions are not the answer. A system of explicit checks and balances is needed.

Humans are creatures of emotion and reason. Head-on collisions of emotion may be devastating, but clashes of thought in debate are nothing to fear. Emotional warfare tears people apart, whereas persisting with rational discussion must eventually lead to some consistent conclusion. Those bureaucrats who reduce themselves to paper-pushing automatons to avoid having to deal with real issues are forgetting that humans do have this rational side and that only by illuminating the differences and similarities between views can a synthesis be reached.

The emotional fiats of the autocratic age disallowed rational discussion, but the public forum is the essence of today's constitutional democracy. How could true participatory rule ever come about if we feared to enter into debate? It may be asking too much to expect children to take part in such discussions, but certainly any persons who have received an education—women included—are well equipped to discern reason from error through debate. Furthermore, it is common knowledge that subjective decisions do not solve anything but, rather, confuse and prolong arguments. They do not uproot the disagreements but actually cultivate them. A neutral third party is a must.

Whether on the international or the individual level, disputes arise from specific causes. They do not just happen spontaneously. True solutions must get to the root of the matter by retracing the course through which the problems erupted and totally eradicating the causes. Judgements must get to the truth and error by relying on principle, not by bowing to anyone's personal authority. There is no other way to solve disputes.

Consider what happens when children get in a fight and adults cannot be bothered to hear out their claims but instead punish both sides. Yes, they may cry themselves to sleep, but not without first having their beliefs in fairness shot to pieces as they learn the terrible "truth" of autocratic domination: "Might makes right." In the same way, I have observed that when disagreements break out between educators, as they often do, just dropping the issue or trying to smooth over hard feelings ends up seriously affecting the efficiency of education. There has to be an agency outside the schools set up expressly for handling such circumstances. Its operations would no doubt be open to various proposals, but the important thing is that it be dedicated to seeing disputes through to a resolution and to tackling problems at their roots. Formalistic decisions that lay down the law as fait accompli without even touching upon the core issues represent nothing more than a demonstration of power politics.

If schools are to operate in the spirit of constitutional rule, the settling of disputes cannot fall to the prejudices of supervisory inspectors who punish both sides because that's the way it's always been done or who rely on clandestinely gathered hearsay. Such unconstitutional practices must be outgrown if we are to increase the overall effectiveness of education and raise the standards of excellence for teachers. We cannot acknowledge constitutional rule as the most rational social system while still accepting the customary bureaucratic ways of settling disputes among educators.

It is just as in the courts. Were trials always open-and-shut cases with definite evidence, a single judge might suffice; but because cases get complicated, and evidence is often circumstantial at best, a jury of persons with no direct connection to the affair is brought in to mediate. This sort of jury system ought to be implemented in education, either as needed or on a regular basis, for certainly educational disputes are complex. One idea would be to form a council of educators who have proven their benevolence over long years of professional experience.

There is a difference, however, between private or criminal cases and putting administrative practice itself on trial. The courts reflect this in distinguishing these as different types of law requiring specialized knowledge and experience on the part of the judges, much as the whole government is divided into executive, legislative, and judiciary powers. Educational disputes raise the difficulties yet another step, particularly when it is ideas that are being debated. There can be no mean wielding of rules; jurors have to be chosen for their perspective on educational thinking. Properly instituted in the spirit of labor mediation boards, this mediating agency would do much to clear the blocked passages to educational reform, assuming that the limits to the powers of this agency would be made equally clear by educational scholars.

The actual power to reprimand must, for example, be vested in a body distinct from that which hands down verdicts. Nor can we simply avoid punishment altogether. Education is serious business with serious social consequences. Educators who act out of pure self-interest not only abuse the trust that society places in them and revoke any real right to membership in the educational community but actually work against education's ideal of creating a cohesive social entity. They are poisoning the seedbeds of culture. And even if by normal social standards of evaluation they were not doing anything so wrong, other more stringent standards of judgement hold within education because of its far-reaching influence. Insidious elements must be gone over with a finer comb, as it were. There must be policing and correction of thinking from self-serving Hinayana alienation, which plunders the system, to true Mahayana constructive participation in the system.[9]

On the other end of the scale, good ideas and practices deserve rewarding, something the mediating agency is not really intended to do. It only passively supports the vindicated parties as an incidental and temporary consequence of the verdict. As important as good, solid human resources are to education and to society as a whole, it stands to reason that we need a separate mechanism to promote creative teaching. This would admittedly be hard to institutionalize, but at least for the time being I can think of no better means than getting together leading figures in education to lend an active voice, a group such as my own Value-Creating Education Society (Soka Kyoiku Gakkai).

Proposed Reforms in the School System

RESPONSE TO THE MINISTRY OF EDUCATION'S REFORM MEASURES

First, it will be instructive to consider the general outline and basic import of the Ministry of Education's original plan for reforming the school system as submitted and approved for adoption at the cabinet meeting of September 1931. In that plan, special emphasis was given to shortening the term of schooling, providing complete education at every level, opening school doors to all citizens, and establishing coeducational university programs. In more detail the ministry's plan includes the following:

1. Kindergarten is to be kept in the present three-year format.
2. Ordinary elementary schools are to be renamed public schools and operate on a six-year program.
3. Higher elementary and middle schools, girls' high schools, and vocational schools are to be renamed high schools and operate on two- or five-year programs. Existing middle schools, however, are to be kept in their present four-year format.
4. Existing higher schools are to be converted into two-year university preparatory schools.
5. Universities are to be kept in their present three- or four-year formats.
6. Graduate courses are to be established above the university level for the benefit of those engaged in special scholarly pursuits.
7. Specialized courses are to be kept in their present three- or four-year formats, with the provision that these may be extended to five years where necessary.
8. Normal schools are to follow a so-called two-pronged approach: The main program of three years is to enroll new-system high school graduates, while an additional two-year preparatory program is to round out two-year high school (prereform higher elementary school) education. Other than this, no special preparatory schooling will be required.
9. Existing higher normal school as well as arts and sciences university programs are to be curtailed and replaced with new four-year normal universities. Separate one-year teacher training centers are to be established for those graduates of specialized courses who wish to become high school teachers.
10. Youth skills centers and vocational training centers are to be grouped under the heading of youth schools, consisting of a regular two-year course and a three-year middle-level course. Moreover, a practical skills course, mainly dedicated to upper-level training, is to be newly established in a three-year format.[10]

Counter to this Ministry of Education plan, the Educational Study

Society has published its own proposal for reorganizing the school system, the first section of which is entitled "Failures of the Existing System" and covers the thirty-odd years since the currently effective Imperial Orders on Schooling and Education were first issued. Over that period, the proposal states, certain changes have been made, but none have been able to meet fully the present demands for education. First, the proposal notes six major shortcomings in the existing educational system:

1. Present educational organization fails to meet demands for equal educational opportunities.
2. Schools from the elementary level on up are operated as preparatory institutions for higher education, effectively sacrificing the interests of the vast majority of students for those of the few who will matriculate to universities or specialist courses.
3. Present education has become enforced uniformity.
4. Present education leans excessively to intellectual cultivation.
5. Unwarranted special privileges accrue to school graduates.
6. Present education often accepts less than exemplary teachers, for lack of an adequate system of teacher training and testing.

Second, the following ten-point plan for correcting the above deficiencies was recommended in the proposal:

1. Universalization of middle-level education
2. Full revision of remedial and supplementary education
3. Founding and expanding of special research and directorial entities to promote the cause of general social education
4. Realization of the special capacities of schools at each level instead of preparatory schooling for higher education
5. Scrapping the mechanical standardization approach and instead allowing greater leeway for free experimentation so long as student needs are met
6. Turning away from education's fixation on intellectual development and instead instilling an engaged working mentality, giving special attention to cultivating the spirit of creativity and training in society-oriented activity
7. Elimination of special privileges for school graduates
8. Shortening the term of schooling

9. Improvement of teacher training in normal schools
10. Rational budgeting of educational expenditures

Third, in a section titled "Outlined Schedule of Educational Reforms," the proposal calls for a school system consisting of elementary schools, public youth schools (currently called remedial schools), middle schools, and specialist courses, while abolishing existing higher schools and universities. Graduate schools are to stand as the highest institutions of learning; all other institutions in the existing system are to largely follow the Ministry of Education's plan.

The Society of Educational Critics (Kyoiku Hyoronka Kyokai) also presented a proposal for reforming the educational system; however, it remains closer to the existing system than the proposal above. This proposal consists of the following eight points:

1. Each school must aim to mold personal character and instill professional competency.
2. Adjustments must be made in both the organization and contents of schooling so as to shorten the period of in-school education.
3. Each school is to complete a full educational curriculum within its respective course length.
4. The entire educational system is to be coeducational.
5. All special privileges for school graduates are to be abolished.
6. Educational expenditures are to be budgeted fairly.
7. Amendments to the educational system are to pass legislative approval.
8. Facilities for general social education are to be developed toward ever more complete educational outreach.

Among the many other views pro and con on the proposed reforms was this excerpt from an editorial in the *Tokyo Asahi Shimbun* (September 2, 1931), which, for the most part, echoes my position:

> The educational community has voiced sharp opposition to the Ministry of Education's proposed school system reforms. . . . Judging from the words and actions of these opponents, however, we seriously doubt if any of them stand on more than their own limited range of information and experience. None seem to have any fundamental recognition of just how grave the shortcomings of today's

school system are. Numerous key issues must be brought up: the reorientation of education to more practical ends and the shortening of the term of study are among the more crucial. Thus, in effect, these educators appear to be opposed to these positions altogether. They are laboring under the misconception that education can be rendered more effective through a complex reworking of curricula, elevating the level of teaching, or extending the term of schooling "even just one year longer." Theirs are the mistaken judgements that come of biased and narrow thinking.

An even more fundamental error lies in thinking that education need be limited to in-school study. We have become prisoners of the conventional view that unless students do their time in school—a sixteen- or seventeen-year sentence—they will not amount to anything. It is unreasonable to assume that the cultivation of each and every citizen, rightfully a lifelong effort, might be fully accomplished through schooling. This is the realization to burst the bubble for all those school shut-ins and hopefully at long last open educators' eyes to the broader spectrum of the life of society as a whole. They just need a little push. Moreover, although the idea of shortening the term of schooling by one or two years can only be a halfway measure at best, their proposal of a year's extension is hardly any less ridiculous. I say that if we're going to go that far, we might as well go the whole way and call for reforms on a scale grand enough to make education extend one's whole life through. Probably the path of least resistance to all concerned is to establish a parallel work-study program, as I will argue below in the section "The Half-Day School System."

REASSESSING THE FAILURES OF THE PRESENT SYSTEM

Surveying the variety of reactions to the prospect of educational reform, I am struck by how far opinions stray for lack of understanding about the present system and of standards by which to plan for the future. I can only repeat my contention that education is a complicated business of far-reaching consequences and interrelationships—one of the most difficult endeavors in human life. Unless we trace minute particulars back to fundamentals, we will achieve no true solutions.

The first thing needed in order to reassess the existing educational system and project a plan of reform to correct for past failures is standards of judgement. In looking at the many views on reform now bandied about, it is unclear just where their various proponents base themselves. The arguments of the proponents fail to convince because they haven't done their homework. Now is the time to dissect current education, analyze it in light of the goal of our survival as a nation, carry out serious evaluation, and give our findings precise expression. The cure must proceed systematically from the base metabolism.

1. Let us observe just how much energy society pours into education. Although more money is spent on education than our society can afford, education, as has been pointed out above, is not managed effectively.

   a. The total cost to the state, to local governments, and to families — to society as a whole — of soaring educational expenditures is staggering. But to what effect?

   b. Out of the sum total of school graduates, how many are meeting society's needs? Does not the rapidly increasing number of unemployed high school graduates constitute a threat to society? What are the causes?

2. The majority of schools merely provide preparatory schooling for higher education, not true education in tune with practical real-life concerns. That is because special privileges accrue upon graduation, and these are considered the only means of access to the good life; hence students matriculate with the exclusive goal of going on to higher institutions. Thus today's education has ended up wholly removed from the broader aims of human life. Unless we put an end to special privileges, all we will have done is construct an alluring trap for our youth. Most persons lack the insight to do anything about what comes to pass. They are merely passive observers of the changing times, so they throng to the schools in the vacuous expectation that these privileges will continue to accrue indefinitely. They are unwittingly making an addiction of education.

3. Education is impractical. It is not a question of whether or not the educational system should aspire to uniformity. Granted, there is little argument that education goes further than necessary in this direction, but it is equally certain that some degree of unification is essential. More important, however, it is education's lack of concern with practical matters that needs correction.

4. Education is unproductive.

    a. Not only should education be more productive in the narrow economic sense, but it also should follow through in all three dimensions of value creation to produce benefit, good, and beauty.

    b. Vocational education must begin from an orientation toward value creation. So-called practical education is all too appealing to today's society, fed up with irrelevant education. Nonetheless, let us not resort to the meanest sort of unmitigated utilitarianism, or we shall veer over to the exact polar opposite of our current dilemma.

5. Are we really overemphasizing intellectual cultivation? Contrary to the popular view, the ineffectiveness of education would indicate an underemphasis. Just where would this supposed overemphasis manifest itself in schooling? If the overemphasis of intellectual education should mean the underemphasis of moral education, this definitely would present a problem. But this is not necessarily the case. Placing the blame for the ineffectiveness of moral education on the emphasis of intellectual education is like being envious of one's wealthy neighbor and attributing one's lowly financial status to the neighbor's neglecting to put forth efforts to improve one's economic situation.

    No, I see the upholding of scholastics as the only basis for realizing moral education. If we cut back on scholastics as a corrective measure, we would only end up that much more ignorant as a people. It is not that we have gone too far with intellectual development but rather that our means run to excessive force-feed methods, and as a result we actually achieve the opposite result, undereducation. Understandably, the amount of time and energy that today's schools expend inefficiently would seem to justify the criticisms of excess. But in terms of actual achievements? Before we lash out against this overemphasis on scholastics, let us recognize the underlying methodological insufficiency it attests to.

6. Leading thinkers and legislators have always been vocal about moral cultivation, but unfortunately, lack of established methods of teaching moral education has led to its being shortchanged. As a result, we now have a morally impoverished citizenry.

7. Long has appreciative education—that is, the cultivation of aesthetic sensibilities—been invoked under the name of emotional refinement, but with no definitive approach set forth. We still hear the same old summons to action, but we remain uncertain about what to

do. My reading of the situation is that because we lack clear educational goals in this direction, we naturally cannot come up with any means of carrying them out.

8. Appropriate planning does not take place, because neither policymakers nor practitioners in education are clear about objectives; hence nothing is seen through to completion. We have been groping in the dark for more than sixty years now and have worked ourselves into a corner. Everyone involved, planners, politicians, and practitioners alike, must look realistically at the whole educational system from top to bottom.

9. Insufficient provision for teacher training and testing not only fails to ensure reasonable staffing but sooner or later turns away toward other professions whatever good teachers might have chanced into the system.

10. Lack of standards for teacher employment and promotion leaves these crucial matters entirely to the whims of administrators.

11. No set directives govern teacher coordination or leadership. Administrators freely overstep their authority to interfere and pressure, squelching any teacher initiative. Hence education cowers at the lowest common denominator of efficiency.

12. Educational policy has yet to be established in any of the above areas. Moreover, no provision yet exists for a review board to consider such matters of policy.

13. There is not even any facility for studying or testing educational methods as a basis for establishing educational policy.

Ultimately, in order to propose decisive and systematic reforms in the educational system, we must resolve certain key issues. Having thus far merely responded to the ever-changing demands of the times, our educational apparatus has heedlessly expanded into an unmanageable behemoth, a huge bureaucratic structure in sad need of repair. We could race about patching leaks as they spring up, and fix this and that, but it would consume all our time and money. The whole works are rotted through from foundation to pillars. It makes more sense to simply pull the whole thing down and build again from scratch. We can thus replace the old uneconomic construction with a brand-new order. As a minimum, we will need to undertake the following moves:

1. A thorough reassessment of the effectiveness of the Meiji educational system.

2. Comparative study of the educational systems in the more advanced nations of Europe and in America as in the past, of course, but also of the systems in more backward countries, such as China, that have tried the same course as Japan and are just now encountering the same dead-end predicament we already face.

3. All involved must bring their own special knowledge and professional experience to bear, but even more important, everyone needs a systematic and scientific grasp of the raison d'être of education.

In other words, we must duly reflect on our experience over the past half century, come to a critical understanding of our ideal, and pull into consideration reference materials from at home and abroad. We must attack problems from three sides by uniting the expertise of persons representing society, practicing teachers, and educational theorists.

Our present predicament is due partially to our having become caught in an autocratic framework that exacts divisions of labor to keep people in their place — teachers following the dictates of the Ministry of Education to the letter and nothing more, administrators considering only their immediate jurisdiction without question. It is precisely because no one steps out of line to take in the larger picture that no one ever puts forth any opinion on reform. And even should someone directly involved in the business of education venture an opinion, the big shots or politicians are quick to make it clear that criticism is off limits to mere teachers. So practitioners just stick to what little they need to know, with nobody saying a word, nobody wanting to know anything more.

Yet what is the meaning of our constitutional rights of suffrage in this day and age when all are expected to lend an active voice in constructive criticism if it is not to call each and every one of us, regardless of position or class, to freely take up a national cause such as this? Now is the prime opportunity in which to contribute to fundamental reform. It is to be expected that building anew will necessarily first entail tearing down. And even if one's own past efforts or those of major figures and politicians are criticized or overturned in the process, making the task less than pleasant, we must think of our nation's future and our children's well-being and sweep aside our small personal attachments.

We must be open-minded enough to place options for decision in the public domain, which is where they belong.

With these general assumptions acknowledged, let us take a quick glance at the roots of the major issues involved:

1. Is it not time to break away from the idea of transmitting knowledge and to change to the idea of guiding the acquisition of knowledge? Does this not go hand in hand with an emphasis on value creation instead of mere scholastics?
2. Is it not unreasonable, from both the point of view of the students' own happiness and that of what society requires, to turn young people's entire childhood and adolescence into a study hall at the expense of all else?
3. Although budgeting of educational finances is of course a necessity, isn't that far overshadowed by the need for an economy of learning? And that goes hand in hand with a total revision of teaching materials and corresponding improvements in teaching methods. (This is the main thrust of the system of education set forth in this book.)
4. Should education be run publicly or privately?
5. And another basic logistical question: Who is most qualified to take charge of shaping the final reform proposal?
6. Lastly, the setting of the term of compulsory education is an important issue because it affects school management and the distribution of courses in the curriculum.

GOALS AND GUIDELINES FOR EDUCATIONAL REFORM

The goals toward which I hereby propose a program of reforms in the school system may be summarized as follows:

1. Education is to focus upon providing guidance to the processes of knowledge acquisition and value creation. Instead of crippling students with the scholastic blinders of book learning, an economy of educational means (in the broadest sense) will see them involve themselves in two parallel courses of activity simultaneously, one scholastic and the other vocational. This will entail the total realignment of all levels of schooling—elementary, middle, and higher.

2. Schooling at every level is to be made to meet real-life needs. Improvements must be made so education will prove useful in life, and schools must become a natural extension of living so that attendance does not need to be enforced.

3. Special privileges for school graduates are to be eliminated; a special examination system is to be established for those seeking jobs requiring specific qualifications. This will see preparatory education vanish in due time and likewise obviate the university entrance crunch.

4. In-school education should be closely connected in practice with actual social life so that it can transform unconscious living into fully conscious participation in the life of society. Education integrated into the life of society will yield benefits of well-planned living without the undesirable effect of mechanical uniformity, an inherent danger in standardized education.

5. Education is to meet the needs of the individual without favoring the privileged classes or persons of exceptional ability. In particular, public education must extend aid to the otherwise underprivileged classes in the spirit of equal-opportunity education lest they turn to socially counterproductive behavior.

6. Study of various teaching methods is to be undertaken to ensure ever greater educational efficiency.

7. Teacher training facilities and normal schools are to be made over so as to yield the quality of human resources fit to manage the above improvements in education.

8. Teacher testing and promotion systems are to be improved.

9. Limits are to be placed on administrative powers, and school autonomy is to be assured in the name of educational rights.

10. The various administrative and regulatory institutions in education are to be streamlined or abolished.

11. Special dispute mediation and assistance facilities are to promote the cause of unhindered education.

12. Educational research facilities are to be established.

13. Improvement of teaching materials and methods should be undertaken, beginning with the revision of Chinese-style characters used in Japanese writing.

Next, we will need to consider structural guidelines to be included in the proposal for reforming school education:

1. Types of schools.
   a. Schools are to consist of elementary schools, public schools, and higher public schools.
   b. Middle schools and specialist courses are to be established as necessary to meet the need for vocational instruction in that particular area.
   c. Existing higher schools and universities are to be abolished.
   d. Supplementary forms of education — youth vocational training centers and the like — should be combined.
   e. Scholastic study centers are to be provided at every level, the highest of which is to be graduate school.[11]
2. Instruction at each type of school.
   a. All schools at every level are, as a rule, to operate on a half-day schedule.
   b. Elementary and public school students are all, as a rule, to work at the family business for half the day.
   c. Daytime and night classes are to be offered in vocational guidance at any school where local conditions merit.
   d. The main purpose of higher-level vocational schools should be to offer the results of research into the best vocational education, and they should, as a rule, be open at night.
   e. All of the above educational institutions are to take as their primary mission of operation the guidance and training of students for cooperative socialized living.
   f. Barring other contingencies, all students at every level are to apply themselves to productive occupations outside of instruction in school.
3. Elementary schools.
   a. Elementary schools are to conform to a six-year course of study.
   b. Major revisions in the curriculum, accompanied by an equally major reworking of the selection, arrangement, and coordination of teaching materials, are to allow no loss of efficiency despite the shortened half-day schedule of instruction. Moreover, it should even be possible to cover materials now covered in the middle school curriculum.

Innumerable unresolved questions are bound to come up in the process of seeking to reform middle school and higher education. Decisions here are again governed by the same basic directives and goals. The presumed difficulty of coming to terms with the issues tends to make people postpone dealing with them. Some reform proposals, such as the shortening of the term of middle schools and high schools, proposals that do not deal with basic directives and goals, may be welcomed because of their closeness to the present system. I feel sure, however, that we will ultimately be forced to face the issues of basic directives and goals regardless of how hard we may try to avoid them.

There is one additional element needed to complete this general outline for educational revitalization, which I have considered above. It is so important and so essential a part of my proposal that it merits a whole separate section. This is the idea of the half-day school system, to which we will now direct our attention.

The Half-Day School System

THE VALUE OF HALF-DAY SCHOOLING

In this section I shall propose a major, fundamental change in our nation's schooling, namely that of placing the entire classroom educational system from elementary school through university on a half-day schedule. My aim here is to initiate discussion, for the issue deserves serious consideration. A decision to move in this direction would have far-reaching effects, compelling a major reorganization of education.

The very idea would have at one time seemed blasphemous and brought down censure from the educational community. Thus, I kept this idea to myself for ten years or more. But times have changed. Men with doctorates are now a dime a dozen, and a doctorate is hardly a claim to anything. Indeed, who could have foreseen how worthless degrees would become in today's tight job market?

The sources of this problem can be traced to our present educational system. As the complaints pile up, I cannot help but believe that it is only a matter of time before reform proponents settle on the half-day school system as a logical solution. Already the higher schools are largely without value, and middle schools and girls' schools hardly return their cost in real education. Vocational schools, the laughingstock of the educational community up until quite recently, now point the way to a highly acclaimed and timely "solution"—the conversion of middle schools to vocational training. But then where in the present educational system are graduates of these vocationalized middle schools to go? Even should the educational community, conservative as it is, resist change, the public, who must face the realities of daily life, will not stand by so complacently.

The educational system of half a century has ground to a standstill. Change must come, and it is my belief that adopting the half-day schedule affords the easiest, most effective road to reform. Following is an outline of the necessary changes as I see them:

1. The shift to the half-day system, from elementary schools up to the university level, is intended as an efficiency measure, and it presupposes corresponding improvements in teaching methods whereby what formerly required a whole day to teach might be consolidated into half the time. I believe that methodological studies in value-creating education, to be detailed later in this book, must provide the key.

2. In order to realize a greater economy on the national investment in school facilities and the teacher work force, the school day is to be divided in two or three to accommodate morning, afternoon, and possibly evening courses. This should alleviate the current "examination hell" to get into overcrowded schools, as well as reduce the actual cost of schooling per student.

3. Students are to spend the remaining half day outside the classroom, involved in productive vocational activity. This might be in their parents' trade or in some other line of work suitable to their abilities or even in the further study of a specialization that will later become their means of support. Or again, in the case of clearly gifted individuals, students might receive coaching in some particular scholastic discipline or physical training. In all events, these programs are to be run with the cooperative understanding and funding of state and private citizens alike.

In this way, we may be able to effect a clean sweep of the "examination hell," while planning to avoid occupational redundancy. The half-day system would also replace the separate system of vocational schools, which now function parallel to the regular school system, and would effectively redefine learning as an ongoing lifelong process, not merely limited to youth. Thus, ordinary schooling and vocational training would come to stand side by side as the norm for education, which seeks to nurture healthy minds and bodies. The only thing holding us back is our own repressive attachment to the outdated ways of the past half century.

To sum up the fundamental idea of the half-day school system, study is not seen as a preparation for living, but rather study takes place while living, and living takes place in the midst of study. Study and actual living are seen as more than parallels; they inform one another intercontextually, study-in-living and living-in-study, throughout one's whole life. In this sense, it is not the better economic budgeting of school programs but the instilling of joy and appreciation for work that becomes the main focus of the proposed changes.

These are times when most students pursue book learning to the exclusion of any opportunity for acclimation to physical tasks, so no wonder they develop a negative attitude toward work. Schools must combat this lethargy by cutting back all the empty hours of inept schooling to a trim half day and encouraging students to apply themselves to directed acquisition of practical skills, whether in the family business or at specially established farms, workshops, or extracurricular training centers. All in all, this would round out education in such a way as to reach both mind and body, would coordinate the development of motor and sensory functions to engage the whole person fully—helping to prevent nervous disorders, boredom, and apathy—and thereby would lead youth to active participation in productive social living.

In other words, some handicaps afflict from birth as physiological or psychological dysfunctions. These can only be lived with or treated as medical problems. But some handicaps are produced by improper education—that is, by enforcing an imbalanced pattern of development on the nervous system whereby the sensory nerves grow all too keen while the motor nerves atrophy. This results in a state of hypersensitivity, which we recognize as unproductive nervous energy with no physical outlet. This is an educational problem especially symptomatic of the overscholastic bias of education during the Meiji and Taisho periods (1868–1926). Is it any wonder that we have produced generations of apathetic people?

The reforms in education that took place in the Meiji era (1868–1912) amounted essentially to eliminating training in martial arts for youths of the samurai class and trade apprenticeship for those of the common classes, giving them only intellectual scholastics in return.

Hence the rise in accomplished do-nothings who had lost interest in carrying on the family business, instead tagging onto· the government payroll as official "brains"—an ironic comment on their disembodied status. Worse parasites on the body politic there never were!

The question of how to realize half-day schooling in actual practice is not as difficult a problem as these addicts of Meiji education would like to believe. Indeed, if these "brains" would simply consider how things were before the modern age, they would see that just because there weren't schools like we have today, the children weren't allowed to have a field day. Our forefathers wouldn't have stood for such nonsense.

Today when most urban youths just fritter away their time and regard labor as too demeaning, that minority who have to work are made to feel ashamed of their position. Yet if the opposite were true, if the majority had jobs to take care of, and the idle few were the outcasts, just think how different it would all be. More than anyone would suspect, youths' awareness about the life of society depends on the degree we adults keep them in line. Our worries about the difficulty of managing the half day out of school only prove how little we have addressed the real issues. If students are not responsible enough to live and work in the real world now, when will they be?

Youth is the best time for learning. Lose this opportunity, and nothing can make up the difference later on in life. Failure to acquire work habits at this point makes for a hard time shifting jobs in middle age. Occupations demanding physical labor especially become impossible to just "pick up."

This fact is appreciated better than anyone by business people whose long years of hard knocks have led them to conclude that it is often impossible to make effective workers out of higher-school graduates. The old apprentice system was better, according to the consensus of these experienced old hands. To take the most important, impressionable years and fill them up with only textbook scholarship eats away at vocational training, the argument runs. And I believe that these veteran professionals will join hands with me when they seriously consider the grave future that awaits us if we do not deal decisively with this problem soon.

Business firms, parents, and students themselves are calling for half-day schooling as the way to ensure a fighting chance in the race for economic survival. Mere addition of occupational or vocational training courses to the existing curriculum will not compensate; the problems have gotten too far out of hand. Even agricultural school graduates end up better adjusted to office work conditions than anything else. Why should this be so?

In the old days in Japan, a person came of age at fifteen. Samurai youths were received into adult company, while those of the common classes were considered fully employable. This continued to be the way largely up until my generation. There is no reason to assume that today's youths have any less drive or stamina than those of years past, so why should parents feel ashamed if they aren't able to support their children all the way through to university graduation? Every summer the beaches swarm with young people who seemingly have nothing better to do than to chase their pleasures to and fro. It hurts me to see these signs of decline, but I encounter them everywhere. Whatever happened to the traditional work ethic?

Nor is the idea of full-day girls' school education any less ridiculous. Should not girls' high-school-level education concentrate first and foremost on the practical learning proper to homemaking? Career women aside, is it not a contradiction to drag girls out of the home to teach them home economics, let alone force them to memorize scraps of fragmentary and abstract information? What possible use will knowledge of English and the like have in the home? It only makes a farce of education.

We have radio courses in English. How would it be if we had similar radio courses in home economics with a girls' higher normal school graduate as the regular lecturer-announcer? Every morning right after the physical exercise program, we could have daughters join with grandmothers nationwide so they could get used to working with their mops and buckets, and knives and cutting boards. It certainly would be more effective and more in touch with everyday life than conducting swimming lessons on the carpet. And this is only one example.

Here, then, is the point at which society as an organized force can apply pressures on otherwise wayward youth and turn them toward worthwhile activities that can lead to social improvements and personal happiness. Still, many would hesitate before committing us to what can be seen only as a radical leap from the present school system. But consider what a radical change modern education must have seemed only fifty years ago. What would have been the result if, at that time, instead of focusing their attention on the samurai and wealthy upper classes, our predecessors had made their central concern the life of the common classes who were engaged in farming, crafts, and commerce and so had wrought schooling as a condensation of that experience.

There is no shortage of examples that support the idea of half-day schooling as a real possibility. For one example, there are the army schools that succeed in imparting a regular higher school education plus specialized military training within the regular number of years; and for another, there was the Tokyo Special Normal Elementary School, which adopted a half-day and three-hour night-school program to run through the complete elementary school curriculum — although it was admittedly a somewhat less-than-perfect success — while at the same time providing business fundamentals and actual vocational training. Thus, even poor children had the opportunity to experience a measure of economic independence before their schooling was out — a real success story in my view. The Ministry of Education, however, apparently aiming at total standardization of all schools in the nation, must consider such cases as exceptions to the rule.

The idea is not better simply in terms of improved managerial efficiency or economics, as we have suggested repeatedly thus far, but also because it takes into consideration what best suits human makeup. The negative example can be cited, that nothing proves so supremely inefficient or uneconomic as forcing labor on the bored and tired. One can savor the pleasures of idleness only in the midst of a productively busy schedule, and conversely, a relentlessly busy schedule can be productive only if broken up with intervals of relief. Anyone who has undergone five, eight, or ten years of solid schooling will readily admit just how boring it all can be. A major reason for the success of half-day vocational programs is the judicious provision of outlets for nervous energy, thereby relieving stress and increasing productivity. I would venture to say that even the adult world at large could benefit from an alternating half-day work-study system. I daresay that productivity would be higher and that a six-hour workday would suffice as well as an eight-hour day.

One concern in regard to the system of vocational training that I am proposing in connection with half-day schooling is that it would conflict with child labor laws, which state in no uncertain terms that children under thirteen years of age are not to work. I admit there is clearly a conflict here, but if we pursue the underlying reasoning, we shall see that there is no real attack on the true spirit of the law. The legal limitations placed on physical labor exist to prevent harm from coming to bodies still too weak to handle excessive exertion. The half-day schedule not only prevents such excess by keeping work within a few hours but actually does positive good by providing professional skill in tandem with scholarship at the most important age in life. This is wholly in keeping with the original spirit of the law to protect the interests of youth and is clearly a step forward.

INADEQUACIES OF VOCATIONAL EDUCATION PROGRAMS

Having said this much in favor of half-day schooling, it may come as somewhat of a surprise that I am against what is commonly called vocational education. Let me explain. At first glance, the recent introduction of vocational education into the school as a compensatory measure for what now at long last has been recognized as real-life learning would seem to have filled the bill very well. Nonetheless, I would counter that educators' insistence on running vocational programs in the same show-and-tell way they have always run everything else reduces those programs to mere pantomime. No matter how earnestly a teacher in a suit and tie tries to inform students about real work that demands a shop apron, the result is merely an accomplished sham.

Furthermore, if job hunting continues to get put off until after graduation, there will never be any end to the employment crunch. The decline of business nationwide says nothing if not to point up the negligible impact of vocational education during the Meiji and Taisho eras.

The call to promote vocational education comes behind the times. Vocational education conducted in the spirit of current educational practices will only cause the further atrophy of business. The reason becomes apparent as soon as we examine the failure of agricultural school education, perhaps the closest thing we have today to real vocational training. Do not most graduates of even these schools end up as meager wage-earning assistants at agricultural testing stations or farming associations? And why? Because their schooling gives them a distaste for real work!

Yet nobody seems to notice; nobody checks up on what actually goes on. People somehow naively trust that if students are placed in vocational schools, they will naturally acquire a liking for work, so that the simplistic answer to how to give business a boost is just to build more vocational schools. Bureaucracy seems to put stock in this sort of superficial short-circuit reasoning.

For all the many instant businessmen who were to have been produced by vocational schools from the Meiji period on, just how many derive value from labors in direct production? The fact is that most end up in labor management. This may have been acceptable up to now, but I shudder to think what will happen if this trend continues.

Again, agricultural schools provide us with a prime example of what went wrong. Here I am grateful to Kozui Otani, a major theorist in agricultural education, for his provocative insights on the future of education. Ultimately, he concludes, inasmuch as land and human labor are givens, and the third factor, agricultural know-how, has yet to be satisfactorily met, "there can be no better plan than to further methodological studies in agriculture, and thereby reap increasing benefits."[12] That is true enough as far as it goes; however, that alone is not enough from the point of view of the educator. This line of thinking is supposedly why agricultural schools were built and agricultural education was promoted in the first place. But an essential element is missing here, and that element is practical fieldwork. Little wonder, then, that graduates of these schools have no commitment to actual labor other than through the tenuous connection of labor management.

A further weakness in the contemporary vocational education system is that in focusing on one aspect of childhood and youth, it, by design, totally neglects other important aspects. That is, in focusing on how to make money, it gives no thought to instructing how to deal with that money. Of course, there is no denying that it taps a great demand among the lower classes for education to help with immediate matters of livelihood. But profit making alone brings definite hazards. The drive to become independently self-supporting as soon as possible leaves no room for parental surveillance or guidance, so that when young people start making their own way, they may become fully competent professionally but remain unfinished and personally immature. Thus, the too common outcome of the present system is persons who are inhumanly calloused and unconcerned with others.

4

Educational Methodology

Principal Issues Underlying Educational Methodology

UNTENABLE INDIVIDUALISM VERSUS SYSTEMATIC UNIVERSALITY

The general public is beginning to recognize the limitations and errors of regimented education, yet, in the swing from one extreme to the other, most of the solutions being offered are scarcely any improvement, because the misguided assumptions about the learning process go unquestioned. Particularly there has been confusion and fuzzy thinking about the issue of individuality. Thus, we must go back to basic concepts, examine them in depth, and start over again.

If individuality is understood as that uniqueness differentiating each self from others, all mutually irreconcilable and absolutely unknowable, then we must dismiss any science that begins from the premise of a continuity of affirmations recognizable to all humanity. To attempt to have that other, in the person of the teacher, even try to get through to the student self, which is what education is, would be out of the question. And yet this contradiction that would negate education does not seem to bother the people who speak so glibly of individuality.

Under the banner of that new school of education whose only slogans seem to be "Revere the individual" and "Smash regimentation," we are hearing a hymn to unconditional acceptance of inexperienced teach-

163

ers. Where can this lead? Unilaterally decrying mechanistic regimentation, yet failing to grasp the implications of that individualism they would have as an alternative, the blind would lead the blind from one momentary reaction to the next. This is not a move forward but a perpetuation of the same primitive vicious circle. When this cycle of overemphasis on the individual at the expense of commonalities proves inefficient, it will be back to authoritarian robotics at the expense of the individual. Nothing will have been learned.

Of course, we must oppose the enforced uniformity that would press people into a mold against their nature, in violation of their humanity. Would it not be more reasonable if instead we were to make a thorough study of people in all their individuality, isolate all those characteristics belonging to certain individuals and no others as secondary nonessentials while concentrating on the remaining essentials shared in common by self and other, and apply these laws of commonality to education?

Are commonality (or generality) and individuality mutually exclusive? If we hesitate to respond, let me shift perspectives. Can we seek individuality apart from humanity? If the answer is yes, just what might this inhuman individuality be?

The answer plain and simple is that no matter how exalted we make individuality out to be, we are unable to pursue it except within our humanity, that is, within the context of our self-awareness and self-acceptance of membership in the human community. This much being admitted, the pursuit of individuality becomes a pursuit common to all humanity. A difference between self and other without a common basis in humanity is an autistic solipsism, utterly inaccessible to others, and nothing with which we need concern ourselves. This kind of individuality should not even figure into serious educational discussions.

If, however, the argument persists that present regimented schemes of education suppress the development of individuality, then we rightfully should have only to look back on the days before education for a golden age of individuality. And we know that that just isn't true, for, if anything, education has presented whole generations with possibilities that were unknown before. At least, it is clear that the biological fact of hereditary individuality cannot be tampered with very much through external influence, whether from parents or society or education. For better or worse, no more than superficial regimentation is possible by outside pressure. We are obliged instead, by the recognition of more-significant morphological and physiological (and psychological) similarities between individuals, to come back to viewing the differences in terms of degree or scale, not of kind—distinctions representing diversity within unity. Almost paradoxically, such individuality as differences of degree can be recognized only within a group or social unit. Durkheim makes this clear when he says that the divisions of labor within society arise not because individuals want to be different but because of the needs of the group. Society's demands come first, and only then do people find a place in the framework suitable to their individual leanings. Doubtless everyone would like to do just what he or she pleases, but the necessities of life must first be met. Individuals must belong to a society capable of dividing up the labor so as to free its members from want. Fundamentally speaking then, the division of labor is something society itself undertakes for its own well-being, and education is one means of directing society's members to their optimum roles therein.

Having brought the discussion this far, my insistence on clarifying our views on individuality might seem unwarranted, but if we are to avoid plunging education into the chaos of simultaneously pursuing the contradictory ends of unmitigated individualism and universalized scientific method, we must cease to equate liberal education with an uncritical fixation on individuality. We must think things through and deductively arrive at practicable teaching methodologies, the only passive restraining condition being that individual motivations to learning are in no way deterred.

Perhaps the best expression of this ideal is the old adage "A normal human being with some one point of personal excellence." In this view, individuality consists in a special difference over and above the norm. A shortcoming such as would place a burden on other members of the community, however, is the sort of individual difference that society wishes to eliminate. Thus, in terms of educational theory, individuality is of two kinds: that which education wishes to promote and extend, and that which it seeks to correct and curb.

We should note here that people left to their own ends—in their "untamed" natural state, as it were—tend to develop not what society would uphold as strong points but shortcomings it would prefer to strike clean from the slate. We all have such shortcomings; hence in our consideration of individuality as a basis for developing educational methodologies, the main focus should be how to reduce errant individuality. Education in this model starts from a normalization of untamed individuality and ultimately achieves the distinction of extranormalization. Rather than asking how to inculcate individualism, the far more pressing issue becomes how to extend individual possibilities beyond partial foci toward ever greater human wholeness. To start from the idea of individualized teaching is, in any case, to attempt to work from the top down, from the outermost branches back toward the trunk. This is no way to figure out how to get from our present dead-end to where we really want to be in education. This is nothing but starry-eyed dreaming. Only after we have established a comprehensive foundation for expanding upon our common humanity will we be qualified to talk of advancing individuality.

We must, then, proceed through method. And this demands as a minimum that we eliminate impracticable fantasies and concentrate solely on that which is actually possible. Short of this there can be no bridging the real to the ideal. Unfortunately, it is often teachers themselves who stand as the greatest obstacles to the scientific approach to educational methodology. To cite one extreme instance, once when I was lecturing to a group of young teachers in Tokyo on the theory of Value-Creating Education, there came a startling question from the floor: "Do you really think it is possible to establish a set of universally applicable truths of education as a framework within which to develop educational methods suitable for any and all children?" The inquirer was no doubt earnest about seeking to understand the logic of educational theory and was certainly more compelled in this search than the others in the seminar, who probably bore the same doubts but dared not speak out. I was taken aback at first but knew that the question required a firm and immediate response, for it surely indicated a firm belief in the supremacy of individuality stubbornly persisting among proponents of so-called liberal education. "Have you ever caught cold?" I asked the questioner. "And did you not then go to see a doctor?" The answer to both, of course, was yes. "Well then, was that not an acknowledgement on your part of the existence of universally applicable truths in the medical sciences? Why, then, do you doubt like truths in education?" Many more instances come to mind, and this is, perhaps, an indication of how far we have yet to go before everyone accepts the idea of conducting education on inductively established bases.

DEFINING EDUCATION

Force-feeding or self-enlightenment? Organizing information or arousing interest? Which is it to be? Educators can cram information or instill awareness, transmit bits of knowledge or guide the learning process. We can choose to focus on scholastics field by field or selectively develop human character. But what we choose will prove the single most important factor toward reforming the school system and, even more, in shaping our entire conception of the how of education.

Curiously enough, probably no one would claim to favor force-feed education outright. But what if we changed the wording to the *transfer of knowledge*? Many would go along with that. And so before any of us were aware of it, the whole of Japanese education from the elementary schools on up to the universities have come to be run on the solitary standard of the level of factual knowledge quantified through examination and subject to pass-or-fail judgements. This is all the more to be deplored when we consider that we are talking about mental phenomena that, like the unified allover fluidity of liquid or gaseous matter, cannot be taken apart and analyzed bit by bit as solid materials can.

As we have noted previously, it was a Herbartian innovation to hold that the accepted notion of using interesting teaching methods as a means to the end of implanting knowledge was in error and that the bestowing of information must rather serve the ends of arousing interest. Why is it then that some thirty years after the blossoming of Herbartian studies, Herbart is seldom mentioned in educational circles? Why is it that after numerous policy shifts and changes, we are still laboring under the mantle of force-feed thinking? If it is the proper role of education to transmit bits of knowledge from teachers to students, then there is no need to be concerned with educational methodology because all teachers need do is provide students with books. But if, on the other hand, the purpose of education is that of arousing the interest of students, then the teacher's role is primarily that of guiding the learning process, and we have to deal with the technical problems of what constitutes interest and how to arouse it.

With the advancement of humankind and the development of culture, the amount of knowledge to be taught continues at an accelerated rate, yet the period of schooling must for all intents and purposes remain fixed. Within this set period we can never hope to match the pace, no matter how hard we try. The only thing we can do is cultivate abilities to use one's own powers to meet needs as they come up. In other words, we must take up the Herbartian approach, that is, not make the acquisition of information the ultimate objective of education but instead cultivate interest whereby people will be motivated to learn for themselves.

The aim of education is not to transfer knowledge; it is to guide the learning process, to put the responsibility for study into the students' own hands. It is not the piecemeal merchandizing of information; it is the provision of keys that will allow people to unlock the vault of knowledge on their own. It does not consist in pilfering the intellectual property amassed by others through no additional effort of one's own; it would rather place people on their own path of discovery and invention. The words have been resounding in the ears of educators like ourselves since the days of Comenius and Pestalozzi, but they have yet to be put into real practice.

Education consists of finding value within the living environment, thereby discovering physical and psychological principles that govern our lives and eventually applying these newfound principles in real life to create new value. In sum, it is the guided acquisition of skills of observation, comprehension, and application.

Thus, if one possesses the keys to unlock the vault of knowledge, it becomes possible to obtain for oneself all the learning one will ever need in life without having to memorize endless volumes of scholarship. What with the highly developed state of printing and publishing these days, all one needs are powers of comprehension to search out information on one's own. Furthermore, given today's advanced divisions of labor, who can say just when a particular bit of information might come in handy? There is no reason to overload our lives with mountains of useless and trivial information that we may never need.

The idea of transmitting knowledge en masse inevitably came down to the practice of teacher modeling. If the presence of a teacher does necessarily invite copying, better then to let the teacher serve as a model of education in practice, of educational method, not of a finished example or embodiment of learning. The teacher must represent a demonstration of education as a process, not stand as product. Otherwise, it becomes a case of haughty showmanship and smug pose that drags the children down in its undertow. The teacher must assume a humble attitude before students. The teacher must guide and encourage students as an elder wayfarer on the same path of learning as they, only a little further along perhaps. Not "Here, try this on for size," as if a teacher could hand over a finished character. To try to do so is the most flagrant hypocrisy.

The most urgent order of business is thus for teachers who are completely in the dark about their proper mission to come to a realization of themselves as learners and of their relationship to others over and above this as that of a guiding aide. It was precisely for lack of an accurate grasp on these fundamental concepts that education ground to its present standstill. To have attempted to undertake as excruciatingly difficult an endeavor as the cultivation of human resources with only the most naive and rudimentary idea of education was like setting sail on a transoceanic voyage without a compass.

These cardinal principles with respect to the relationship of teachers to the learning process may be summarized as follows:

1. Teachers are not retailers of cheap bits of information obtained from elsewhere; they are to serve as thinking experts who guide students in their studies and daily lives.
2. Unlike technicians and artists who seek to create material value of benefit and beauty from material resources, teachers deal with the spiritual growth and development of human resources, directing them in the creation of character values whereby they in turn might create material value. Thus, education stands as the highest technology or art.
3. Accordingly, teachers must not fall prey to the simplistic perception that views them as goal markers or finished products before their students but must themselves tirelessly strive to further their own discipline, and so draw students into the ongoing progress toward rationality. Teachers must outgrow their own holier-than-thou self-importance.
4. Teachers must come down off their thrones and serve; they are to stand not as the pattern to be followed but as accessory agents helping implement the pattern.
5. Teachers are to leave the fact-feeding to books and instead take a supporting role to the students' own learning experience.

How on earth can teachers who cannot even understand how they themselves ought to study be expected to direct students on how they should study? How can teachers ever serve as role models if they can't even be emulated in how they themselves conduct their own learning in the first place? Teachers have no business getting up in front of a class if they do not understand what learning means themselves.

Studies in Educational Methodology

BACKGROUND METHODOLOGICAL STUDIES

Thinking is of little value if we do not think correctly; if we do not know how to go about thinking, it hardly matters what we think about. Before sculptors begin their carving, they make sure their tools are well honed. Similarly, farmers thoroughly prepare the soil prior to planting. The consideration of methods of educating children likewise demands a certain fundamental rigor if we are to weigh things properly. Short of this, our investigations will end up in pointless arguments, one opinion pitted against another.

The most typical hazards are associated, as we have noted elsewhere, with confusions between cognition and evaluation, with putting the latter before the former. There are times when emotion prevents people from noticing the irrationality of their response, or their confusion between cognition and evaluation. Yet, even irrationality has a generalizable regularity to it.

One common pattern is that we stand by our allegiances in spite of counterindications. We do not move to verify the facts, or else we ignore them. Or even worse, we distort and obliterate facts to forge a counterproof. This attitude is a hindrance to learning. Thinking and learning necessarily include listening to the views and ideas of other persons and relating those views and ideas to our own experience. When we shut our minds to what others can offer to us, we limit our own growth.

Another common error follows the exact opposite pattern. Instead of machinations to falsify what we are told, we swallow just any piece of information as readily as an addict. This becomes particularly problematic when we accept reportage of news from places beyond our personal acquaintance or an official line without critical examination.

A third type of error is well illustrated by the following amusing anecdote I once read in the writings of Charles De Garno, an American Herbartian. It seems a German newspaper reporter once found himself seated across from an American in a small compartment aboard a France-bound train. The American scrutinized the German and proceeded to write something down in his journal, at which the German felt compelled to respond by jotting a comment in his. That night when they lodged in the same inn and came to be on better terms, they compared notes. What the American had originally written was, "Germans continue to wear their overcoats even when they're sweating from the heat," while the German had secretly responded with "Americans put their pencils to their lips as they examine the subject they're writing about." Both had a good laugh and erased the offending passages. This is a good example of the dangers of generalizing from irrelevant specifics without complete data.

A fourth pattern, a corollary of the above, is that of drawing conclusions from one case and then extending them to another when there is no essential parallel between the circumstances. This is aptly expressed in the Japanese proverb "Once scalded by hot food, some persons will even blow at a vinaigrette to cool it off." Or country folk may come to the big city, have an unfortunate experience with one con artist, and then refuse to trust any city dweller thereafter.

Yet a fifth pattern is our tendency to write off actual occurrences when they are far removed from our common experience or everyday norms. We tend to stand by our preconceptions, disallowing proofs to the contrary, and going so far as to doubt even the persons who would present such proofs. Contradictions of this kind are rife in sectarian disputes and must be dealt with on objective grounds before real thinking can take place.

Finally, when things veer too far from what we want to believe, we simply fall back on the oldest scheme of self-justification—that of "Might makes right"—for fear that even discussing an issue on equal grounds with an opposing view lends it legitimacy.

Whatever the avowed reasons, the underlying patterns all amount to emotional defenses of mistaken hypotheses based on one's limited knowledge up to that point that prevent us from looking at realities outside those limits. Our eyes are colored by attachments to personal loss and gain. Either we avoid all recognition of the facts, or else we pick up only data we consider favorable while discarding the rest.

But no matter how extensively we extrapolate beyond the narrow confines of previous experience and present mental schemata, there is no sure way of predicting the unlimited expanse of unknowns that lie ahead. Although it is a simple matter to dismiss the shallow preconceptions of the undisciplined, it is, paradoxically, none too easy to accept the realization that predictions based on a solid body of scientific evidence may not be foolproof either. We often hear great scholars warn that the sum total of human knowledge is but a drop in the vast ocean of unknowns. Yet, short of the minute incremental expansion of knowledge achieved through cognition, tempered by a hard and true scientific attitude, we would be forever condemned to leaping into petty emotional evaluations from the fixed, minuscule bounds of our own imaginings. We would never be free from self-aggrandizement without the humbling realization of just how little we do know.

What matters is that we establish measures and scales of evaluation. And then, with the true humility associated with the scientific method, we must take care not to get ahead of ourselves. There is no weighing kilograms on a gram scale. Everything must be done in minute particulars. It is not easy to throw away our preconceived scales of generalization. The human leaning toward laziness and self-vindication would just as soon cover up the issues, I am sure, though nothing could be so damaging to a scholar's reputation. There can be no excuses. We must earnestly wipe the slate clean of preconceptions.

Up to now the conviction of educators has been that we need only study the nature of children for educational methodologies to emerge, out of the woodwork as it were. Hence, most educators have been eager to hang on to the coattails of child psychologists. Why, then, has nothing come of this approach? Because that is the wrong place to start looking, the wrong object of study. If understanding children were all there were to the how of education, then it stands to reason that parents would be the best teachers of all, for who know children better than their parents? Yet we should hesitate to emulate doting parents.

Let us consider, by way of further illustration, the case of the carpenter. If it were indeed true that we had only to look far enough into the recipients of our labors in order to derive a sense of method, then the carpenter with the best knowledge of wood should by all rights prove the most competent workman. To be sure, such knowledge is not out of place, but it is by no means the entire picture. More important are the special skills of craftsmanship matched to the best utilization of each variety of wood. Here is a lesson for teacher and parent alike. Even if we were to observe the children in our charge from morning to night, nothing much would come of it. Again, it is more important to keep a watch over their hungry minds, to see where their mental makeup seeks nourishment. It is unnecessary to point out how difficult this is to carry through to application, for though the need has been recognized for more than three thousand years, we have yet to come up with guiding principles to meet those needs. There is as yet no easy way for the inexperienced young teacher to acquire veteran expertise. The best we can do is to gather examples of educators' past successes in adequately nourishing hungry minds, contrast these examples with our own failures, and thus learn how to better our own efforts.

This amounts to a shift in the focus of our studies, from the child as such to understanding how teaching materials can be successfully and variously utilized in developing the potential of each child. It might have been possible at one time to make the rounds in a study-tour of veteran teachers' classrooms, but in this day and age such information is to be had more simply and economically by means of a scientific survey of teaching materials to extract and universalize methods. If anyone knows a better way, I would be most anxious to learn of it.

We must, then, first take stock of our goals, focus our critical standards, analyze each and every element of our methods to determine whether they are appropriate to our ends, and thus establish causal rules. In order to come up with ways to teach others, teachers themselves must discover their own ways of learning. And, as suggested earlier, once they find the most cogent method, they will understand it to be the very method for guiding children. Teachers must, in other words, reflect upon a scientific course for discovering truth, then proceed as scientists on the basis of their findings.

Nonetheless, there is considerable variance within the scientific method. Considering the poles of transcendental deduction, traditionally the exclusive method of the normative sciences, and experimental induction, transcendental deduction's methodological counterpart in the natural sciences, it is doubtful whether either approach alone is adequate to guide the whole of education, inasmuch as education must embrace both theory and practice. Faced with this dilemma, the postwar German educational community has branched out in several directions in an attempt to render the greatest coverage, the three main approaches being the comprehensive method, which begins from a grasp of reality and proceeds to build a conceptual framework around it; the dialectic method, which endeavors to grasp reality from the standpoint of antithetical ideas; and the phenomenological method, which looks on both practice and theory from a higher level and carries out both efforts in tandem.[1] Needless to say, none of these methods is fully perfected; thus no system of education can yet be established on these bases at this time. These are still fragmentary attempts, far from conclusive.

In the view of Eduard Spranger,[2] who employed the comprehensive method to deal with educational issues in psychological perspective, that method amounts to a search for explanatory principles or else an inductive departure from the immediate reality at hand. More than this, however, it understands the meaning of any given in terms of its relationship to a larger whole. That is, the comprehensive method differs from pure experimental induction in that a given object's status as a compositional element in an inclusive system of values is more important than the object itself. Here we find value structuring superimposed over a basic view of reality.

Dialetics as a conceptual means of pinning down truths through the synthesis of opposites would seem a straightforward method of value structuring were it not that when seen from an epistemological vantage point, the thought patterns are tantamount to a scheme of grasping reality.

Phenomenology analyzes real objects in order to disclose that transcendent objectivity immanent in their intentional existence as willing phenomena. It resembles the dialectic method in that it analyzes real existence and objectivity, but it takes that analysis only far enough to establish a symmetry without subsuming the relationship into syncretic conceptual schemata.

It should strike us immediately from this brief survey of German educational philosophy that scholars are not at all clear in their approach to determining the objects of study. They are really at a loss for values to tell them what should take precedence in study. Or conversely stated, they are not clear as to just whom they should be aiding as a result of their research. Thus, their efforts can be regarded only as very preliminary fundamental efforts that are still far from direct application to guiding educational methodologies. Be that as it may, they do raise basic doubts about the existing system of studies.

Such scholarship for scholarship's sake would be harmless enough were it not that educational practitioners have felt compelled to accept this sort of abstruse hypothesizing, unwittingly dragging themselves out to extremes far removed from the actual business of teaching, just to keep abreast of some scholar's personal interests but with no intention of deducing rules or principles actually applicable to their work. I say this because no significant educational discovery has come to us by this means, that is, by some scholar first presenting a hypothesis and then educational practitioners finding a valuable rule based on that hypothesis. Rather, it has always been the case that new ideas for educational reform have come out of the actual experiences of educational practitioners. Neither Comenius nor Pestalozzi nor any other educational reformer has ever made major discoveries by first paying dues to the scholarly community. Actual experience may give rise to flashes of insight or discoveries that sweep the world over, but only rarely do these ever end up renovating practice. Even the boom in Herbartian studies has left little mark on education in the schools. Most educators have little understanding of Herbart's ideas; they may engage in some formalistic mimicry of the tenets, but these, too, will be forgotten in time.

I have said it before, and I will say it again: The educational theories that teachers are taught in school hardly ever relate to practice. To this day, philosophers' ideas are applied to the realm of classroom education only with difficulty. We continue to push scholarship without any value-born view of whom exactly we are to be benefiting. We have not given enough thought to the object of our efforts.

Although we may realize that the existing mode of philosophical studies is of little worth, and so fervently search for alternatives, we somehow cannot bring ourselves to cut off our past attachments. From which I can only conclude that educational studies, by reason of our own fixation on philosophy, remain in the hands of philosophers who care precious little for the hardships of practitioners. Hence it's more of the same for any foreseeable future. It is my belief that the longer we delay in breaking out of our habitual rut of following philosophers and educational theorists who put off taking the initiative in studying the causal relations at play in human occupations and their associated technologies, the more indefinitely we forestall the establishment of those guiding principles of educational methodology so anxiously awaited by educational practitioners.

In all areas of human endeavor, soon after people began some line of labor with regard to their environment, there also developed a related tradition of technique. This goes far back into prehistory. By contrast, scientific research came much later, really only quite recently. Thus, the notion that technology exists as the application of science is mistaken. Rather, it was only because explaining the principles on which technology is based seemed a convenient way of transmitting an understanding of existing technologies to later generations that recent schooling has resorted to this long-winded process. Such was not the case in times past, for through countless successions of master-disciple apprenticeship, explanations were left until last. The deductive tradition, if it may be called that, actually goes against the greater part of the history of ideas.

Furthermore, just as technology was transmitted master to apprentice, scholarship concerning technology does not so much deduce principles of explicative science as systematize knowledge through comparative observations on the state of the art in existing technologies, together with reviewing their historical development and following this up with rigorous testing toward proofs of the inherent truths of these technologies. How much more, then, should this be the case in education? I have continually counseled against subjective thinking and accepting isolated cases of accidental success in practice, which individual educators would hold up as showpieces. Education is doomed to stagnation if it does not stand on method or develop its ideas methodically. As I have stated repeatedly before, education is perhaps the most complicated of all technical sciences in human life, dedicated as it is to the advancement of human life itself, and there are bound to be many slipups along the way that will require correction and reassessment on the part of scholars to come.

Haphazard and arbitrary subjective evaluations cannot be tolerated. New ideas must be given the benefit of methodical trial. They must be tentatively accepted and tested in faithfully conducted experimentation before any decision is reached. If borne out, so much the better; if found wanting, there must ensue a painstaking analysis of the causes of failure. Nothing is to be left to chance, nor are snap judgements to be acceptable. Again we are here discussing only the aspect of methodology in education, having agreed from the beginning that educational aims are to be based on common human goals that are revealed by psychophenomenological studies of human nature.

In concluding this section, I would like to quote a passage from Durkheim that supports the approach I have used in my own studies of educational methodology; that is, I have studied educational techniques, rather than educational facts, and by observing, comparing, and classifying them have attempted to find causal laws in them.

> While scholars of morals cannot claim to have derived their theories from some *a priori* principle, they do presume to label their morals "scientific" for reason of having deduced them from propositions culled from one or more of the corroborative sciences, i.e.,

biology, psychology, sociology, and the like. The methods I choose are nothing of the sort. I do not attempt to draw morals out of science, but rather would seek to create a science of morality. The two notions could not be more different.[3]

THE ATTITUDE FACTOR IN EDUCATORS' METHODS

The days when it was thought that educators had merely to force-feed information in the form of subject materials and that education would then take care of itself are past. We have now come to recognize that the essence of education consists in how teaching materials are employed so as to guide the students' own learning processes. As we have seen, this demands concerted studies in various methodologies. But to take this one step further, before even discussing methods of teaching others, we may note, as John Dewey argues, that teachers' attitudes toward their own studies provide a good predictive factor of teaching effectiveness.

If this be the case, the investigative study of educational methodology must depend in no small part on the earnestness with which teachers apply themselves. Of course, one widely acknowledged view would go so far as to say that teaching methods come naturally if only one is earnest enough, and they hold up Pestalozzi as the example par excellence. Although there is no doubt some degree of truth to the claims, we should not ignore the fact that even the most earnest teacher might head off in a totally wrong direction. Pestalozzi was indeed earnest, yet we must not forget that he did not content himself with merely burning with intensity but continually applied that intensity throughout his entire life to the hard discipline of studying educational methods. This is not to say that we should ignore teacher character or reject earnestness. Far from it, for they are the bases for making any kind of progress; they underlie all that we wish to achieve. But how may we best assess this earnestness? As a beginning, I would propose the following four-level scale of evaluation:

1. Teachers whose primary motivation is monetary remuneration
2. Teachers whose primary motivation is status
3. Teachers whose primary motivation is the love of children
4. Teachers who work out of an interest in education itself

The first category, teachers who are entirely mercenary in their ethics, are placed lowest on the scale. For although the complexity of the teacher's art demands continual practice and refinement to perfect, this type of teacher really has no interest in the calling itself but rather is temporarily attracted by the prospect of money, essentially a side benefit. Such teachers may easily waver in their dedication to their jobs as wages fluctuate, and they may even quit at a moment's notice. This is hardly the devotion to children's development and accomplishments expected of a teacher but is rather a self-serving, egotistical orientation. Not only can we not depend on such teachers or make long-term plans based on them, but their singularly cold attitude does a disservice to parents and nation alike. By comparison, teachers motivated by the prospect of rank and advancement probably represent a more "normal" attitude, given that in our present-day capitalistic society it would be next to impossible to do away completely with the notion of fame. Even so, what are we to think when that becomes the main aim or when education takes a back seat to that end? Is that not an even colder attitude? Finally, even the teacher whose primary motivation is altruistic concern for children as fellow human beings still has a long way to go to become a technically good practitioner. In other words, anything short of a steady and continuous dedication to the actual business of teaching itself will be an insufficient basis for a teacher's motivation.

Judging inductively from my lengthy experience as an elementary school principal, I can say quite conclusively that one can clearly recognize an able or unfit teacher just the same as with practitioners in any of the arts or technical fields. Unfortunately, this point has largely escaped the notice of teacher training and supervisory organs. Apparently satisfied with the mercenary mentality, their complacency in not setting up directives has allowed some frightfully unfit persons to gain employment. In the general run of technical occupations in private enterprise there is fierce competition for survival, but in the teaching profession the government extends its umbrella of administrative protection so far that even the most unworthy can survive and entrench themselves in the community—no matter how adversely this affects the children in their charge. A misshapen piece of china made by a clumsy craftsman will never even reach the market, but what can be done about delinquent persons created by the hysterics of an unfit teacher? They can only survive to trouble society. Here is a cause that the minister of education, politicians, and educators alike have overlooked in their planning. Instead of spending enormous sums on the rehabilitation of delinquents, why not try an ounce of prevention and pay a little more attention to the question of teacher influence on children and youth? To merely ignore the great potential for good or bad vested in teachers can only spell disaster for society.

Laxity is the enemy of all educators who would strive to develop an educational methodology that will prove of actual use in real life. Lazy and complacent attitudes must be replaced with directed, planned activity. We must be quick to reject easy approaches that would claim to extract some form of practical educational principles from facile ideas perfunctorily gleaned from child psychologists or from simple mental factors noted or experienced as casual stimuli in the course of everyday living. How much more, then, must we reject the adulation of philosophical inquiries far removed from the realities of practice!

These are not concerns we can begin to think about only after we have children placed before us. If they were hospital patients, they would die on us before we got around to treating them. Civilized people's addiction to scholarship causes them to lose their bearings in ways primitives never did. We need to set aside the books and return to "primitive observation" of the human factor in achieving results. We might follow others' paths in this, but why go out of our way to cultivate an attitude of dependence when educators need to develop the resolution to stand before their students as exemplars of serious dedication to the learning process? This is, as nothing else, the living image of education. Short of this, no amount of telling can do much good.

First and foremost, we are looking for a method of teaching that will not become obsolete too quickly and that we will not tire of in the course of day-to-day professional teaching activities. Thus, the most immediate thing to do is to take the business of daily teaching activities as our object of study, tirelessly comparing planning to results, estimated effects to actual outcome, bridging back to new directions in planning — a veritable casebook in the inductive method. And, of course, there is ample room for comparison with similar experiences of our colleagues in order to seek out causal connections not apparent in the narrow range of our own personal experience.

Teachers must also practice and experience in their own lives the principles and techniques of learning that they are seeking to help their students understand and acquire. One necessary condition is that we must not addict ourselves to scattered and random information skimming. Our reading must have depth and focus. Nor is there any particular benefit in seeking out imported ideas in translation when more directly applicable materials are already available closer to home. If indeed there is any truth to my claim that education is an applied science, then it stands to reason that instead of the medieval fixation on trying to deduce ideas from tomes of philosophy, psychology, and other fields, we should go straight to studying educational technique, which is more highly evolved than such scholarship in the first place.

If all we do is force-feed knowledge into ourselves, what else do we know but to force-feed children with like knowledge formulated by others? But if we ourselves are engaged in our own self-initiated study, the process of formulating our own ideas becomes an outline of how to guide students in their studies. Pestalozzi himself was proud that in thirty years of teaching he did not even keep one book at hand—not the sort of statement a lazy teacher might make lightly!

My criticism of teachers who mindlessly absorb poorly understood philosophical ideas without giving attention to the principles and techniques that can grow out of their own teaching should not be interpreted to mean that there is no place for books written by other people as a guide for our own self-initiated study. There certainly is. Reading is more economical than gaining knowledge through observing other teachers' classes. Furthermore, knowledge gained through reading is easier to organize in one's own study than that which is obtained through other means. Reading, however, should supplement rather than replace our own firsthand search for effective teaching principles and techniques through analysis of our own and our colleagues' teaching experience.

I have dwelled on this matter of the study of educational methodology at some length because I wish to emphasize that self-study on the part of the teacher is the primary preparation for a competent method of teaching students. Without this sound orientation toward learning upon the part of the teacher, study of methodology will, I am afraid, be wasted effort.

ORDINARY AND SPECIAL MEANS IN EDUCATION

By way of review, the system of value-creating education set forth in this book reveals present schemes of education by force-feeding as both inadequate and harmful and aims, instead, to guide people toward the good life through integrating values of benefit, good, and beauty. It does not address itself to disparate cognitive and emotive faculties but brings guidance to bear on the comprehensive activities of the individual student as a whole being through a program fully coordinated between the three component areas of education.

If existing schools were asked to accomplish all that this entails, it would require many times more operating costs and labor than it already does. Moreover, they still probably would not be sufficient to the task. In this connection we may note that education in school, education in the home, and education in the community all aim to provide the individual with guidance for living; the only differences between them are in their respective time frames and means. In the days before there were schools, the prevailing method of guiding young people to the proper roles in the general scheme of life was an extended home life, whereby one apprenticed at the family trade throughout one's formative years, with this training supplemented by things learned from the local community. Then came the Meiji period with its modern education and the spread of schools that were created to provide some measure of additional knowledge beyond the three R's. Everyone was taken by the hand and dragged off to schools, and soon the other two schemes of learning fell into disuse. This was the age of the school reigning unchallenged and omnipotent. Only in recent years have we come to see the grave error of our ways and tried to fill in the gap with various kinds of adjunct education and youth groups for extracurricular activity.

From this point on, school education must be aware of its own share of the educational role of awakening individuals to their own powers, to all they themselves are capable of doing. It must cooperate with the other two areas of education, the home and the community, each with its own expertise and with conscious awareness of the overall picture of the ultimate goals of education as a whole. These three areas of education must link together in an orderly system of mutual complementarity.

My proposal earlier in this book for the establishment of a comprehensive half-day school system was based on this idea of cutting back on ill-managed education that eats into valuable work-learning time. If we return to the other two areas of education much of their premodern territory in overall life guidance, only the remainder need be taught in the schools, and in a half day at that. This would at once prove more efficient, and create an organic bond with the other two areas.

Complex, long-range planning inevitably involves a division of labor over many procedural levels from proposal to completion. At every level, implicit mutual understanding and cooperation is of the utmost importance:

1. Planning—educational scholars
2. Facilitating—government
3. Management—public and private administrators
4. Technical implementation—teachers
5. Critical evaluation—educational critics

It is not that any of these positions is currently nonexistent or vacant, but they are far from effective or cooperative in their interaction. There is no inclusive principle of planning to tie them together in their own respective thinking. Each tends to carry on isolated functions, distrustful and even spiteful of the others. There is no unity. Only when we come to the fifth step do we get any kind of overview of what everyone is doing.

As I have suggested before, perhaps the closest model of what education must become is to be found in the medical sciences, with their many subsciences. For if education is ever to truly cover the vast range of value creation, guiding the development of every kind of ability to create value, it must break down horizontally into numerous subdivisions, which are then to be cumulated vertically into a hierarchy of expertise. In short, it must achieve a highly ordered structure, just like a hospital's optometric, dental, surgical, pediatric, obstetric, and other departments wherein professionals of all levels work, from nurses and doctors to researchers. At the same time, we must be careful to avoid the pitfalls of Western medicine when it loses sight of the patient as a whole person. In this sense, traditional Eastern medicine has much to say.

Education must prove a sister science to medicine. But where medicine takes the biological life of the person as its highest concern, education's concern is for the total life of the individual: education in the home passively guarding against obstacles to growth on the physiological side, school and social education actively seeking to guide mental growth. And all this is to be perceived as a basic task in the life of society, that is, the fostering of human resources with the drive to create value.

AN OUTLINE OF METHODS IN EDUCATIONAL GUIDANCE

Everything in this book up to now has in a sense been preface. We now must undertake the formulation of a comprehensive plan for value-creating learning. Included must be the following:

A. *Teaching materials.* A complete reexamination of subjects to be included across the whole of the natural and social environments is needed. Such a reexamination would seek answers to the following questions:
1. What is to be the coverage of teaching materials?
2. By what standards are materials to be selected?
3. By what standards are selected materials to be arranged?
4. How are they to be unified?
5. How are the items thus brought together to be structured into various curricular subjects?
6. Are the teaching materials consistent with the principles of the historical evolution of teaching materials?

B. *Implementation of teaching materials in guided study.* Attention must be directed to our role as teachers in encouraging self-initiative among students, instead of forcing teaching materials upon them.
1. The basics of the teacher's role should be consistent with the historical evolution of teaching methods.
2. Guidance provided must embrace three aspects:
   a. Guidance in cognition.
   b. Guidance in evaluation.
   c. Guidance in value creation.
3. Research into the levels of teaching as reflected in the processes of guided study is needed.
4. Criticism of the progress in teaching (or lack thereof), as well as of practice teaching, is needed.

C. *Sociological considerations in educational management.* Modern schools can be regarded as a model society in which students are divided into groups and subgroups according to their ages and other criteria and live a kind of community life. One result of this development is that mutual influence in the forming of character among students has emerged as a new educational element in modern education. Within this context, the old definition of education, "the intentional transfer of knowledge from the mature to the immature with established methods," is no longer valid. Thus new perspectives are required for guiding a variety of groups whose members possess different backgrounds and interests. In particular, educators need to consider the following:

1. Sociological management of class levels.
2. Sociological management of schools.
3. Constitutional supervision of schools.

We also must establish methodologies for problem teaching above and beyond methods that suffice in normal cases. In other words, we must stand ready with an array of ordinary and special means.

A. Types of education according to stages of student development
   1. Elementary education
   2. Secondary education
   3. Higher education

B. Types of education according to normality of students
   1. General education
      a. Superior students
      b. Ordinary students
      c. Inferior students
   2. Special education
      a. Handicapped students
      b. Impaired learners
      c. Retarded students

C. Types of education according to sex of students
   1. Male students
   2. Female students
   3. Coeducation

D. Distinct environments for education
   1. School education
   2. Education in the home
   3. Education in society at large

E. Types of education based on generalized or focused approaches
   1. General education — aimed at rounding out the whole person
   2. Civic education, adult education — aimed at developing specific parts of the person

F. Types of education according to special characteristics of various curricula: methodological differences as required to teach knowledge and skills related to various items of the curriculum, such as history, geography, grammar, and so on

Let us now consider the question of special or remedial education in closer detail. This can be an extremely touchy subject, for no one likes having his or her faults pointed out by others — mental shortcomings probably even more so than physical disabilities. Many physical ailments once thought incurable — infantile paralysis, club feet, and the like — now have remedies. Mental and emotional disorders present a more difficult problem. There can be no artificial limbs or other material aids as for physical disablement, because problems of this kind are integral with the person's life. Still, inasmuch as the life of the body is the life of the mind, there is no reason to assume that mental and emotional ailments should not be as treatable as outward physical incapacities. The key factor here is the will to be cured or the confidence that one can be cured. Without this, not even the most famous doctor can effect a cure. When will is lacking, recovery is painfully slow, but when the individual's will and self-confidence work in cooperation with the efforts of others, growth toward health and productive living can occur.

And this is, in the final analysis, what value-creating education is about. It is our responsibility as teachers to enable every student, regardless of background or individual capacity, to discover and develop those unique abilities and interests that each student possesses by virtue of heredity and individual circumstances. Unlike other members of the animal kingdom, human young can experience this kind of healthy, normative growth only through wise and patient guidance by persons who understand basic principles of human learning and growth. It is within this context that I have stressed the need for teachers to develop understanding of the principles of learning through objective, scientific examination of their own and other teachers' experiences.

5

Teaching Materials

The Selection of Teaching Materials

In March 1931 the Lower House of the Legislature of Japan declared that "in regard to the changing times, the Government is to proceed with reforms on the system and contents of education with all due haste." To which a Tokyo newspaper ran an editorial that sharply criticized the whitewash of generalities. Specifically, it pointed out that

> (1) School subjects themselves are in need of reorganization and unification; (2) the various subjects need to be balanced and interrelated; (3) a great many elements within each subject obviously merit greater or lesser relative emphasis to counter insufficiencies and excesses . . . . Many have been the conferences held up to now on the issues of educational reform, but most merely assembled ineffectual authorities. There is, of course, nothing wrong with conferences to discuss generalities. But what is demanded today is a thorough investigation of the above three points and the next step toward concrete proposals. It will not happen in just one meeting. No reform that fails to take into account the current state of society, or that neglects to solicit the views of experts in every field to participate in detailed consideration of the issues at sub-meetings, can be called a reform in any true sense of the word.[1]

187

So how are we to go about filling in these gaps? We are at the point at which we can no longer avoid overhauling our selection and organization of teaching materials. And this, once again, comes down to the basic question of fundamental principles and the purpose of education. Perhaps it is only natural that those outside education should imagine they have only to ask for changes and then those ideals will be swiftly realized by educators in the field—after all that is their job. Most educators, however, are in the dark about what they should be doing and end up going solely on their own intuitive experience.

Here we see the real danger of committee discussions that never conclude anything. A majority conclusion derived from unfocused viewpoints is no way to arrive at an accurate picture of anything. Hence my call to base decisions on happiness as the purpose of education and on its component principles of benefit, good, and beauty values.

The standards for selecting materials to be taught must come down to questions as mundane as, What will have meaning in the lives of common people—the children of mere farmers, daughters of the small merchant, the classes that had no contact with schooling in the days before equal-opportunity education? To this day, foreign language courses are blindly maintained, the holy of holies to the educator. By such a route, students might end up at the college level shoulder to shoulder with that select few who can vainly pride themselves on their ability to read a handful of obscure books. But where does that get most people? Who can look back on his or her own school days and not regret the precious time wasted on such academic nonsense?

Again, how are we to select and reject particular elements of our environment as proper or improper to study? By what standards? We have come to the dead end of unrealistic subjectivism. To allocate school time and funds to foreign languages and arcane mathematics is the height of the traditionalist bourgeois mentality. Unlike some people, the majority of students have to worry about their future livelihood.

Thus, we are back to the issue of purpose in education and who is to formulate goals for the common citizen. Purpose in education must come from the recognition of existing goals of human life, from the observation that consciously or unconsciously people are already advancing toward something in their own living. On analyzing these observations, we find that everyone is looking for some permutation of benefit, good, and beauty. Thus, I hold that these values should stand as principles for the selection and organization of teaching materials as well as for teaching practices.

Looking around the world we live in, we can distinguish two general realms of phenomena:

Natural phenomena—roughly divisible into celestial, terrestrial, and human realms
    astronomical phenomena
    land phenomena
    aquatic phenomena
    atmospheric phenomena
    biological phenomena
    inorganic phenomena
    human phenomena
        means of living
        means of grouping
        social groups
        social classes
        division of labor in society
        political phenomena
        economic phenomena
        educational phenomena and transfer of culture

To guide students in how to live their lives in harmony with the natural world and the human world is to guide them in creating value in these many areas. To show how, in desiring relations with these things of the real world, people evaluate, discard, and select, and eventually enjoy or suffer things according to tripartite standards of beauty and ugliness, loss and gain, and good and bad is to demonstrate how we all live in worlds of value of our own making and remaking. Education serves to increase people's powers to create such values. As means, subject material can be aligned to focus on the following three areas: subjects for the economic valuation of life, subjects for the moral valuation of life, and subjects for the aesthetic valuation of life.

Once established, subjects must be placed or given relative standing according to standard valuative principles. Likewise, the extent of coverage must also be tempered by considerations of value. That is, we should not turn our backs on the process of children's mental development and forget there are limits on how much they can understand at any given time. This suggests an arrangement and organization of subjects into an orderly progression from simple to more complex. There is an economy to learning that does not jump around erratically. Students develop their own powers of reasoning from each step to the next, providing they are not stifled by rote memorization. Thus the ordering of texts and other subject materials can make a crucial difference in fostering student abilities to reason their way to the life of value. An excellent example of teaching materials based on these principles is Josei Toda's *Suirishiki Shido Sanjutsu* (A Deductive Guide to Arithmetic).[2] Teachers who have used this text report remarkable progress in the development of mathematical understanding upon the part of their students.

Structuring the Curriculum

THE ORDER OF TEACHING MATERIALS

Conducting children through their studies in an orderly manner according to a set, graduated program does not merely refer to proceeding in sequence from one school term to the next but means touching upon all subjects throughout the school year every school year. The presentation of materials to be taught must follow in this spirit.

Such matters of curriculum ought to be immediate concerns for Japan's educators as they go about their daily business. Yet, in the Japanese educational system, subject selections, teaching plans, and the like are not made with any comprehensive vision of the curriculum as a whole. Rather, they stand as a word-for-word translation of the German system as adopted after the reforms of the 1890 Imperial Elementary School Order, with no consideration of basics versus peripheral matters, no organic connections from top to bottom, left to right. Whether it has value or not, whether the children understand or not, the curriculum stands, a string of materials that someone perhaps believes necessary for living, although no thought is given to just how the children are to apply it in their own lives. It can only be called a form of violence.

Thus, I propose the following three-step structuring of the curriculum:

1. A fundamental direct-observation course—guided studies in direct

observation of the actualities of living on the students' own home
ground
2. Specialized skill courses—classroom studies in various intermediate
disciplines
3. Comprehensive summary courses—directed studies in real-life applications toward total citizenship

At the mere mention of a home-ground course, some senior members of the educational community are bound to seize the opportunity to
denounce it as an additional course when the curriculum is already too
full. But these are the very persons who would uncritically uphold the
existing Meiji-period standards of education. It only convinces me more
that their idea of education has no point contiguous with the actualities
of living.

In the history of human education we observe the development of a
formative process of human learning. Present-day science did not just
come out of nowhere. Looking back over the path whence we came, we
clearly recognize a branching upward and outward. At first, human life
was a chaotic bluster of blind reactions to an environment neither wholly
understood nor very consciously perceived. Then, one by one, we singled
out particular elements that were somehow related and focused our attention on them, contrasted them with other elements in like relationships, and so discovered which elements were essential. From such
primitive beginnings modern science was born. Education should follow
a similar developmental course if children and young people are to arrive
at any true cognizance of their environment. Leading educational
thinkers from the time of Comenius on have declared that education
must obey nature inasmuch as nature dictates a natural course of
growth. Yet when I look at the current distribution and ordering of
subject materials in Japanese education, what I see goes against any such
scheme. From the first year of elementary school, we have a lineup of
courses that includes morals, spelling, and math. It should be simple
enough for anyone to see what a waste of students' most impressionable
learning years such present practices amount to. Not only are such advanced concepts as nation and state thrust upon children barely ten years
old, but they are then plunged into the history of that state authority
back twenty-five hundred years.[3] No wonder the children are less than
interested; it is as if a complete novice were suddenly enrolled in a specialist course.

What I propose instead is a home environment course to serve as grounding for the later teaching of existing courses by taking beginning students on a guided tour of the local world into which they were born. At the very least, such direct observation offers a key to preventing isolated specialists from reducing education to piecemeal abstractions at the cost of distancing children from any awareness of the value of work. I have continued to grow more convinced of the basic soundness of the idea of a home environment course ever since it first occurred to me more than twenty years ago. Here, I can only hope to outline the contents and methods of such a course, pending such time as I can write a separate book.[4]

While the idea of a home environment course has been a long time coming, it can be seen in retrospect to have a sound basis in the overall evolution of concepts pertaining to teaching materials. Thus, we can identify four specific periods in regard to use of teaching materials: the age of exclusive reliance on written-word texts, the age of reference to pictorial illustrations, the age of reference to actual objects and models, the age of direct observation of the environment as teaching material. I submit that once the insufficiencies of the first three stages are realized, the fourth stage is inevitable.

SUBJECT COVERAGE OF COURSES

The good life can be realized only through the fulfillment of the individual, and this goal of happiness can in turn be attained only through the fulfillment of the group on which the individual depends for life and livelihood. Thus education, as a means of assisting the individual in gaining understanding of how to realize the good life, must provide specific guidance toward adequate living according to the expectations of his or her society. But even more, it must foster competencies that will enable the individual to contribute actively to the greater good of society. It is a serious discredit to the present educational system that no systematic attempt is made to instill an awareness of society in light of these higher goals.

Although supporters of the present system argue that a major effort is made for the fulfillment of the individual life, no effort is made for consciously organized guidance toward the creation of real benefit values. True, there have been some efforts, but they have been all too fragmentary. But because the well-being of the common citizen — that is to say, almost all of us—has much to do with daily economics, and economic independence is the primary foundation of human life, there should be little objection to education's taking up the subject of economic means. Of course, thorough study above and beyond existing course divisions must first explore a variety of alternatives as to just how this is to be done.

When education realizes its important responsibility to conduct students in the creation of benefit values, it will look at the natural and human realms with different eyes in its search for subjects to teach. Mere cognitive intellectual interest will no longer be a sufficient criterion; the view to cultivating powers of benefit-value creation will come to the fore, bringing the curriculum around to include evaluative and appreciative courses on means of benefiting oneself. Countless possibilities present themselves in many fields: courses on the utilization of nature, organic and inorganic, toward benefit-value creation in such primitive means of production as agriculture, livestock farming, sericulture, aquaculture, hybridization, and forestry or in various industries utilizing their products as raw materials toward extended value creation or in the transport of these goods and further upgrading of value through trade and commerce. Of course, existing courses in science, geography, crafts, agriculture, and so on, surely fit into this picture, but not in the isolated fragmentary way they do now. Again, comprehensive planning is necessary.

Let us now consider what sort of courses should be instituted with regard to the fostering of abilities to create good. Immediately subjects like morals, history, geography, and the national language come to mind, and we see how much these are emphasized—perhaps even overemphasized. Why, then, are these not tied together with the core concept of society? Why do we give students partial views but not the whole picture? Why must they chase shadows, the resultant operant phenomena, yet not apprehend the essential body? Is this any way to get children to appreciate the concept of nation? Even history, like just any story, will be remembered only for occasional interesting scenes if it is not clearly connected with an overall presentation of society. Likewise, in geography, it is not enough just to describe the map of the surface of the earth for the purpose of fostering patriotism. Geography should contribute to clarification and awareness of the interdependence of our lives. Teaching practices must change to reflect this comprehensive orientation.

How about courses to guide students' aesthetic life? We already have a number of courses intended to encourage and direct such value creation: crafts, gardening, drawing, chorus, and so on. Nonetheless, these are not clearly unified in relation to goals in human life; hence they are not seen as preparations for anything. They are not conducted as evaluative activities, so they amount to blind or random cognitions of the environment. Guidance toward value creation, yes, but in bits and pieces. Without giving students much of a clue as to how to consciously unify the threads, the general picture fails to come alive for them. By contrast, I have heard that in America, children's art classes are taught not just as self-expression or fine art but as a part of real-life concerns. That is, they are taught to meet their aesthetic demands in items of real use, items that also provide practical benefit—beautiful yet functional things. Thus, children learn to create and appreciate value in a connected way.

By way of summary, I offer a four-part framework within which to critically evaluate and restructure the present curriculum in order to provide more effective learning:

1. Courses aimed at guiding the creation of benefit values: existing courses in crafts and sewing need extensive supplementation with life-skills guidance.
2. Courses aimed at guiding the creation of moral values: morals, history, geography, and so forth, with major revisions in their respective contents.
3. Courses aimed at guiding the creation of aesthetic values: drawing, chorus, crafts, and so on, again with major revisions in the methods of teaching.
4. Courses intended as general guidance in value creation to provide foundations for the above courses: (Japanese) language, arithmetic, physical education, and so on, with rethinking of their objectives and redirection of associated contents.

People who are unacquainted with the psychology of learning may seek to reduce other courses by expanding the Japanese language course on the grounds that the language course covers the materials and contents of other courses. This is, however, a faulty argument because it would eventually become uneconomical in terms of learning time and effort. In the case of the language course, for example, command of language not only makes for economy of learning but also is easily applied in daily life toward social communication, thus facilitating entrance into cooperative living in one's social group. A course dedicated solely to language skills is a must.

In closing this section it may be helpful to note that Herbert Spencer[5] has argued in his seminal work, *Education: Intellectual, Moral, and Physical* (1861), that subjects for teaching should be selected according to the following fivefold approach to education as preparation for the life of happiness, that is, the life of self-fulfillment:

1. Activities directly related to self-preservation = direct provisions for self-preservation = physiology
2. Activities indirectly related to self-preservation = indirect provisions for self-preservation = mathematics, physics, chemistry, biology, sociology
3. Activities leading to the education of further generations = preparation for parenthood = developmental psychology
4. Activities supportive of proper sociopolitical relations = preparation for citizenship = civic history and natural history of societies
5. Activities to fill free time = provisions to round out the life of taste and interested involvement = art, painting, poetry, literature, and so on

Here we find a concise hierarchy of values reflected in concrete subject selections, an important document not to be overlooked. This value-oriented proposal appears all the more significant when we consider that it was offered some seventy-five years ago, making the present educational chaos all the more intolerable.

THE ORGANICALLY STRUCTURED CURRICULUM

The various component courses of the elementary and middle school curricula must represent a summation of knowledge. They must be united around some central concern if we are to prevent the fragmentation of personal character. Only when the many branches of study, the disciplines and subdisciplines that have been built up over the years in both the East and the West, are seen as means to reach back to some central starting point will an organic system of knowledge take shape.

For too long we have neglected this starting point. And what do we have to show for it but the meaningless, unrelated bits and pieces of knowledge that students gain from their time spent in school, or else the meager opportunities for applying this knowledge in real life, or, again, improper application of this fragmented knowledge? Does this not go a long way toward accounting for the rise in crime in our society despite increases in education? Show miseducated youths a motion picture with several violent or pornographic segments, for example, and out of the entire plot, most will be left with a fragmentary impression of just those segments, giving them a twisted outlook on human life and human behavior. I cannot emphasize it too strongly! We must always bring education back to bear upon the central issue of human happiness and the good life within an overall perspective of value creation.

Inasmuch as happiness stands as the goal of human life and hence the goal of education, and further, because happiness is, in effect a summation of the result of life engaged in creating values of benefit, beauty, and good, education must therefore engage students in appreciative and evaluative activities in these three directions. Education must provide a systematic approach to living. All persons long at the depth of their being to proceed through life in a safe, sane, and orderly manner. And herein lies the possibility for education to play a proper role in our lives. Through their studies, children must be brought to that point of awareness wherein by the time of graduation—the culmination of their curriculum—they can look back over the courses they have studied thus far and get some sort of total picture of it all. Their schooling should make sense to them, at least in retrospect. At the upper levels of education, their courses should draw things together for them; students should reach an understanding of how every part fits in as a means to bring them to this point. Thus, in advancing level by level through the curriculum, students should be internalizing an overall idea structure of means and ends.

While they are yet children, students should be reflecting on the goals toward which they advance, on the reason they go to school each day, on what sort of value they have been creating. It should all come together to form a clear network of ideas for them. This is as possible as it is necessary. What this will amount to is the formulation of a coherent view of human life: Is it all for money and property, or fame and position, or for something else? Can this something be attained by oneself alone or only through the cooperative life of the community?

Once these objectives in life are recognized, the next step is to have each student compare his or her way of life with that of others in order to hone the critical faculties. No course in morals will have any meaning in children's real life unless it comes to this point. And what applies to elementary school subjects applies to all other levels as well. Only as studies are made to relate in a cumulative way to the life students live in their particular environment will those studies come alive for students. Only then will we see real attainments in learning.

So how are we to go about realizing this? And to whom does the task fall? For the time being, no matter who does the thinking on the issue, the task comes down to the preparation of material from the state-edited textbooks and its presentation by the teacher. This makes it all too easy to fall into the same old trap of force-feeding information. Here we see the need for teachers who can teach these ideals effectively, hence the need for stricter teacher selection and improved teacher education. There is a considerable gap between these ideals and current realities, and it goes without saying that there will be many difficulties—but not insuperable ones.

Generally speaking, courses intended as a means toward the goal of happiness through creative living must include three stages: first, courses to guide in low-level evaluative activities not requiring much awareness; second, courses to guide in advanced reevaluation through the cognitive processes of understanding the nature of things in terms of value; third, courses to guide in applied value creation as the ultimate point of return. This is the way we must unify the curriculum, causally relating part to part so as to build up a wholly organic systematization.

We are, indeed, already partway toward realizing that goal, for essentially no one stands in disagreement about what is ultimately expected of education, any more than about what is thought to be the meaning of life. We complete our original birthright, fulfill our mission in life as humans by attaining values of living in harmony with the natural and social environments of the place we call home. That is, we create values of benefit, good, and beauty according to our individual proclivities and offer them to the culture of our society. If education succeeds in directing students to this realization, it will have met our expectations of value-creating education.

In an organically structured curriculum, every course should have its contributive function, and every individual purpose its own corresponding course—just as each organ of the body is there for a reason. Therefore, we must not go eliminating courses right and left simply because appearances tell us there are too many, without properly investigating the raison d'être of each respective course. By the same token, the uniqueness of each course and its particular purpose does not mean that each course should be allowed to pursue its own separate end, any more than an organ might declare independence from the rest of the body. If anything, that is the problem of today's curriculum — a body divided against itself.

How, then, do we give each course its due measure of autonomy and yet check the tendency to divide off indefinitely? Let us, for this purpose, define autonomy in terms of three major groupings of courses needed in order to instill standards for living. These are areas of knowledge that students must first have if they are to be healthy and whole and to develop the ability to work and proceed toward individual life goals. These three requisite curriculum components may be thought of as keys to establishing laws of human life. As complementary systems of knowledge, they may be organized in a tripartite structure at every level:

I. *Knowledge of natural laws.* Science to foster an understanding of natural laws and their applied technologies.

II. *Knowledge of social laws.* Morals, history, geography, and so forth to foster respect for social laws and their application.

III. *Knowledge of values relating nature and humankind.* Systematic coverage of ways to express values created in one's inner life.
   A. Direct expression through physical activity: play, physical education, dance, and so on.
   B. Three-dimensional creative expression: productive courses in crafts and the like.
   C. Two-dimensional creative expression: drafting, drawing, mapmaking, and so on.
   D. Linguistic expression.
       1. Audio-vocal knowledge and skills: speech, singing, and other items related to the rest of the curriculum.
       2. Visual-notational knowledge and skills.
           a. Writing, spelling, reading, and so on.
           b. Numbers, arithmetic, and so on.
           c. Musical notation and music reading.

Each of the above subjects has been selected for a purpose, and all function in complement. All work to support and develop a proper balance of physical sensibilities. To simply reduce or arbitrarily combine subjects for appearance' sake can only result in shutting off one or more of the five senses from the full range of its potential capacities.

The organic structuring of the curriculum also has the added benefit of providing students with the most economical means of covering the range of studies by merit of rendering them connected, that is, in accordance with the tenets of modern-day psychology, which holds that the retention and recall of knowledge can be made more efficient by tying down ideas to several grounding points. Of the countless ideas floating around in our brains, associations do not manifest themselves randomly but enmesh in a decided order at particular points of connection. Hence we are able to bring the right idea to mind at the right time for it to prove useful in our lives, if the fabric of our thinking but connects up in the appropriate ways. In this view, the virtually limitless gradations of human acumen depend on nothing so much as the degree of integral connectedness of their ideas. And if this much be admitted, it should be an easy matter for anyone to see that a network of ideas does not necessarily organize itself competently if left to its own devices.

Accordingly, if in the teaching of various subjects, conscientious and consistent efforts are made to connect the starting points and conclusions of presentations to direct observations in the home environment, then from that stream of stimuli that children receive over long years of schooling there will develop a consistent and interconnected body of knowledge, a system of knowledge that begins and ends in the world they see around them. In so doing, we are not forcing information on students but rather providing them with their own mental bookshelves and filing systems. Each student thus becomes his or her own master librarian, who can use the system for expanding the library itself. Here we can recognize one major criterion of unified learning: that the body of knowledge available to the student will always be completely and organically connected at every stage, and later additions can take the previously rooted home environment course as a core for further branching out like a tree.

As can be seen in the following diagram, then, the home environment course should ideally occupy the seat of central importance in a growing curriculum:

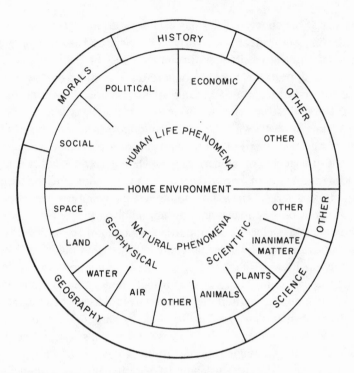

Fig. 1. Visual diagram of the home environment course.

This is but one possible scheme of course distribution. The important thing is that even and equal coverage be given to all subjects at all times. Since the primary goal of instruction is that of honing basic mental powers, the emphasis is not on the quantity of information, but on a balance of disciplines. There have been many schemes put forward for achieving this balance, most of which chose one specific subject, such as religion, or some distillation of several subjects, and organized all other subjects around that subject as the core of the curriculum. But all these schemes have problems built into them. Particularly, I have noticed that wherever one or more subjects are contrived to serve as the unifying factor of the curriculum, the going gets difficult. No matter how hard scholars try to justify their own particular brand of belief structure as *the* way to draw things together for children, the reality is that abstract ideas relate poorly to young minds. Thus, each of these schemes for developing meaningful and effective learning programs, one after another, has enjoyed its day of popularity, then faded away without effecting any significant long-range changes in educational policy or practice.

These observations brought me to the idea of a home environment course as a more reasonable way to organize basic curriculum subjects. Instead of authoritarian implantation of a central theme from above, to which children cannot relate, it occurred to me that children already have a considerable wealth of basic material and ideas from which to begin. If educators were to take all the things, both tangible and intangible, with which children have had to become familiar in their own home environment — stimuli they can in no way escape or forget — and connect all other material to those things, beginning to end, the result would be the most natural and, I am convinced, the most effective scheme of unification imaginable. This is the future I see for curriculum organization.

Afterword

A PHILOSOPHICAL APPRAISAL

Ironically, Tsunesaburo Makiguchi's distinction in Japan as the founder of Soka Gakkai (a Buddhist lay organization committed to value creation) has obscured his life's work as teacher, philosopher of education, and educational reformer. It is to direct attention to the highly significant results of this work that Professor Dayle Bethel presents Makiguchi's central educational theories and proposed reforms in this volume.

Western readers—perhaps to their surprise—will not be hindered in their access to Makiguchi's ideas by a culture gap. The ills in Japanese society that Makiguchi traces to deficiencies in Japanese education are replicated in the United States and other Western nations today. And although his proposed reforms are in some cases radical, they reflect understandings that are lodged in the foundations of Western culture. Specifically, Makiguchi works with conceptions of human being, of the individual, of good growth, and of worthy living that first found expression in the eudaimonistic philosophies of Socrates, Plato, and Aristotle. I will try to make these roots of Makiguchi's thought explicit, attesting to the profundity and durability of his themes while at the same time allowing Makiguchi's work to alert us to the continuing vitality of classical understandings today.

Consider first some of the ills of Japanese society that Makiguchi regards as the direct or indirect result of miseducation:

203

The Japanese people preponderantly identify the good life with material rewards; "happiness" is conceived egoistically and economistically.

Increasing numbers of people "loudly claim their rights but ignore the responsibilities that accompany them."

Values and evaluation are thought to be each individual's private concern, for which no education is needed; each person's valuations are thought to be as sound as anyone else's.

Character development is ignored as irrelevant to the goals of life or is narrowly conceived as training in nationalist loyalties.

Learning is identified with the classroom and is neglected after the first two or two-and-a-half decades of life.

Makiguchi identifies the following maladies within the educational system itself:

The entire educational system is run on the primary standard of the level of factual knowledge acquired, as measured by examination.

Children's inherent love of learning is commonly extinguished by adolescence as the result of force-feeding. While some learning disabilities are inborn, many more are produced by miseducation.

Educational practice is caught between the polarities of excessive uniformity and excessive permissiveness.

The pattern of formal education consisting of twelve to sixteen years at one sitting is at odds with the metabolism of young people and with their avidity for direct contact with the world. It disserves the ideal of lifelong learning by generating the belief that one's education is complete with the diploma or degree.

Prevailing theories of education come from scholars and researchers who are remote from primary and secondary teaching; as a result of this divorce, educational theory is largely inapplicable in the classroom.

If Makiguchi mirrors for us our own condition, then we have found our points of contact with his proposed reforms. I will first enumerate some of the more central or striking ones and then introduce the philosophical understandings that knit them together and invest them with enduring substance.

Clearly the most striking reform is Makiguchi's proposal that classroom schooling at all levels be confined to half days. The intention is to integrate the classroom and the world and to restore to community and home their full partnership in the work of education.

Correlative to the above, formal education must expand its concern from the mind of the student to the whole person. Specifically it must assume responsibility for cultivating good moral character. This requires that to the preoccupation with facts and truth be added the cultivation of young people's capacities of value recognition, evaluation, and, ultimately, value creation. Because valuation has an inseparable emotional component, the education of feelings is involved. The commonsense supposition that feelings are simply had, and are not teachable, is one of the mistakes perpetrated by supposedly value-free education and its neglect of character development. As Aristotle held, the deepest aim of education is learning to take pleasure in the right things.

Teachers must primarily be, not suppliers of information, but helpful guides to students' own learning initiatives. They should "leave the fact-finding to books and instead take a supporting role to the students' own learning experience." It must be recognized that the basic moving force in education is students' own interest: It can be channeled, redirected, and focused, but it must never be ignored or suppressed. The supreme importance of this point will justify, I think, my inclusion of the following anecdote by an American teacher. It pertains to university teaching, but we can readily recognize that it applies even more urgently to primary and secondary education.

> Some years ago I found myself teaching a mathematics course with Ptolemy's *Almagest* as a text. In the beginning I assumed that the students would be familiar with the motions of the heavens that can be seen with the naked eye — the diurnal circular motion of the fixed stars about the pole, the wandering of the planets, and the change in the position of the sunrise, for example — and I launched out at once on Ptolemy's explanation of them. I shortly discovered that none of the students had had occasion to really see these things, as they certainly would if they had lived in a less urban culture than ours. I found myself offering elaborate and ingenious explanations of phenomena which the class, to a man, did not know existed, and which, consequently, they felt no need to have explained. The experience was traumatic, and I have since been careful to see to it that a sense of the need for an explanation preceded the explanation itself.[1]

Education must seek to engender social consciousness and identification with the social good. It should endeavor to cultivate "the personal character needed by the members of a society which will enable them to become creative participants in that society." Individuation is of vital importance but must be conceived, not egoistically, but in terms of the kind of social contribution each person shall make.

In light of the priority given to social consciousness, primary education should begin with home environment courses, that is, on-site and classroom studies of the local community as the unifying ground. Makiguchi argues that because this ground of integration is natural to children, it is far preferable to abstractly conceived integrations "imposed from above."

Each of the indicated reforms has, of course, implications for reforms at secondary and tertiary levels, but it will be more useful now to turn to the conceptual framework from which the reforms draw their substance. As indicated earlier, the key understandings concern the nature of man, the nature of the individual, the question of what constitutes worthy living, and the nature of good growth. I can best indicate the wisdom and profundity of Makiguchi's ideas by pointing to their support in the eudaimonistic thought of Socrates, Plato, and Aristotle and their successors in this tradition of Western philosophy down to today.

But it is imperative to point out that Makiguchi's philosophy did not derive from these sources: It developed from his reflection on his own and others' experience in teaching Japanese school children. This must be emphasized, first, because of Makiguchi's insistence that the sources of Japanese thought and culture must be Japanese, and not imports from Europe and the United States. Additionally we have earlier noted Makiguchi's contention that Japanese education is debilitated by being obliged to struggle to incorporate philosophies of education promulgated by scholars who are remote from the practice of primary and secondary teaching. Rather than the derivation of Makiguchi's ideas from classical sources, what we are witness to is a remarkable confluence in the work of independent thinkers—Socrates, Plato, and Aristotle on one hand and Makiguchi on the other. Such confluences are exciting moments in the history of thought—independent arrival by Leibniz and Newton at differential calculus, independent arrival by Wallace and Darwin at the theory of evolution of species by natural selection. I know of a case closely comparable to Makiguchi's that involves my acquaintance with Abraham Maslow. Out of his clinical studies, and wholly without reference to Socrates, Plato, and Aristotle, Maslow arrived at conceptions of human nature, of good growth, and of full functioning in human beings that were identical to theirs. Given that philosophy, by the nature of its problems, cannot be (and should not try to become) an exact science, such confluences are what philosophy affords in the way of independent confirmation of hypotheses.

The backbone of Makiguchi's philosophy of education is his thesis that the ultimate goal of education is happiness. To arrive at his meaning, we must avoid two immediate pitfalls of misunderstanding. In the first place he does not mean (as we shall be prone to suppose) that education's aim is the future happiness of students: It is the happiness of students now that is to be sought. To be sure, their future happiness is likewise to be sought. But in effect Makiguchi's argument is that training in deferred happiness leads to an adulthood of deferred happiness. However, this is the less egregious of the two pitfalls, and it will be best to begin with the source of severest misunderstanding.

It occurs when we read our commonsense meaning of *happiness* into Makiguchi's declaration. For what we—Americans and Japanese alike—ordinarily mean by *happiness* is pleasure in the long run, and a happy period in our lives is one in which the sum total of pleasures significantly exceeds the sum total of pains. And *pleasure* is defined as the feeling of gratified desire. Doctrines that uphold pleasure (and happiness) as the supreme good at which all persons necessarily aim or ought to aim are grouped as variants of hedonism.

But Makiguchi holds that happiness in this sense affords no guidance to right living, because pleasure affords no such guidance. The reason is that pleasure attends the gratification of all desires indiscriminately and therefore can do nothing with regard to the crucial distinction between right and wrong desires. Together with happiness, Makiguchi holds the primary goal of education to be the development of personal character. This is because the two are inseparable: Happiness in Makiguchi's meaning is the subjective reward of living well, and to live well for a human being is necessarily to develop in personal character, because for all of us in the beginning (as infants and young children), what is good in us subsists as unactualized potentiality.

Development is a kind of change, but it is not random change; it is directed change. The trouble with raw desires is that they are omnidirectional and contradictory. This is transparently the case in small children, where it is to be expected. But it is also prevalent in adulthood—for example, in a person who wants a new car but equally wants not to deplete his savings or go into debt; or the person who lusts after a neighbor's spouse while wishing to preserve a good marriage—and here it is evidence of the lack of the development of personal character to which Makiguchi gives priority in education.

Persons who lack self-knowledge will frequently desire what is bad for them, and pleasure will attend the gratification of these desires. Individuals who seek to evade self-responsibility, including their rightful social responsibilities, will be pleased by success in such evasions.

Moreover, hedonism masks the important distinction between what I will term productive desires and recipient desires. By *productive desires* I mean desires that can be gratified only through the efforts of the person whose desires they are, while one's *recipient desires* can equally be gratified by others. My desire for a new car, for example, will be abundantly gratified if you make me a present of one. But no one can confer a better character on me; my desire for character development, though it may be supported (or obstructed) by others, can be gratified only through my own efforts. It was predictable that loss of the distinction between productive and recipient desires has resulted in a preponderantly recipient orientation in which persons' self-conceptions are made up largely of what they believe themselves entitled to receive. It is this that Makiguchi refers to when he speaks of persons who "loudly claim their rights but ignore the responsibilities that accompany them." From the developmental point of view, it may be noted that in childhood the primary question is, What shall I receive? whereas the pressing question in adolescence is, What shall I do? From this standpoint the shift to a recipient orientation (or consumerism, as it is sometimes called) indicates developmental arrest or regression.

By giving primary emphasis to the development of personal character, Makiguchi emphasizes productivity over recipience. Another way to state this is that responsibility is accorded logical priority over rights. It will be remembered that in *The Republic*, Plato's primary conception of justice is each person's doing what he or she is best suited by innate nature to do. Recipient justice derives from this: Each person is entitled to what he or she needs, in order to do what is his or hers to do. And Aristotle defined *happiness* productively, as "activity in accordance with virtue." Makiguchi's conception of the essence of personhood is identical to Plato's and Aristotle's. To be a person is to be an innate potential excellence requiring to be actualized, and responsibility for such actualization is the foundation of moral life. "Something innate . . . guides the life of each individual," and, accordingly, happiness is "a sense of becoming." From this it follows that "educators must actively work to show each child his or her potential to realize an ideal life."

An important implication is that the well-lived life is one's basic work, namely the work of self-actualization. This sets Makiguchi in opposition to the modern conception of work as an unpleasant necessity that everyone would avoid if he could and that must be compensated for by material rewards and leisure. Makiguchi calls for education to "instill joy and appreciation of work" (as Henry Thoreau insisted in "Life Without Principle" that work should be "inviting and glorious"[2]).

The reason that work is regarded as an unpleasant necessity is that persons, by innate disposition, differ greatly from one another with regard to the work that is theirs to do. For each person there are many kinds of good, useful, productive work that are nevertheless intrinsically unrewarding. On the other hand, there are a few (usually interrelated) kinds of work that will be experienced as intrinsically rewarding, such that the individual will identify with them and on his or her own initiative invest the best of the self in them. But currently—as for several centuries—no attempt is made to match persons to their meaningful work (or in education, to assist them toward the self-knowledge that such matching requires). In consequence, persons who by accident or good fortune find their meaningful work are extremely few, and the vast majority, having no experience to the contrary, endorse the prevailing view that work is an unpleasant necessity. The work that is one's life and the work by which one earns one's living are analogous cases. When it is the right work (that is, in the former case the right life for the individual one is), its intrinsic rewards are such, as Aristotle said, that one would exchange with no other. (And as Plato stressed, the virulent social and personal corrosive of envy finds no foothold in such a life.) It is the intrinsic rewards of living the right life that Makiguchi identifies as happiness. Integrated within the life that is right for the individual should be the right work in the limited sense of vocation or job, that is, the work-for-pay that the individual experiences as intrinsically rewarding and identifies with.

Makiguchi condemns egoism but without making the compensatory mistake of identifying moral conduct as altruistic (that is, as intended to serve the interests of others to the exclusion of the interests of self). Instead he holds that others' interests and the interests of self, when rightly conceived, are so intimately connected as to be inseparable. This understanding is integral to his definition of happiness as the value-creating life. The well-being of each individual is thus understood as contributory to the well-being of all. The true objective of the individual who is engaged at self-actualization is to manifest objective worth in the world, by no means for the benefit of self alone or primarily, but for whoever is capable of appreciating and utilizing the distinctive kind of worth it is. At the same time, Makiguchi's emphasis on evaluation is training in the appreciation of varieties of value, to enable persons to recognize, appreciate, and utilize a broader spectrum of the diverse kinds of value that value-creating individuals manifest. The carpenter and the philosopher, for example, can each be expected to recognize excellence in his or her own field, but each person becomes useful to the other when each can recognize and appreciate excellence in the other's field as well.

When we get rid of the egoism-altruism bifurcation, we are in a position to recognize that each of the moral virtues — wisdom, courage, and temperance, for example — is both a personal utility and a social utility. Clearly the virtues strengthen a person in the pursuit of personal ends; and just as clearly a virtuous person who lends self to others' ends is a more valuable ally. And if the aim of the virtuous person is, as we have said, to actualize value in the world for whoever can appreciate and utilize the distinctive kind of value it is, then those virtues serve both self and others at the same time. This is the meaning of Aristotle's observation that "every virtue or excellence both brings into good condition the thing (person) of which it is the excellence and makes the work of that thing (person) be well done."[3]

Concrete illustration of the harm caused by the egoism-altruism bifurcation appears in current controversy over various experiments in work reform. Under such names as "job enrichment" and "humanizing the workplace," many experimental endeavors to make work more meaningful have been conducted in the United States and other Western nations over the past thirty years. But trade unions have questioned the intent of the experiments, pointing out that managerial support is enlisted solely by the prospect of increased productivity. In reaction to this, some humanistic work-reformers have sought to display the purity of their motives by eliminating increased productivity from their list of aims. But in so doing they have, predictably, lost the managerial support that they need for the implementation of their proposed reforms. These unrewarding pendulum swings can be arrested only by recovery of the truth by which Makiguchi stands, namely that both enhanced worth in the products of work and increased personal fulfillment of workers result from matching workers to the kinds of work for which their various innate dispositions suit them. Granted, self-knowledge will always be imperfect, even when education is designed to cultivate it; and perhaps some kinds of socially necessary work will be found to be fulfilling to no one. These are problems that call upon human ingenuity for their handling. But by the redirection of social initiatives they can be rendered vestigial, whereas presently the absence both of self-knowledge and of meaningful work is the prevailing condition.

There are few conceptual problems about which we in the United States are more confused at present than the notions of individuality and individualism. These concepts lie deeply embedded in our national heritage, yet critics in mounting numbers ascribe to them what are said to be our ubiquitous ills of alienation, anomie, and narcissism. Here again the wisdom of Makiguchi intercedes. Our predicament is the product of disjunctive thinking—either the individual or society. One must predominate, we suppose, at the expense of the other. But Makiguchi leads us to a reconception of both, such that the prosperity of each presupposes and entails the prosperity of the other.

From what has already been said, it will be clear that Makiguchi is a kind of individualist; the good life for human beings is a value-creating life "according to our individual proclivities." Yet he is vehemently opposed to the kind of individualism that is rampant in his own society (and ours), namely egoistic, economistic individualism that strives ceaselessly for its own material advantage (recognizing no other) in zero-sum competition with all other persons. Moreover, such individualism prizes an autonomy that it conceives as total individual self-sufficiency, in disregard of persons' inevitable indebtedness to the society in which they live and the tradition in which they were reared. By contrast Makiguchi's individualism is consistent with a deep human interdependence that penetrates the identities of persons, uniting them in community as a common bond. Conversely the false ideal of total self-sufficiency denies community by conceiving of the individual as an asocial, atomic entity; egoistic, economistic individualism limits social relations to the purely external relations of voluntary exchange. In the words of one critic, it is a "contest of selfishnesses."

In proposing the cultivation of the kind of moral individualism that finds its fulfillment in its social contribution, one of the pedagogical problems that Makiguchi squarely faces is that persons who have arrived at this understanding of self-fulfillment have typically had the opportunity of "leisurely reflection based on material comfort." For persons whose very subsistence is precarious and day-to-day, self-knowledge stands as an unaffordable luxury; yet it is a necessity to the well-lived, intrinsically rewarding life. Here is a Gordian knot. How is it to be untied? The only possible answer is, by social intervention. And indeed, the first momentous step has already been taken; it is the institution of mandatory universal public education by which children who formerly were obliged to labor in field or factory are afforded several hours per weekday of — potentially, at least — respite from the exigent struggles of life. Broadly viewed, this is a monumental achievement, amounting to nothing less than the socially created space for reflection for all persons. Yet of course this is not how the created breathing space is used. It is used instead for fact cramming in the interest of test taking in the interest of "success" in the world, in the prevailing economistic, egoistic meaning. Thus what might have been breathing space is made to replicate the stifling exigencies of life.

Makiguchi insists that education must be a preparation for living in the world, but more than this, it should be preparation for living well in the world. As we noted earlier, according to Makiguchi, this entails living well now, for a training that postpones happiness to an indefinite future is a training in the postponement of happiness. What we find in Makiguchi is a theory of stages of life — childhood, adolescence and youth, maturity, old age — each with its distinctive kind of fulfillment and therefore of happiness (together, to be sure, with deep strands of continuity running throughout). The values, virtues, and obligations intrinsic to each stage must be fulfilled in that stage, not postponed in one bundle to the adult years. Makiguchi puts the matter emphatically: "It is not the prerogative of professional educators to decide that preparation for adult life should be the purpose of education. . . . [They] must come to realize that schooling which sacrifices children's present happiness and makes some future happiness its goal violates the personalities of children as well as the learning process itself." In particular, force-feeding of facts in disregard of children's interests will in due course extinguish children's native avidity to learn.

But children's native curiosity can and must be sympathetically guided. Concerning the directions such guidance should take, I will confine my comments to just one of Makiguchi's recommendations, but it is the very heart of his educational philosophy, for it is the means by which children can be led to the understanding that was a moment ago noted to have heretofore been the province of the wise, namely that individual fulfillment lies in social contribution. Children will themselves gain access to this recognition, Makiguchi contends, if their education is designed to begin with "home environment" studies, that is, with both on-site and classroom familiarization and understanding of their own community. The purpose is to facilitate, from the beginning, children's identification with the needs and services of the community—not at the expense of their own nascent individuality but as the appropriate arena for the expression of that individuality. The community has for the child the advantage that it is tangible and concrete; it provides the initial context for the idea of value-creative living. As education proceeds, it includes the study of other communities, then one's nation and other nations, and finally the world as the total human community.

In order that the community be not merely the subject of study but also the teacher, Makiguchi proposes to limit classroom learning to half days. His underlying thinking finds significant counterparts in the United States. The 1979 Carnegie Council report on education, *Giving Youth a Better Chance*, includes the following: "Young people receive too heavy a dose of schooling for too long a period, unmixed with knowledge of the world of work or experience in work or community service. Work that takes the form of community service is particularly desirable, giving young people a feeling of involvement in community problems and of contributing to their solution."[4]

With related intent, a succession of influential Americans—from the philosopher William James early in this century and anthropologist Margaret Mead to President Lyndon Johnson and New Jersey senator Bill Bradley—have proposed a National Youth Service, under which young people could at intervals totaling perhaps two years, devote time to a great variety of kinds of national and local service.[5] Six or seven nations currently have such a service, and some of them engage in international exchange of work parties, affording overseas as well as domestic opportunities for experiencing other cultures and life-styles.

And again with similar intent, some American secondary schools and colleges have for several decades been experimenting with work-study programs that alternate a semester in the classroom with a semester of community service or work in the private sector or divide the day between work and study. Former Secretary of Labor Willard Wirtz endorsed this endeavor for its mitigating effects upon the "time traps of youth for education, adulthood for work, old age for nothing."[6]

Amid the many advantages that may be cited for breaking up the conventional pattern of education as sixteen-years-at-one-sitting, we must not overlook the priority that eudaimonism gives to individual development. In its model of development, adulthood begins with the life-shaping choices (vocation, whether to marry or not and whom to marry, whether to have children, avocations, locale of residence, religious and civic commitments, and so on), and adolescence is the time for exploration of the available alternatives with respect to these choices. The classroom cannot suffice as the setting for these explorations. It is one thing to read about Alaska and a very different thing to live there; it is one thing to read about a vocation or life-style and a very different thing to practice it; and people are legion who have discovered that the practice of their vocation is altogether different from their classroom preparation for it.

Presently, much that passes for choice with respect to these life-shaping matters is pseudochoice. The challenge is to facilitate genuine choice, based upon self-knowledge, by enhancing each person's practical knowledge of alternatives. Self-knowledge is cultivated by this means, for it begins in discovery of those productive options that one experiences as intrinsically rewarding.

Among Makiguchi's many important contributions to this framework of understanding is his persuasive demonstration that education for productive, intrinsically rewarding living must begin in earliest childhood. Many eudaimonistic philosophers have supposed that if only we can avoid suffocating children's innate incentive to grow and to learn, then the truly constructive work begins in adolescence.

My task in this appraisal has been to connect Makiguchi's philosophy of education and his proposed reforms with a deep strand in Western philosophy—Greek eudaimonism—that is still very much alive today. Indeed, there is evidence that increasing numbers of Western thinkers are turning to this strand to extricate us from some of our ubiquitous maladies that are the harvest of modern—less profound, more opportunistic—conceptions of the individual, society, and the good life for humans. But I know of no contemporary thinker who approaches Makiguchi's achievement at developing the implications for education, and most notably primary and secondary education, of the enduring eudaimonistic understandings.

DAVID L. NORTON
Professor of Philosophy
University of Delaware, Newark

Notes

Introduction

1. For a comprehensive analysis of the impact of industrialization on human societies, see Alvin Toffler, *The Third Wave*, William Morrow, New York, 1980. See also C. Wright Mills, *The Power Elite*, New York, 1956, and *The Sociological Imagination*, New York, 1959.

2. *Soka Kyoikugaku Taikei*, vol. 1, book 1 (Soka Kyoiku Gakkai, Tokyo, 1930), Seikyo Shimbunsha, Tokyo, 1972, p. 25. This insistence that there be a close relationship between education and the practical side of people's lives can be found throughout Makiguchi's writings. The following statement, quoted from the inaugural address of a newly appointed director of the department of architecture at Armour Institute of Technology in Chicago, November 20, 1938, echoes this concern. It provides both a summary of Makiguchi's position in this regard and support for that position:

> All education must begin with the practical side of life. Real education, however, must transcend this to mould the personality. The first aim should be to equip the student with the knowledge and skill for practical life. The second aim should be to develop his personality and to enable him to make the right use of this knowledge and skill.
>
> Thus true education is concerned not only with practical goals but also with values. By our practical aims we are bound to the specific structure of our epoch. Our values, on the other hand, are rooted in the spiritual nature of men. Our practical aims measure only our material progress. The values we profess reveal the level of our culture. Different as practical aims and values are, they are nevertheless closely connected. For to what else should our values be related if not to our aims in life? Human existence is predicated on the two spheres together. Our aims assure us of our material life, our values make possible our spiritual life.

3. Makiguchi, *Soka Kyoikugaku Taikei*, vol. 1, book 2, p. 134.

4. Makiguchi, *Soka Kyoikugaku Taikei*, vol. 1, book 2, p. 169.

5. At this point a note of caution is in order. This condemnation by Maki-

guchi of egocentric preoccupation with immediate personal materialistic gain would seem to contradict his general value orientation, in which he places personal gain at the center of his philosophical system of beauty, gain, and goodness. Upon closer examination of his ideas, however, it becomes clear that although pursuit of personal gain is recognized, even sanctified in a sense, as a good and wholesome element of life, that pursuit is always in the context of and balanced by the values of beauty and goodness. Thus, a single-minded drive for personal gain, whether in material wealth or in status and power, was for Makiguchi a cancerous, destructive element in human life that, he came to believe, was at least partially if not totally a consequence of the existing educational system.

6. Makiguchi, *Soka Kyoikugaku Taikei*, vol. 1, book 1, p. 19.

7. Makiguchi's position here should not be confused with the self-oriented value system that developed in Western cultures and came to form the core of American "rugged individualism." The difference between the two positions is profound. Makiguchi's position is that the individual whose learning experiences nurture appreciation for and understanding of self and the self's sustaining communal network of interrelationships will naturally strive to develop the inherent creative potential of the self to the utmost limits in order to contribute value to that sustaining community and its members. (Here Makiguchi is in the company of a long line of philosopher-psychologist-educators that extends from the philosophers of Greece through such recent and contemporary thinkers as Abraham Maslow, Robert Theobald, David Norton, Erich Fromm, and Carl Rogers.) In contrast, America's rugged individualism, with its origins in British individualism and social Darwinism, imbues the individual with the conviction that life centers in developing the creative powers of the self for the self's gain and aggrandizement. The outcome of this value system and life orientation—what David Norton describes as "maximization of benefits" for the self—Makiguchi condemned as self-destructive both for individuals and for societies. This outcome, he insisted, was one of the legacies of the Japanese educational system. In this connection, see David L. Norton, *Personal Destinies: A Philosophy of Ethical Individualism*, Princeton University Press, 1976, pp. 315–18.

8. Makiguchi, *Soka Kyoikugaku Taikei*, vol. 1, book 1, pp. 19–20.

9. Makiguchi, *Soka Kyoikugaku Taikei*, vol. 1, book 1, pp. 28–29.

10. Makiguchi, *Soka Kyoikugaku Taikei*, vol. 1, book 1, pp. 49–51.

11. Makiguchi, *Soka Kyoikugaku Taikei*, vol. 1, book 1, pp. 36–37.

12. Makiguchi, *Soka Kyoikugaku Taikei*, vol. 3, book 4, (Soka Kyoiku Gakkai, Tokyo, 1932), Seikyo Shimbunsha, Tokyo, 1979, pp. 250, 252.

13. Tsunesaburo Makiguchi, "Soka Kyoikugaku ni Motozuku Kokugoka (Yomi-kata, Tsuzuri-kata) Kyoju no Kenkyu Happyo" (Study of teaching Japanese [reading and writing] based on value-creating pedagogy), in *Makiguchi Tsunesaburo Zenshu* (The complete works of Tsunesaburo Makiguchi), vol. 5, Tozai Tetsugaku Shoin, Tokyo, 1965, p. 467.

14. Dayle M. Bethel, *Makiguchi the Value Creator*, Weatherhill, Tokyo, 1973, pp. 72–73, 95–96.

15. Makiguchi's preface from volume 1 of *Soka Kyoikugaku Taikei*, published in 1930, is presented as the preface to this book.

16. Makiguchi was encouraged and assisted in his efforts to reform education at this time in his life by friends and former students who were convinced of the value of his ideas. Out of their shared interests and concerns emerged an informal organization named Soka Kyoiku Gakkai (Value-Creating Education Group). It was within the fellowship of this group that Makiguchi attempted to integrate and further develop his ideas and to prepare his notes for publication. See the Preface for further details.

17. A note at the end of volume 4 of _Soka Kyoikugaku Taikei_ refers to a fifth volume, which was to have been titled _Methods of Guiding Value Creation._ A complete table of contents is included in the note; thus, it appears that Makiguchi had already finished the preliminary writing. No manuscript of the volume has ever been found, however, and it is assumed that if he did write it, it was lost during the war.

18. It is my conviction that Makiguchi's proposals for educational reform merit the attention of international educators and that objective testing of those proposals should be designed and carried out. The schools that Soka Gakkai has established in Tokyo, Osaka, and elsewhere in Japan, from elementary through university levels, are presumably engaged in such testing and application. However, it is not known to what extent they have actually been able to incorporate Makiguchi's ideas and proposals for educational reform into their educational practice, which would mean radical departures from existing educational policies and practices, and to what extent Soka Schools have simply had to conform to educational realities in Japan. Objective studies of Soka Schools in this regard have yet to be made. Insofar as I am aware, the limited implementation of Makiguchi's proposals that I have been able to do at The International University Center in Osaka, Japan, represents the only attempt at testing other than that being carried on in connection with Soka Schools. I would be most interested in any other testing of Makiguchi's ideas that may have been undertaken.

19. Bethel, _Makiguchi the Value Creator_, pp. 83–87.

20. Koichi Mori, _Study of Makiguchi Tsunesaburo: The Founder of Soka Gakkai_, doctoral dissertation submitted to the Graduate Theological Union, Berkeley, California, 1977.

21. Mori, _Study of Makiguchi_, p. 206.

22. Mori, _Study of Makiguchi_, pp. 200–215.

23. On the other hand, some things that Makiguchi wrote suggest that he was not unaware of the role of existing power structures in denying to individuals opportunity for creative growth and well-being. See particularly his reference to the "soulless power of suppression," his criticism of government policy, and his view that "the socio-economic situation in our country has become imbalanced in the extreme and that the time for change is upon us," pp. 26–32 in _Soka Kyoikugaku Taikei_, vol. 3, book 4.

Chapter 1

1. Ooka Tadasuke (1677-1751) attained such fame during the Edo period for his ingenuity in settling disputes that a whole volume, the *Ooka Meiyo Seidan* (Famous judgements of Lord Ooka), was compiled of his rulings. For historical background, see Edwin O. Reischauer and John K. Fairbanks, *East Asia: The Great Tradition*, Houghton Mifflin Company, Boston, 1960, p. 623.

2. For a description of the English curriculum in Japanese schools during this period, see Yoshikichi Omura, *Eigo Kyoiku Shiryo* (Materials for the history of English teaching in Japan), Horei Shuppan, Tokyo, 1980.

3. Immanuel Kant (1724–1804).

4. The Confucian Five Relationships were the loyalty of minister to lord, the piety of son to father, the fidelity of husband and wife, the respect of youth for age, and the mutual trust of friends. See Reischauer and Fairbanks, *East Asia*, p. 28.

5. The source of this quotation is not indicated.

6. The insight Makiguchi is pointing to here may seem to be nothing more than simple common sense. It is, however, as Alfred North Whitehead insisted years ago and as an increasing number of educators are recognizing today, an insight that has been ignored by human beings for three hundred years. It was Whitehead's main theme that our modern scientifically oriented industrial societies are based on misguided assumptions about location, time, space, and causality and that these misguided assumptions have been built into our educational systems. Robert S. Brumbaugh has commented on Whitehead's views:

> A case in point that Whitehead discussed is the acceptance of the technical notion that space functions only as an insulator. For small material particles, it is useful to assume that any two do not influence each other unless there is some kind of contact. But when we generalize this notion of all kinds of things and all kinds of spaces, the result is clearly mistaken. In the interests of a supposed "realism," we can treat every nation as a unit radically insulated— except for contact along frontiers—from every other. The result is irrational nationalism and imperialism. We apply the model to individuals in society, and the result is irresponsible egoism. We extend it to cosmology, and the result is a materialism that seems to make any reconciliation of reality and religion an impossibility.

See Robert S. Brumbaugh, *Whitehead, Process Philosophy, and Education*, State University of New York Press, Albany, 1982, pp. 1–6.

7. *Jinsei Chirigaku* (The geography of human life), Fuzanbo, Tokyo, 1903, pp. 673–77. The translation of this chapter from Makiguchi's earlier work was done by Dr. Stanley Ohnishi and Dr. Hope C. Bliss.

8. Makiguchi's reference here was to Ward's *Applied Sociology*, Ginn and Co., New York, 1906.

9. These ideas were cited from *Sei no keishiki* (Forms of life), a Japanese translation of the original title (1920) by Eduard Spranger (1882–1963), and *Ippan Kyoikugaku* (General pedagogy), a Japanese translation of the original title (1806)

by J. F. Herbart (1776–1841). Spranger classified human motivation into six parts: economic behavior, logical behavior, aesthetic behavior, political behavior, social behavior, and moral and religious behavior. Herbart's six modes of interest were observational or informational interest, inferential interest, aesthetic interest, social interest, moral interest, and religious interest.

10. For a further discussion of Auguste Comte's ideas on the development of human knowledge, see Kenneth Bock, *Human Nature and History: A Response to Sociobiology*, Columbia University Press, New York, 1980, pp. 106–108, 170–172. See also William E. Drake, *Intellectual Foundations of Modern Education*, Charles E. Merrill Books, Columbus, Ohio, 1967, pp. 230–231.

11. Kuan-tsu (d. 645 B.C.) was prime minister of the state of Ch'i during China's Spring and Autumn period. As a legalist philosopher, he emphasized practical abilities and economics.

Chapter 2

1. Henri-Louis Bergson (1859–1941), French philosopher. The exact source from which Makiguchi paraphrased is unknown.
2. Wilhelm Dilthey (1833–1911).
3. Hermann Heinrich Gossen (1810–58), German economist.
4. First stated in the Confucian *Analects* (*Lunyu* 15:23) in defining *reciprocity*.
5. Paraphrased from an unidentified sourcebook, *Platonic Philosophy and Education*.
6. Wilhelm Winderband (1848–1915).
7. Cengzi, or Cengshen (ca. 505–436 B.C.), a disciple of Confucius.

Chapter 3

1. Paraphrased from a quotation by Honma Toshihara (1873–1943), Japanese Christian social worker.
2. Makiguchi mentions specifically an article, "Nijuseiki No Sekai to Nippon Seinen" (The world of the twentieth century and Japanese youth), by Soho Tokutomi, in connection with this view.
3. Jean-Jacques Rousseau (1712–78), John Amos Comenius (1592–1670), and Johann Heinrich Pestalozzi (1746–1827).
4. "*Nijo fusabutsu, yo fujobutsu.*" The two vehicles referred to here are two levels of spiritual awakening: realization (J. *engaku*, Skt. *pratyeka*) and learning, that is, hearing the Word from a teacher or Buddha (J. *shomon*, Skt. *shravaka*).
5. From the Confucian *Analects*.
6. The source of this article is not indicated.

7. Established in 1924, the Educational and Cultural Policy Council was to "be under the suprvision of the Prime Minister and respond to his inquiries by conducting investigations and deliberations on important matters of educational and cultural policy."

8. "Examination hell" refers to the experience of some students in Japan who undergo excessive emotional pressure while studying to pass the entrance examination to enter a particular school or university.

9. *Hinayana* (Skt.: lesser vehicle) is a derogatory term used by later Mahayana (Skt.: great vehicle) Buddhists to refer to early schools of Buddhism that concentrate exclusively on individual salvation. Mahayana Buddhism is distinguished by, among other things, the introduction of the so-called Bodhisattva Vow to save all other sentient beings before one's own enlightenment.

10. The youth training centers, established in 1926, employed military training methods. See *Makiguchi Tsunesaburo Zenshu* (The complete works of Tsunesaburo Makiguchi), vol. 6, Daisan Bunmeisha, Tokyo, 1983, pp. 185, 228.

11. Just how these scholastic study centers envisioned by Makiguchi were to be organized and what their precise nature was to be are not clear. In regard to the training of teachers, however, the following reference, included among a collection of random notes, provides some insight into what he had in mind:

> Ultimately, more than mere craft or technique, education should be understood as a Way (*do*) as profound and rigorous as any transmission in the Japanese tradition, such as Kendo (the Way of the Sword) or Chado (the Way of Tea). These are disciplines requiring practice of techniques, of course, but also a comprehension through study and personal command through a unified character. Accordingly, it only stands to reason that teacher candidates should first work out at a proving ground for a few years before they are granted certification, just as in any of the other Ways. In this case, the proving ground would be an intensive educational center.

12. Kozui Otani, *Nogyo Rikkoku Ron* (National stability through agriculture). Other books by this author have been located, but the volume referred to by Makiguchi is not now in existence in Japan.

Chapter 4

1. Takeya Fushimi, "Saikin niokeru Doitsu no Kyoikugaku" (The recent pedagogy in Germany). This article appeared in the journal *Teikoku Kyoiku* (Imperial education), published by Teikoku Kyoiku Kai (Imperial Education Society), October 1931.

2. Eduard Spranger, *Lebensformen: Geisteswissenschaftliche Psychologie und Ethic der Persönlichekeit*. Verlag Max Niemeyer, Tübingen, Germany, 1921. Makiguchi refers to a Japanese edition of the book, published under the title *Sei no*

Keishiki (Forms of life), trans. Kozaburo Tsuji, 1926. No copy of the translation is now available in Japan.

3. Emile Durkheim, *Shakai Bungyo Ron* (Division of labor in society), trans. Hisatoshi Tanabe, Moriyama Shoten, Tokyo, 1932, pp. 38, 64; originally published as *De la Division du Travail Social.*

Chapter 5

1. The newspaper is identified as the *Tokyo Daily Newspaper*, but no date is given for the quotation.

2. Josei Toda was Makiguchi's closest disciple and the second president of the organization that he and Makiguchi founded. The initial name of the organization was Soka Kyoiku Gakkai (Value-Creating Education Society). When Toda reorganized the organization following World War II, the name was changed to Soka Gakkai (Value-Creating Society).

3. During the prewar years and until the end of World War II, Shinto mythology of the divine descendence of the Japanese imperial family from the sun goddess Amaterasu-Omikami was taught as literal fact. The divine authority of the imperial lineage from the mythical emperor Jimmu was especially emphasized by the military leadership of the country.

4. Insofar as is known, the book referred to was never written.

5. Herbert Spencer (1820–1903), English social philosopher.

Afterword: A Philosophical Appraisal

1. Blair Kinsman, *Wind Waves*, Dover Publications, Mineola, N.Y., 1984, p. 5.

2. Henry D. Thoreau, "Life Without Principle," in *Reform Papers*, ed. Wendell Glick, Princeton University Press, 1973, pp. 155–79.

3. Aristotle, *Nichomachean Ethics*, book 2, 1106a, lines 15–17.

4. Carnegie Council, *Giving Youth a Better Chance*, Jossey-Bass, San Francisco, 1979, pp. 94–95.

5. See Michael W. Sherraden and Donald Eberly, *National Service: Social, Economic, and Military Impacts*, Pergamon Press, New York, 1981.

6. Willard Wirtz and the National Manpower Institute, *The Boundless Resource: A Prospectus for an Education-Work Policy*, New Republic Books, Washington, D.C., 1975, p. 9.

Index